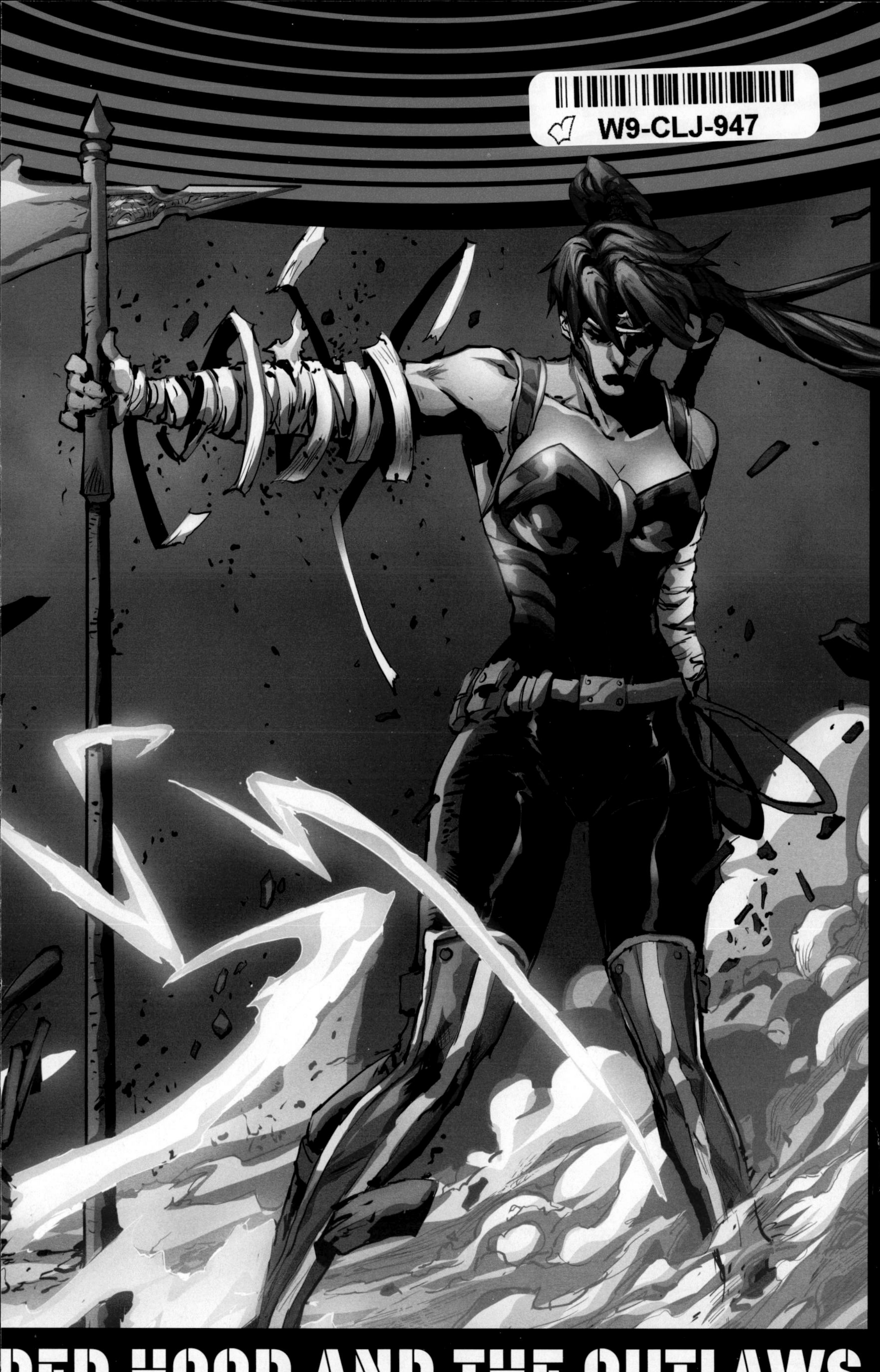

RED HOOD AND THE OUTLAWS

VOL.2 WHO IS ARTEMIS?

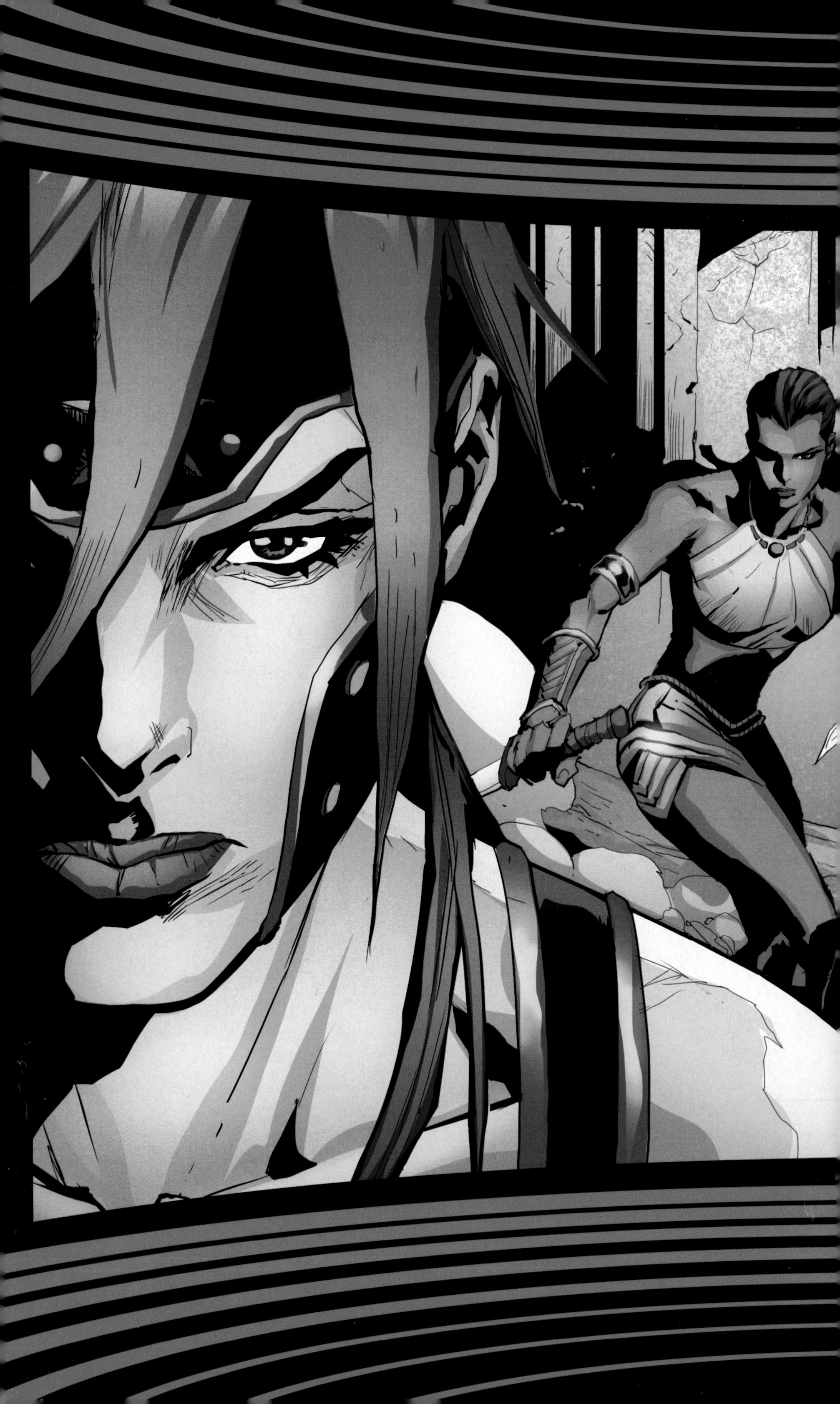

RED HOOD AND THE OUTLAWS

VOL.2 WHO IS ARTEMIS?

SCOTT LOBDELL
writer

DEXTER SOY

MIRKO COLAK * TOM DERENICK * KENNETH ROCAFORT
artists

VERONICA GANDINI

DAN BROWN
colorists

TAYLOR ESPOSITO
letterer

NICOLA SCOTT & ROMULO FAJARDO JR.
Collection cover artists

ALEX ANTONE Editor – Original Series ◆ **BRITTANY HOLZHERR DIEGO LOPEZ** Assistant Editors – Original Series
JEB WOODARD Group Editor – Collected Editions ◆ **LIZ ERICKSON** Editor – Collected Edition
STEVE COOK Design Director – Books ◆ **MONIQUE GRUSPE** Publication Design

BOB HARRAS Senior VP – Editor-in-Chief, DC Comics
PAT McCALLUM Executive Editor, DC Comics

DIANE NELSON President ◆ **DAN DiDIO** Publisher ◆ **JIM LEE** Publisher ◆ **GEOFF JOHNS** President & Chief Creative Officer
AMIT DESAI Executive VP – Business & Marketing Strategy, Direct to Consumer & Global Franchise Management
SAM ADES Senior VP & General Manager, Digital Services ◆ **BOBBIE CHASE** VP & Executive Editor, Young Reader & Talent Development
MARK CHIARELLO Senior VP – Art, Design & Collected Editions ◆ **JOHN CUNNINGHAM** Senior VP – Sales & Trade Marketing
ANNE DePIES Senior VP – Business Strategy, Finance & Administration ◆ **DON FALLETTI** VP – Manufacturing Operations
LAWRENCE GANEM VP – Editorial Administration & Talent Relations ◆ **ALISON GILL** Senior VP – Manufacturing & Operations
HANK KANALZ Senior VP – Editorial Strategy & Administration ◆ **JAY KOGAN** VP – Legal Affairs ◆ **JACK MAHAN** VP – Business Affairs
NICK J. NAPOLITANO VP – Manufacturing Administration ◆ **EDDIE SCANNELL** VP – Consumer Marketing
COURTNEY SIMMONS Senior VP – Publicity & Communications ◆ **JIM (SKI) SOKOLOWSKI** VP – Comic Book Specialty Sales & Trade Marketing
NANCY SPEARS VP – Mass, Book, Digital Sales & Trade Marketing ◆ **MICHELE R. WELLS** VP – Content Strategy

RED HOOD AND THE OUTLAWS VOLUME 2: WHO IS ARTEMIS?

DC Comics, 2900 West Alameda Ave., Burbank, CA 91505
Printed by LSC Communications, Kendallville, IN, USA. 9/1/17. First Printing.
ISBN: 978-1-4012-7399-6

Library of Congress Cataloging-in-Publication Data is available.

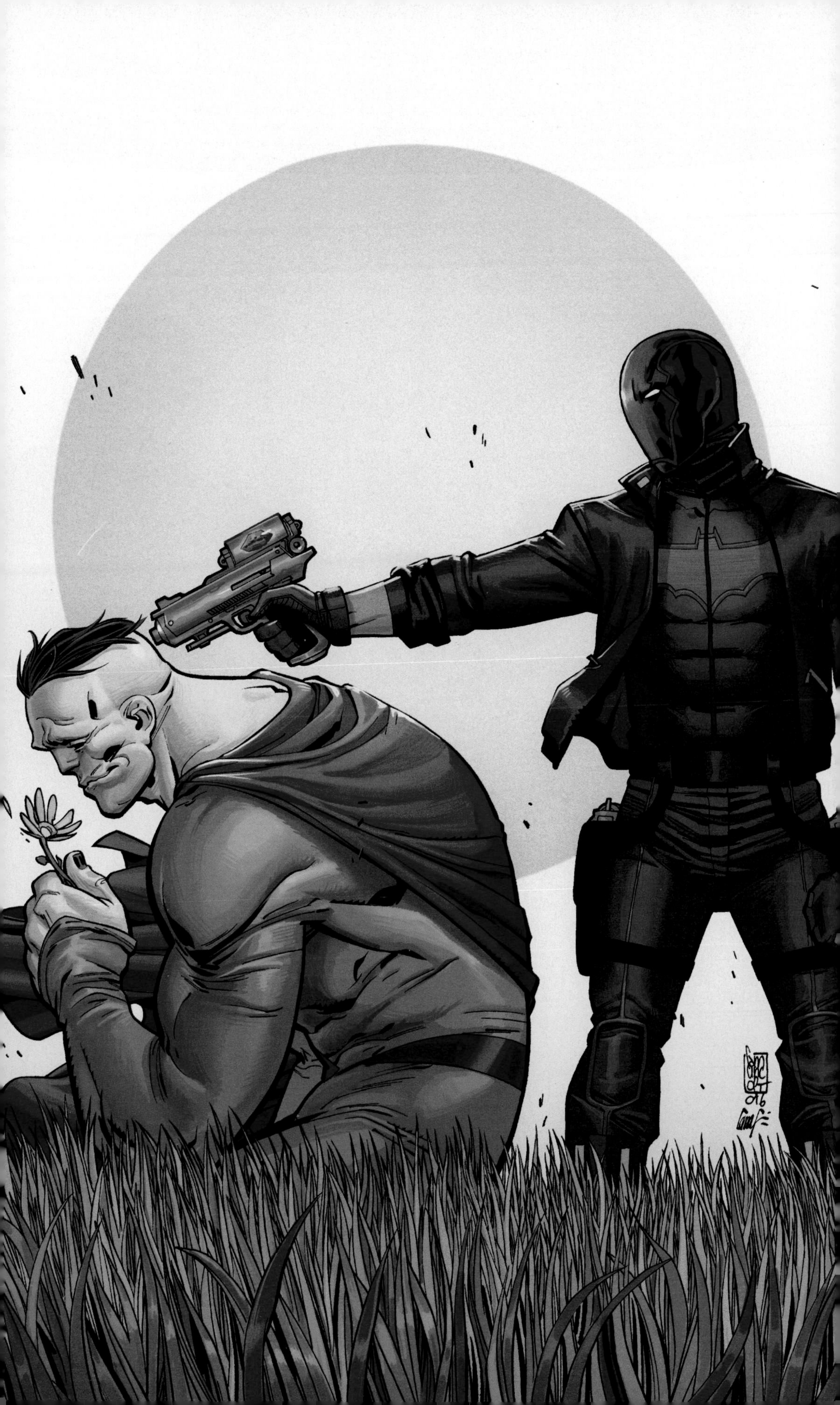

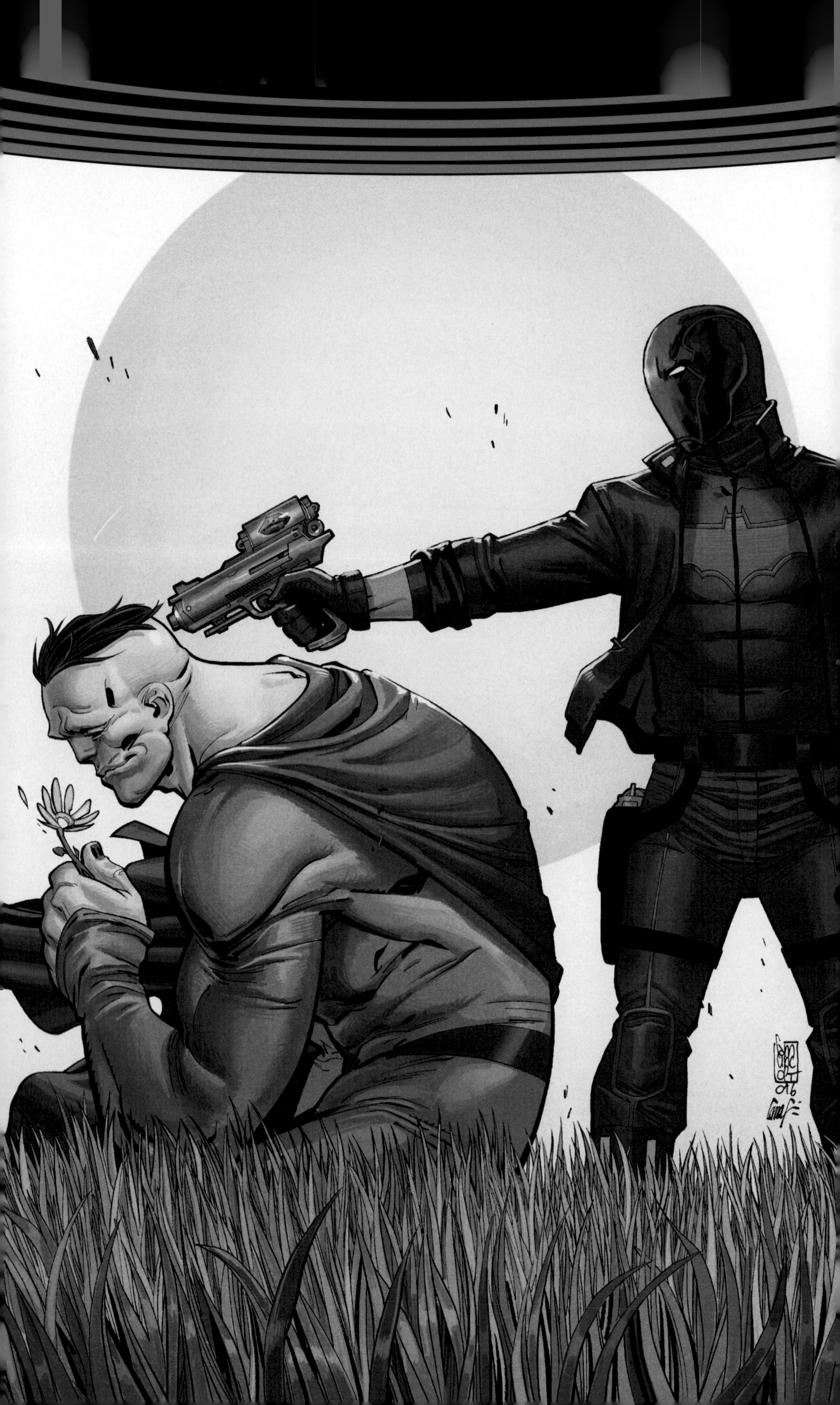

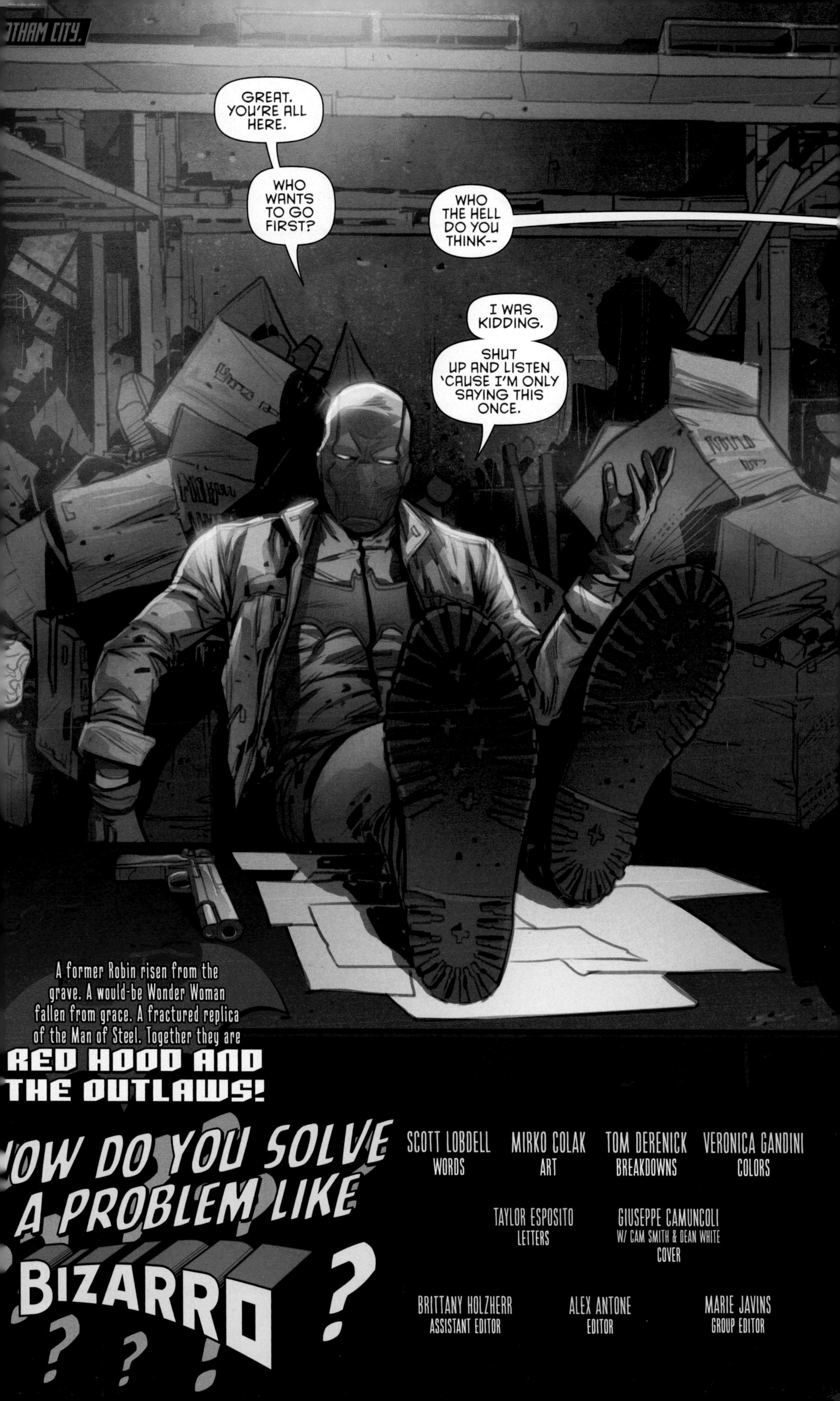
THAM CITY.
GREAT. YOU'RE ALL HERE.
WHO WANTS TO GO FIRST?
WHO THE HELL DO YOU THINK--
I WAS KIDDING.
SHUT UP AND LISTEN 'CAUSE I'M ONLY SAYING THIS ONCE.
A former Robin risen from the grave. A would-be Wonder Woman fallen from grace. A fractured replica of the Man of Steel. Together they are

RED HOOD AND THE OUTLAWS!

OW DO YOU SOLVE A PROBLEM LIKE BIZARRO ?

SCOTT LOBDELL WORDS
MIRKO COLAK ART
TOM DERENICK BREAKDOWNS
VERONICA GANDINI COLORS

TAYLOR ESPOSITO LETTERS
GIUSEPPE CAMUNCOLI W/ CAM SMITH & DEAN WHITE COVER

BRITTANY HOLZHERR ASSISTANT EDITOR
ALEX ANTONE EDITOR
MARIE JAVINS GROUP EDITOR

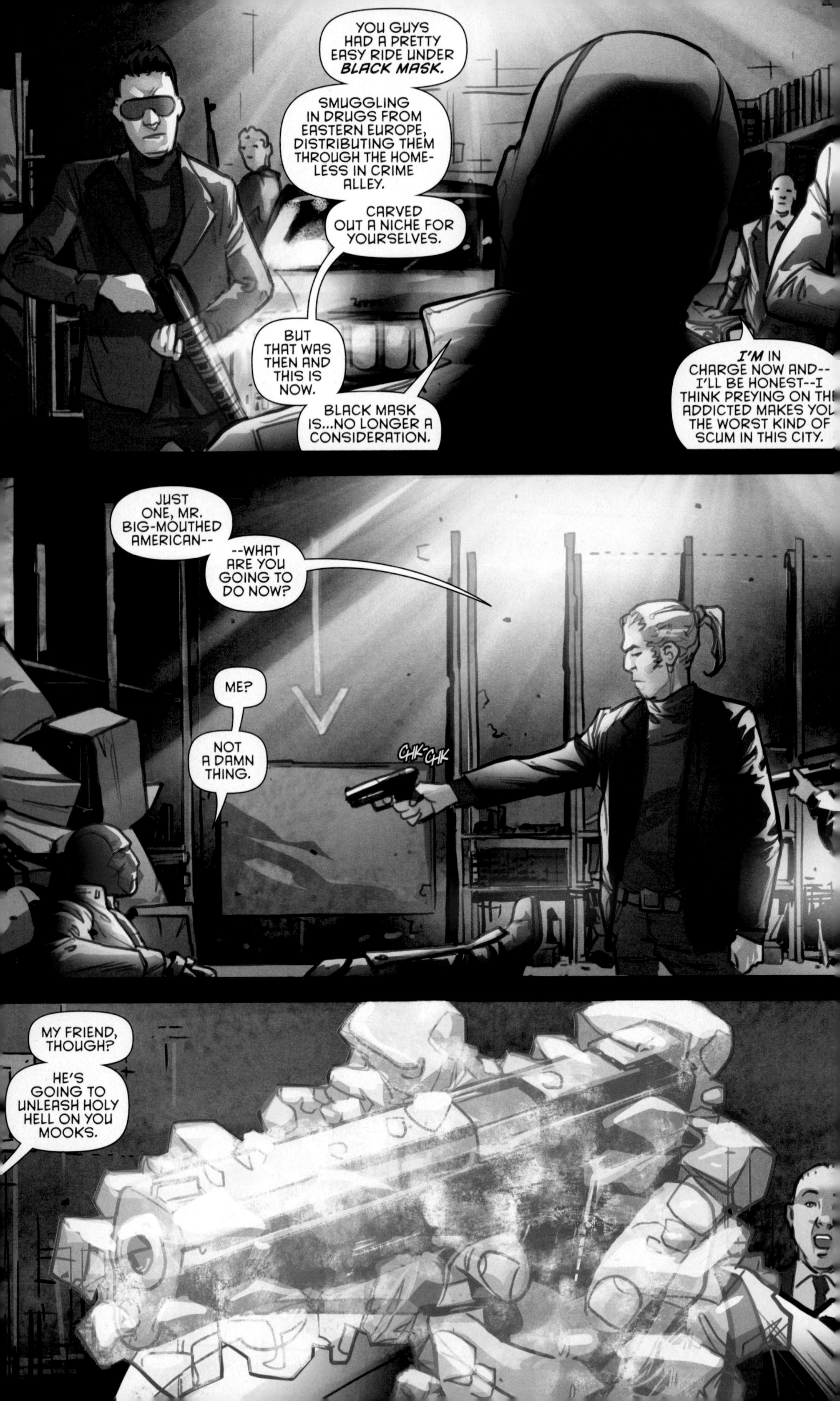
YOU GUYS HAD A PRETTY EASY RIDE UNDER BLACK MASK.
SMUGGLING IN DRUGS FROM EASTERN EUROPE, DISTRIBUTING THEM THROUGH THE HOMELESS IN CRIME ALLEY.
CARVED OUT A NICHE FOR YOURSELVES.
BUT THAT WAS THEN AND THIS IS NOW.
BLACK MASK IS...NO LONGER A CONSIDERATION.
I'M IN CHARGE NOW AND--I'LL BE HONEST--I THINK PREYING ON THE ADDICTED MAKES YOU THE WORST KIND OF SCUM IN THIS CITY.
JUST ONE, MR. BIG-MOUTHED AMERICAN--
--WHAT ARE YOU GOING TO DO NOW?
ME?
NOT A DAMN THING.
CHK-CHK
MY FRIEND, THOUGH?
HE'S GOING TO UNLEASH HOLY HELL ON YOU MOOKS.

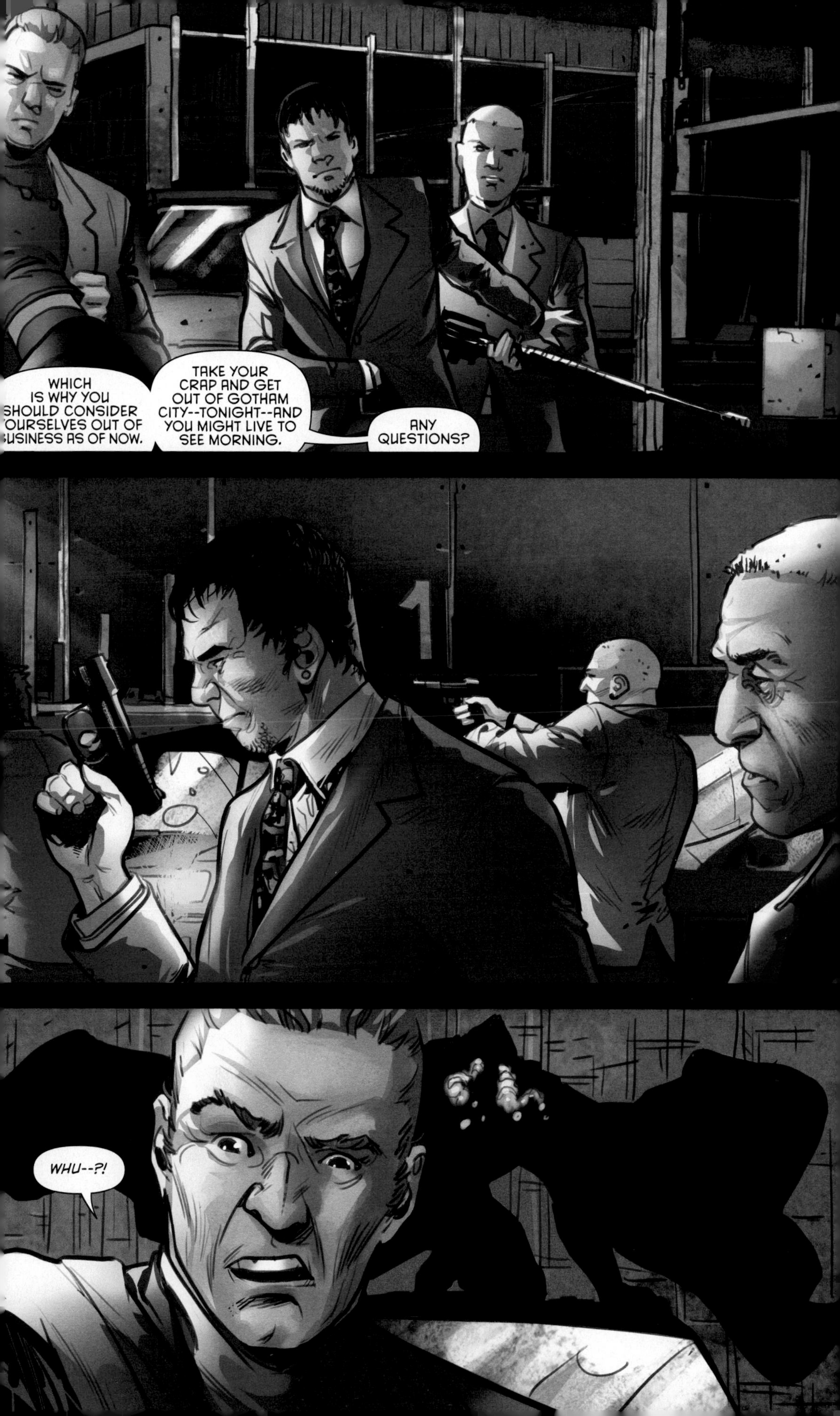
WHICH IS WHY YOU SHOULD CONSIDER YOURSELVES OUT OF BUSINESS AS OF NOW.
TAKE YOUR CRAP AND GET OUT OF GOTHAM CITY--TONIGHT--AND YOU MIGHT LIVE TO SEE MORNING.
ANY QUESTIONS?
WHU--?!

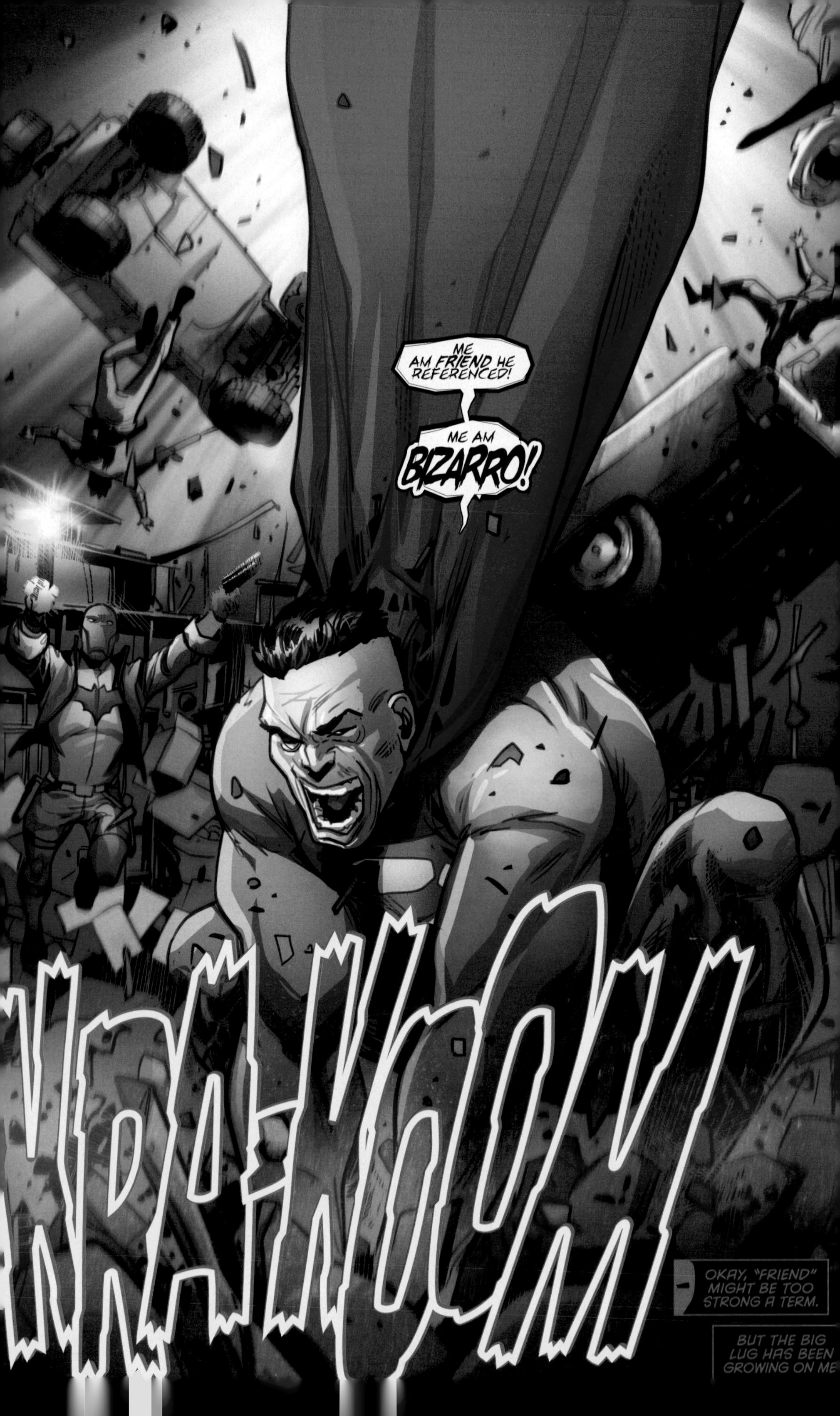
ME AM FRIEND HE REFERENCED!
ME AM BIZARRO!
KRAKOOM
OKAY, "FRIEND" MIGHT BE TOO STRONG A TERM.
BUT THE BIG LUG HAS BEEN GROWING ON ME

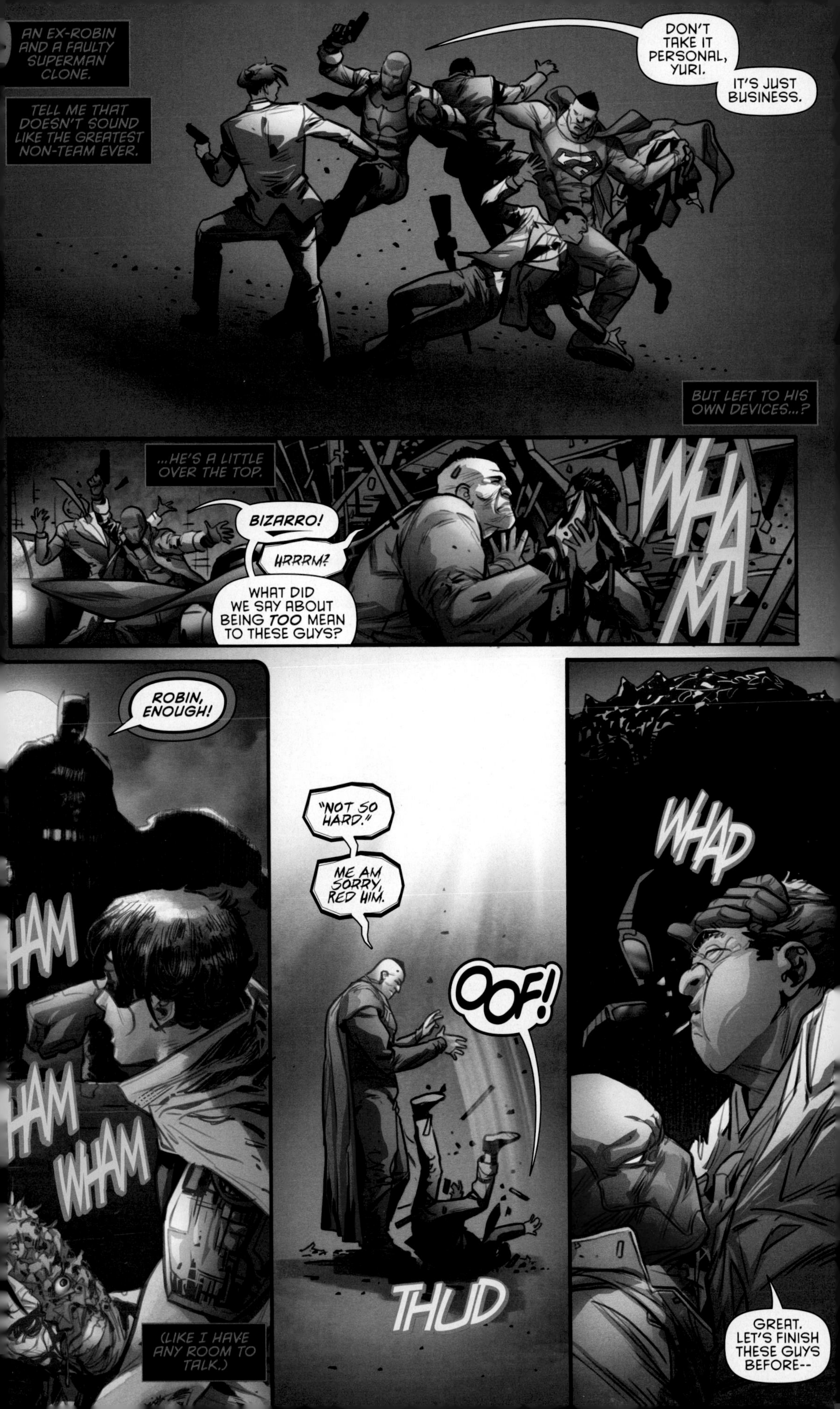
AN EX-ROBIN AND A FAULTY SUPERMAN CLONE.
TELL ME THAT DOESN'T SOUND LIKE THE GREATEST NON-TEAM EVER.
DON'T TAKE IT PERSONAL, YURI.
IT'S JUST BUSINESS.
BUT LEFT TO HIS OWN DEVICES...?
...HE'S A LITTLE OVER THE TOP.
BIZARRO!
HRRRM?
WHAT DID WE SAY ABOUT BEING TOO MEAN TO THESE GUYS?
WHAM
ROBIN, ENOUGH!
HAM
HAM
WHAM
(LIKE I HAVE ANY ROOM TO TALK.)
"NOT SO HARD."
ME AM SORRY, RED HIM.
OOF!
THUD
WHAP
GREAT. LET'S FINISH THESE GUYS BEFORE--

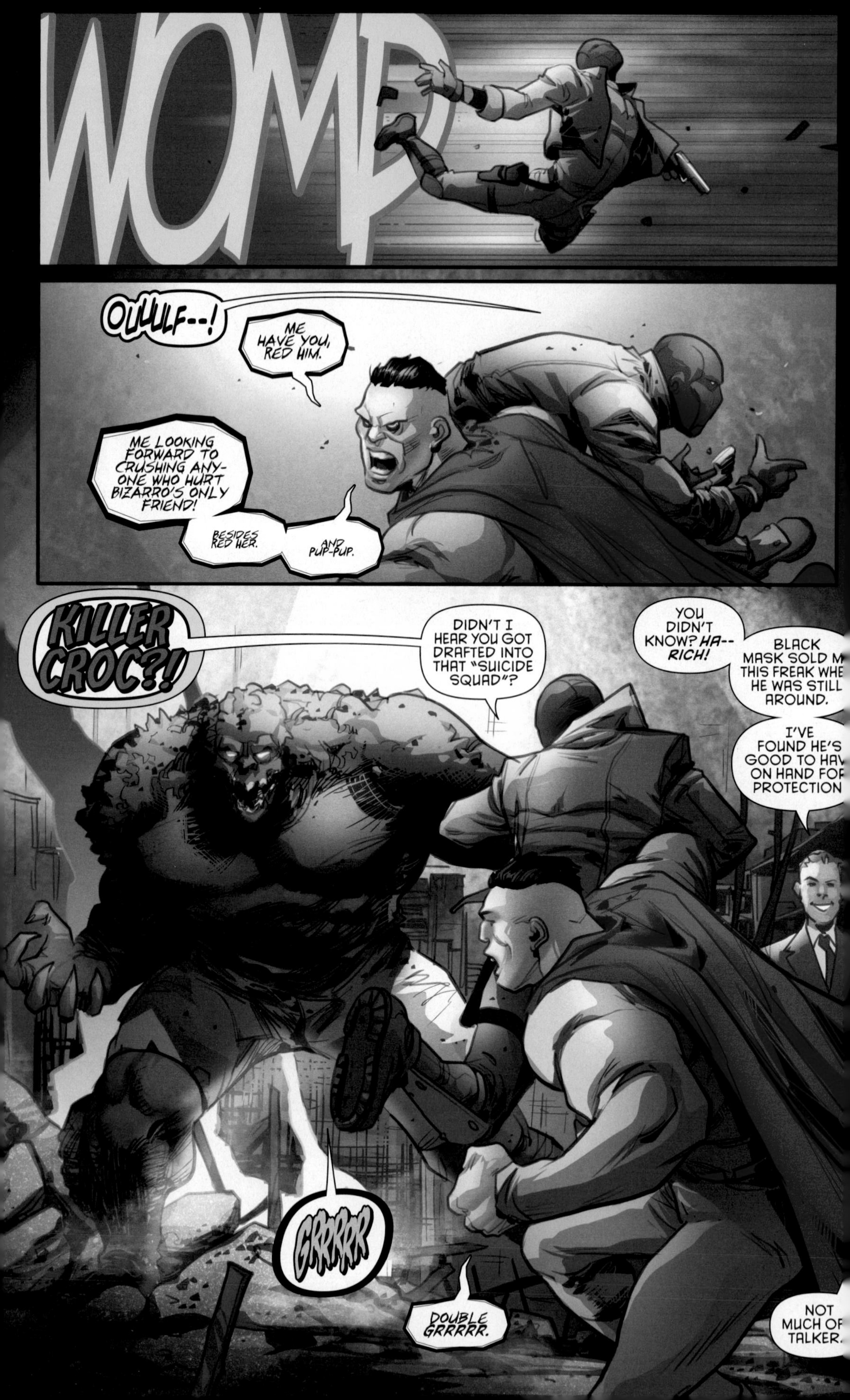
WOMP
OUUULF--!
ME HAVE YOU, RED HIM.
ME LOOKING FORWARD TO CRUSHING ANYONE WHO HURT BIZARRO'S ONLY FRIEND!
BESIDES RED HER.
AND PUP-PUP.
KILLER CROC?!
DIDN'T I HEAR YOU GOT DRAFTED INTO THAT "SUICIDE SQUAD"?
YOU DIDN'T KNOW? HA-- RICH!
BLACK MASK SOLD M THIS FREAK WHE HE WAS STILL AROUND.
I'VE FOUND HE'S GOOD TO HAV ON HAND FOR PROTECTION
GRRRRR
DOUBLE GRRRRR.
NOT MUCH OF TALKER.

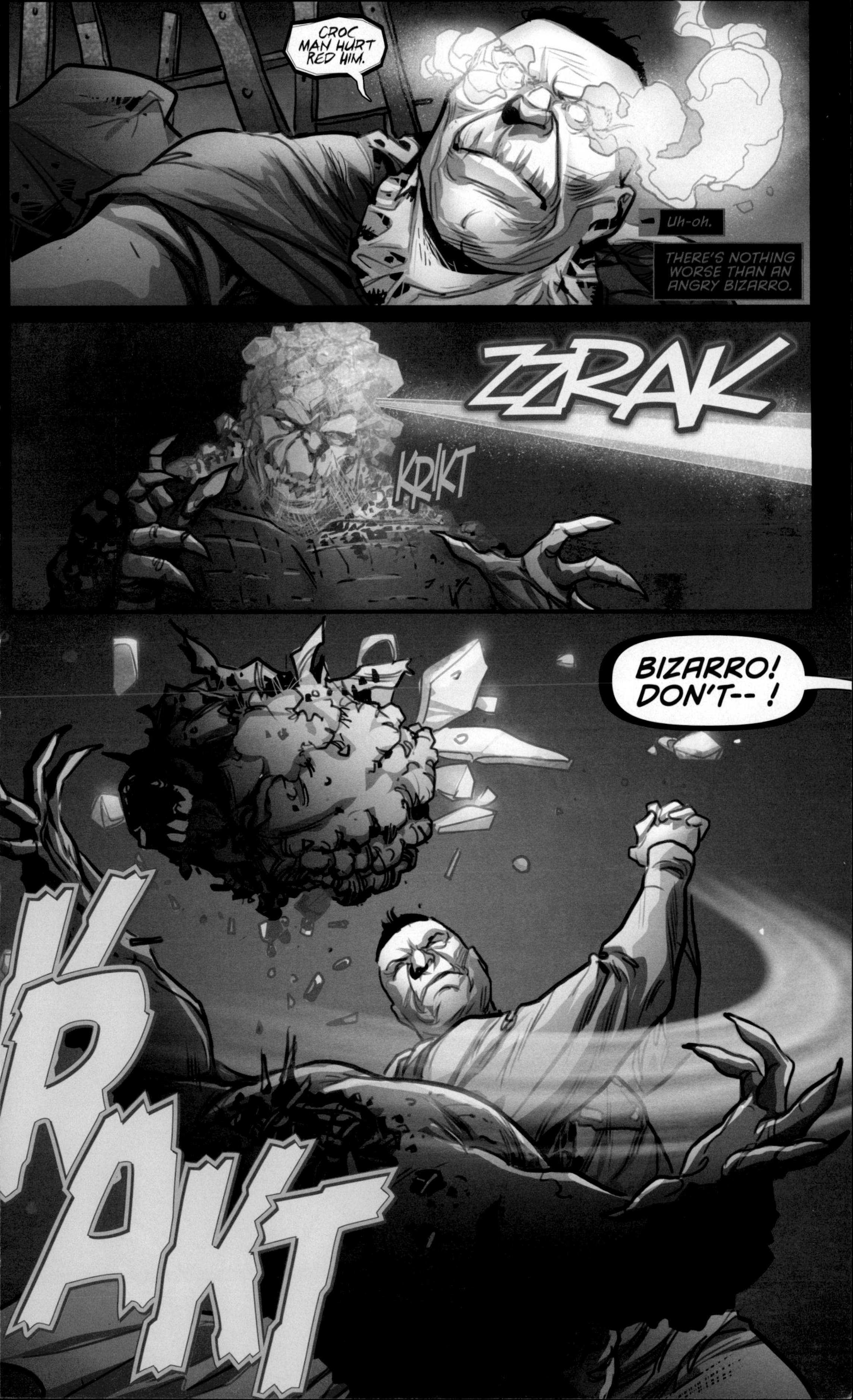
CROC MAN HURT RED HIM.
Uh-oh.
THERE'S NOTHING WORSE THAN AN ANGRY BIZARRO.
ZZRAK
KRIKT
BIZARRO! DON'T-- !
RAKT

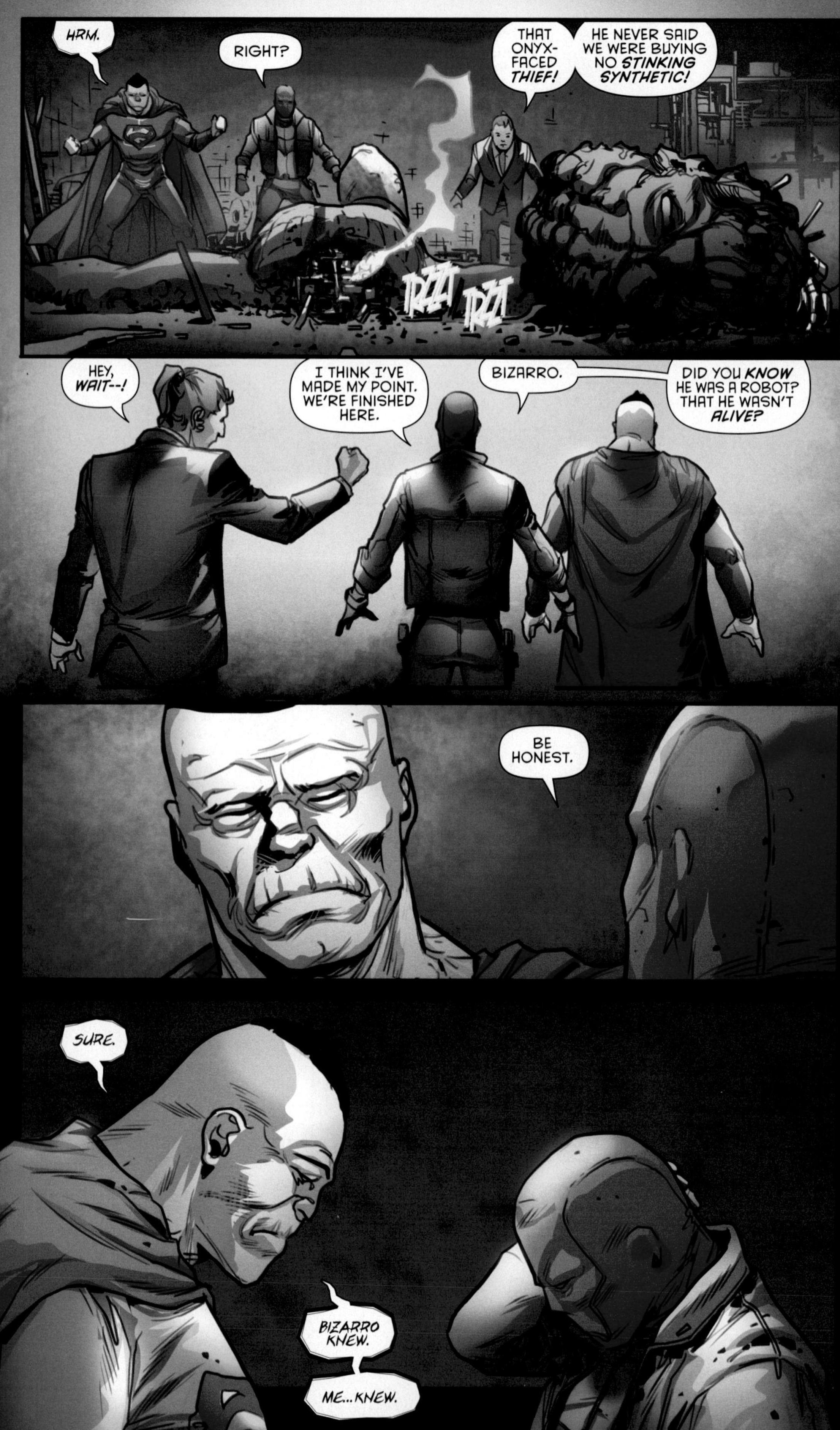
HRM.
RIGHT?
THAT ONYX-FACED THIEF!
HE NEVER SAID WE WERE BUYING NO STINKING SYNTHETIC!
TRZZT TRZZT
HEY, WAIT--!
I THINK I'VE MADE MY POINT. WE'RE FINISHED HERE.
BIZARRO.
DID YOU KNOW HE WAS A ROBOT? THAT HE WASN'T ALIVE?
BE HONEST.
SURE.
BIZARRO KNEW.
ME...KNEW.

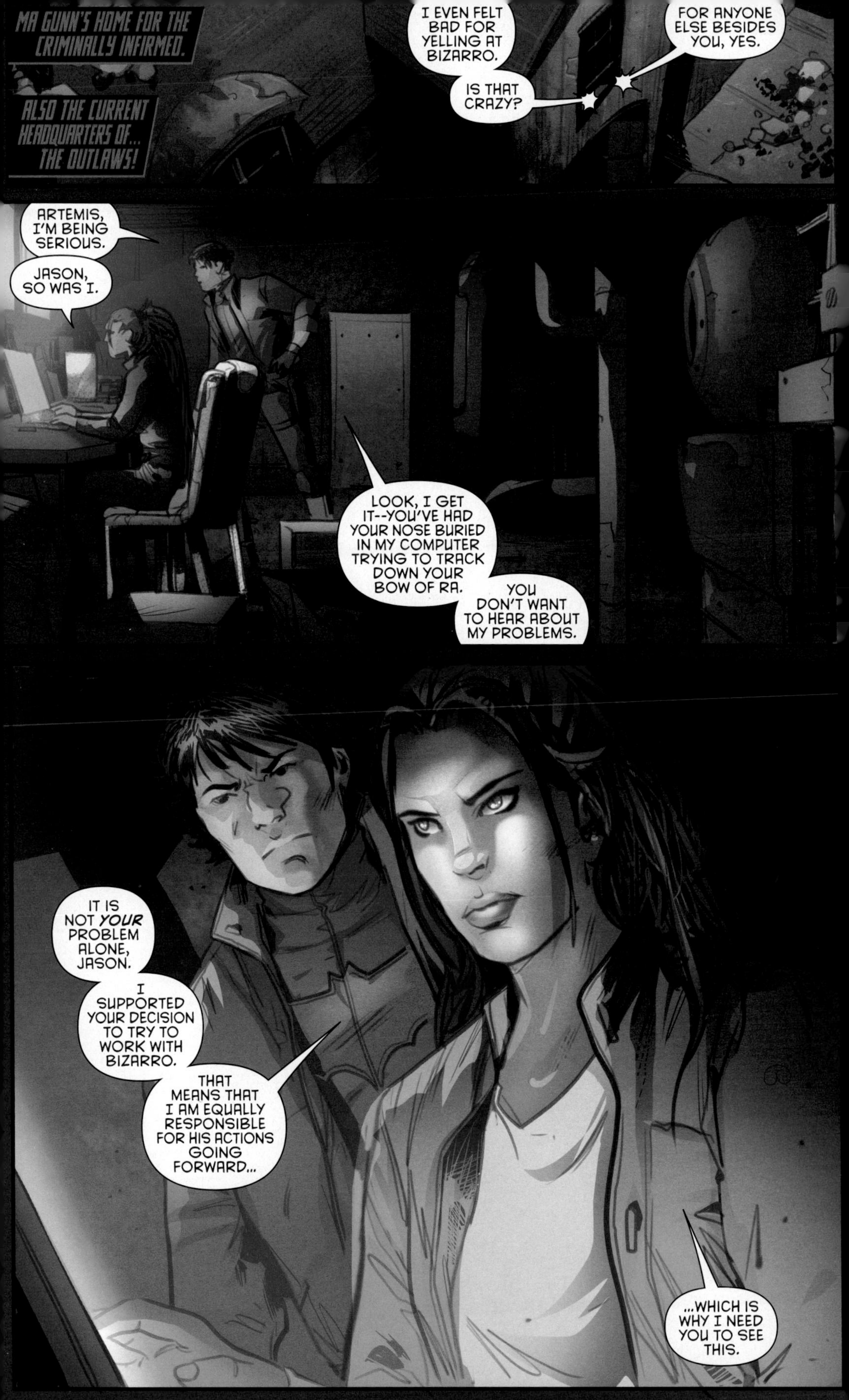
MA GUNN'S HOME FOR THE CRIMINALLY INFIRMED.
ALSO THE CURRENT HEADQUARTERS OF... THE OUTLAWS!
I EVEN FELT BAD FOR YELLING AT BIZARRO.
IS THAT CRAZY?
FOR ANYONE ELSE BESIDES YOU, YES.
ARTEMIS, I'M BEING SERIOUS.
JASON, SO WAS I.
LOOK, I GET IT--YOU'VE HAD YOUR NOSE BURIED IN MY COMPUTER TRYING TO TRACK DOWN YOUR BOW OF RA.
YOU DON'T WANT TO HEAR ABOUT MY PROBLEMS.
IT IS NOT *YOUR* PROBLEM ALONE, JASON.
I SUPPORTED YOUR DECISION TO TRY TO WORK WITH BIZARRO.
THAT MEANS THAT I AM EQUALLY RESPONSIBLE FOR HIS ACTIONS GOING FORWARD...
...WHICH IS WHY I NEED YOU TO SEE THIS.

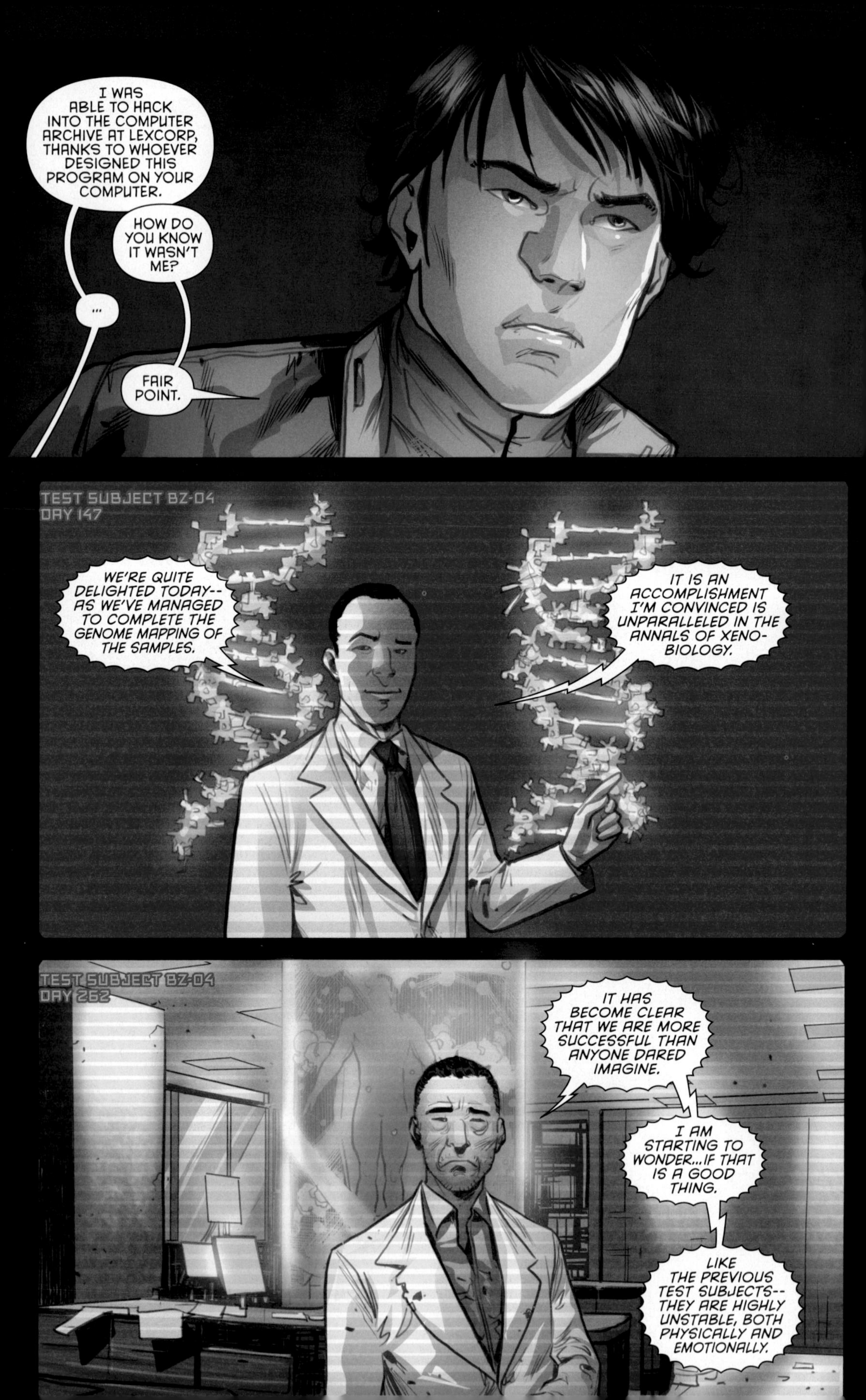
I WAS ABLE TO HACK INTO THE COMPUTER ARCHIVE AT LEXCORP, THANKS TO WHOEVER DESIGNED THIS PROGRAM ON YOUR COMPUTER.
HOW DO YOU KNOW IT WASN'T ME?
...
FAIR POINT.
TEST SUBJECT BZ-04
DAY 147
WE'RE QUITE DELIGHTED TODAY-- AS WE'VE MANAGED TO COMPLETE THE GENOME MAPPING OF THE SAMPLES.
IT IS AN ACCOMPLISHMENT I'M CONVINCED IS UNPARALLELED IN THE ANNALS OF XENO-BIOLOGY.
TEST SUBJECT BZ-04
DAY 262
IT HAS BECOME CLEAR THAT WE ARE MORE SUCCESSFUL THAN ANYONE DARED IMAGINE.
I AM STARTING TO WONDER...IF THAT IS A GOOD THING.
LIKE THE PREVIOUS TEST SUBJECTS-- THEY ARE HIGHLY UNSTABLE, BOTH PHYSICALLY AND EMOTIONALLY.

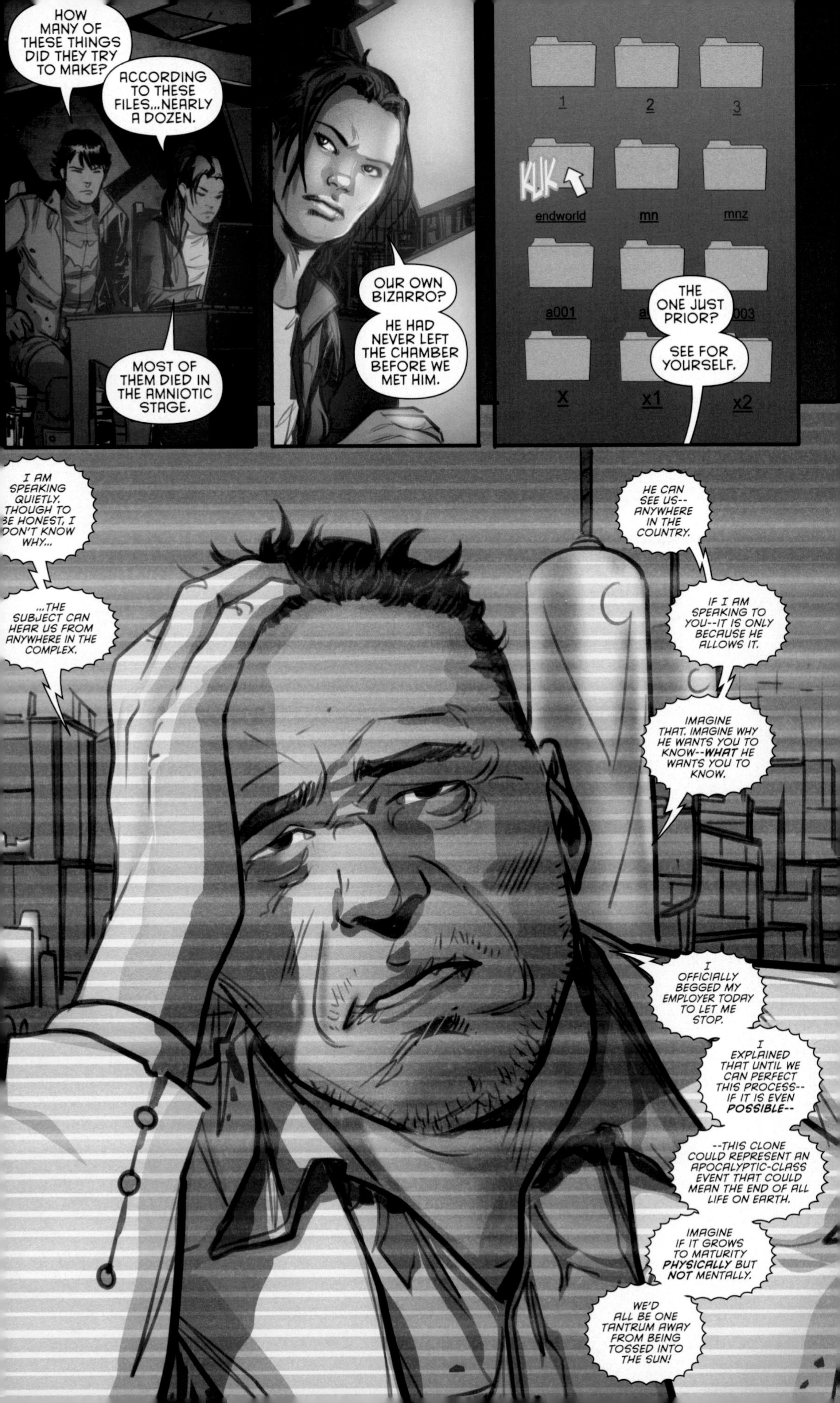
HOW MANY OF THESE THINGS DID THEY TRY TO MAKE?
ACCORDING TO THESE FILES...NEARLY A DOZEN.
MOST OF THEM DIED IN THE AMNIOTIC STAGE.
OUR OWN BIZARRO?
HE HAD NEVER LEFT THE CHAMBER BEFORE WE MET HIM.
1
2
3
KLIK
endworld
mn
mnz
a001
003
x
x1
x2
THE ONE JUST PRIOR?
SEE FOR YOURSELF.
I AM SPEAKING QUIETLY. THOUGH TO BE HONEST, I DON'T KNOW WHY...
...THE SUBJECT CAN HEAR US FROM ANYWHERE IN THE COMPLEX.
HE CAN SEE US--ANYWHERE IN THE COUNTRY.
IF I AM SPEAKING TO YOU--IT IS ONLY BECAUSE HE ALLOWS IT.
IMAGINE THAT. IMAGINE WHY HE WANTS YOU TO KNOW--WHAT HE WANTS YOU TO KNOW.
I OFFICIALLY BEGGED MY EMPLOYER TODAY TO LET ME STOP.
I EXPLAINED THAT UNTIL WE CAN PERFECT THIS PROCESS--IF IT IS EVEN POSSIBLE--
--THIS CLONE COULD REPRESENT AN APOCALYPTIC-CLASS EVENT THAT COULD MEAN THE END OF ALL LIFE ON EARTH.
IMAGINE IF IT GROWS TO MATURITY PHYSICALLY BUT NOT MENTALLY.
WE'D ALL BE ONE TANTRUM AWAY FROM BEING TOSSED INTO THE SUN!

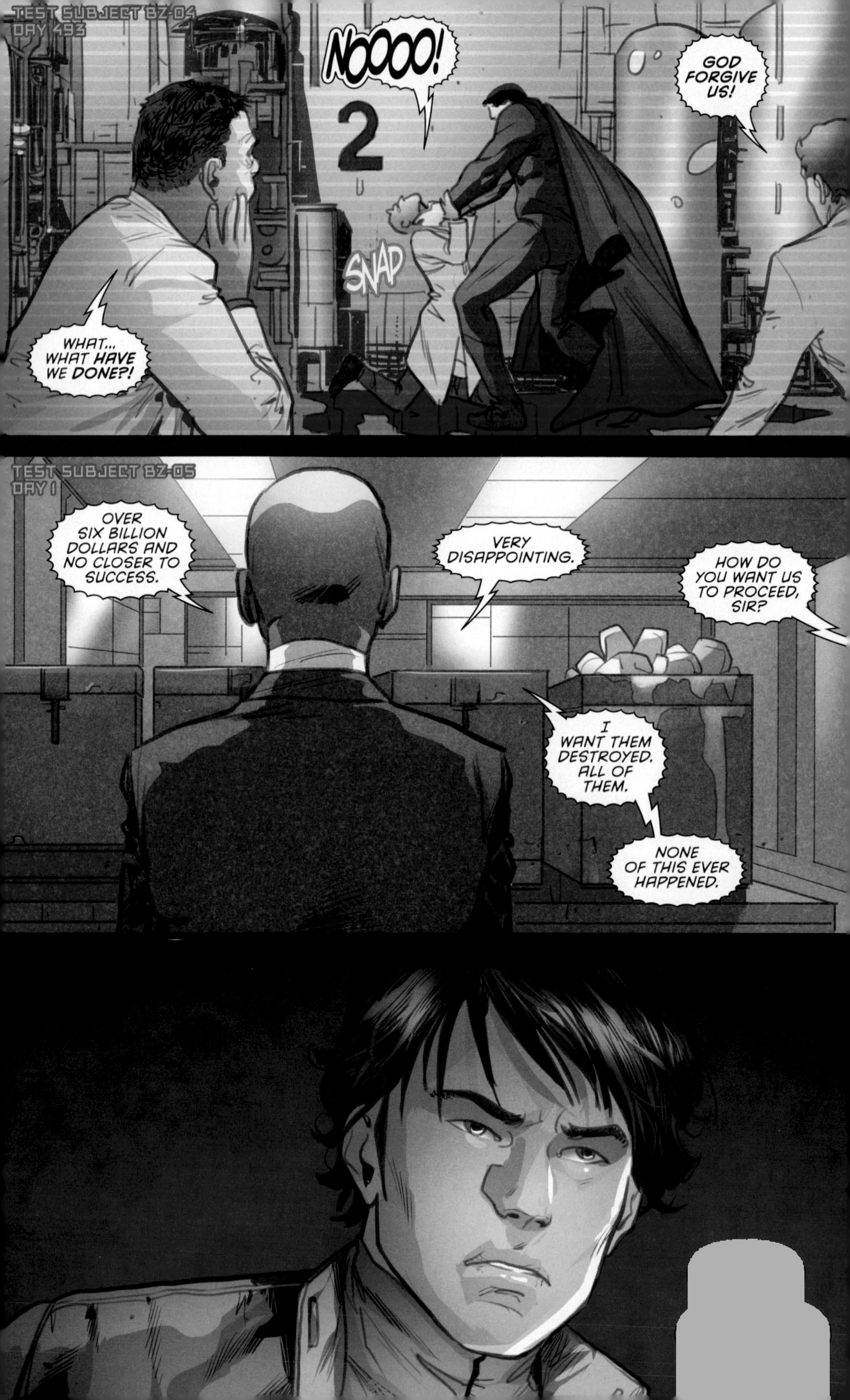
TEST SUBJECT BZ-04
DAY 493
NOOOO!
GOD FORGIVE US!
SNAP
WHAT... WHAT HAVE WE DONE?!
TEST SUBJECT BZ-05
DAY 1
OVER SIX BILLION DOLLARS AND NO CLOSER TO SUCCESS.
VERY DISAPPOINTING.
HOW DO YOU WANT US TO PROCEED, SIR?
I WANT THEM DESTROYED. ALL OF THEM.
NONE OF THIS EVER HAPPENED.

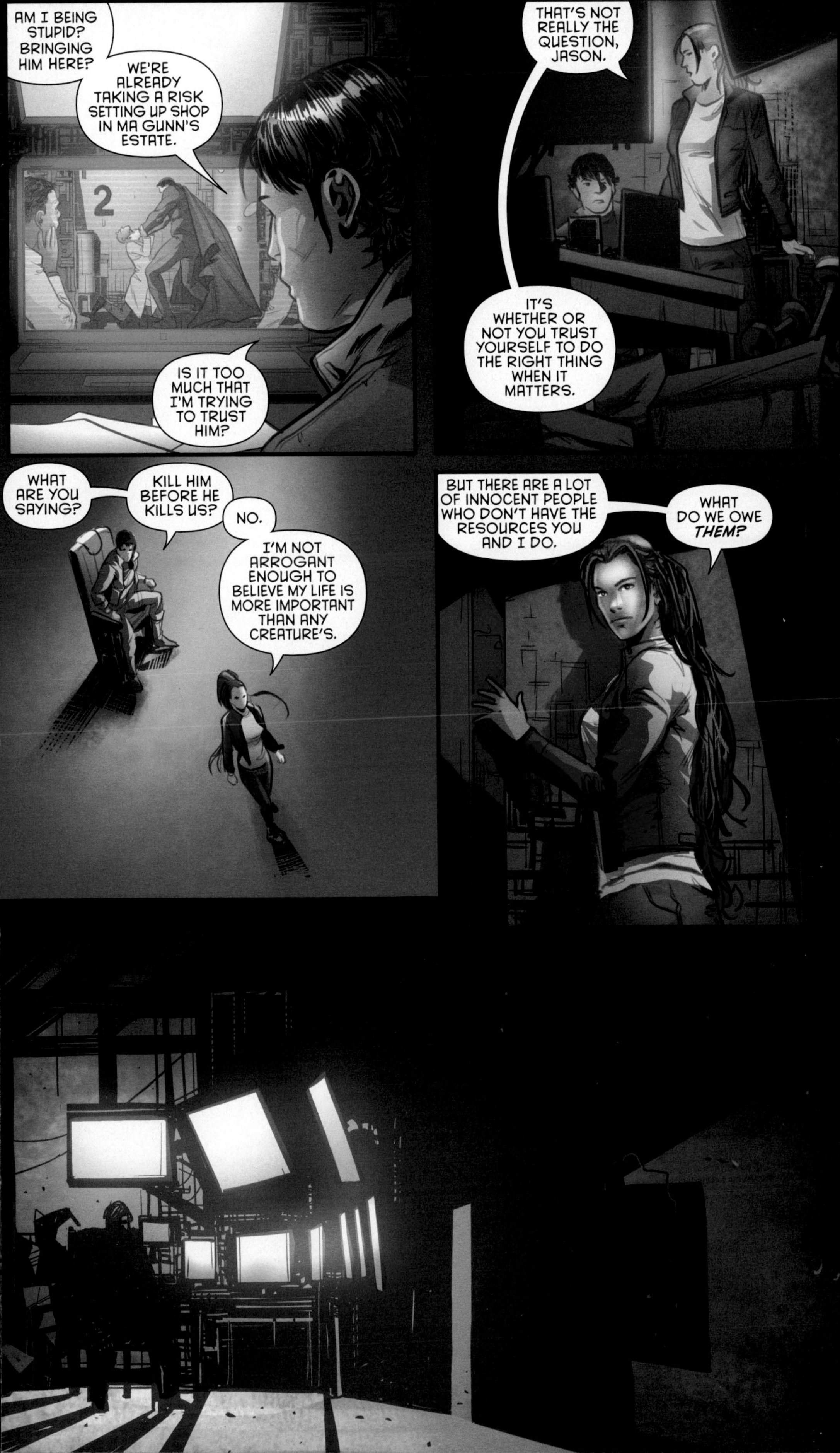
AM I BEING STUPID? BRINGING HIM HERE?
WE'RE ALREADY TAKING A RISK SETTING UP SHOP IN MA GUNN'S ESTATE.
IS IT TOO MUCH THAT I'M TRYING TO TRUST HIM?
THAT'S NOT REALLY THE QUESTION, JASON.
IT'S WHETHER OR NOT YOU TRUST YOURSELF TO DO THE RIGHT THING WHEN IT MATTERS.
WHAT ARE YOU SAYING?
KILL HIM BEFORE HE KILLS US?
NO.
I'M NOT ARROGANT ENOUGH TO BELIEVE MY LIFE IS MORE IMPORTANT THAN ANY CREATURE'S.
BUT THERE ARE A LOT OF INNOCENT PEOPLE WHO DON'T HAVE THE RESOURCES YOU AND I DO.
WHAT DO WE OWE *THEM?*

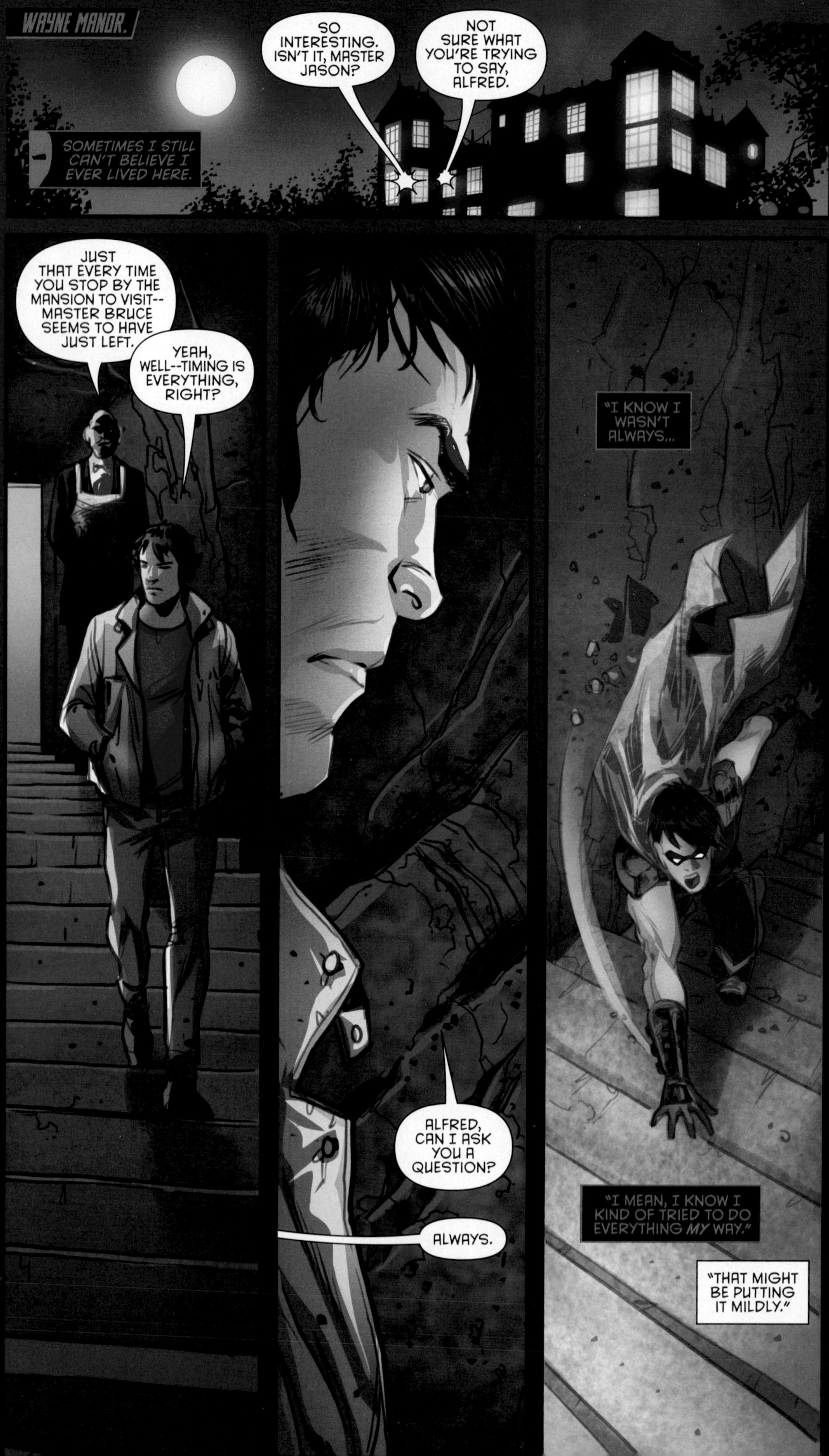
WAYNE MANOR.
SOMETIMES I STILL CAN'T BELIEVE I EVER LIVED HERE.
SO INTERESTING. ISN'T IT, MASTER JASON?
NOT SURE WHAT YOU'RE TRYING TO SAY, ALFRED.
JUST THAT EVERY TIME YOU STOP BY THE MANSION TO VISIT--MASTER BRUCE SEEMS TO HAVE JUST LEFT.
YEAH, WELL--TIMING IS EVERYTHING, RIGHT?
ALFRED, CAN I ASK YOU A QUESTION?
ALWAYS.
"I KNOW I WASN'T ALWAYS...
"I MEAN, I KNOW I KIND OF TRIED TO DO EVERYTHING *MY* WAY."
"THAT MIGHT BE PUTTING IT MILDLY."

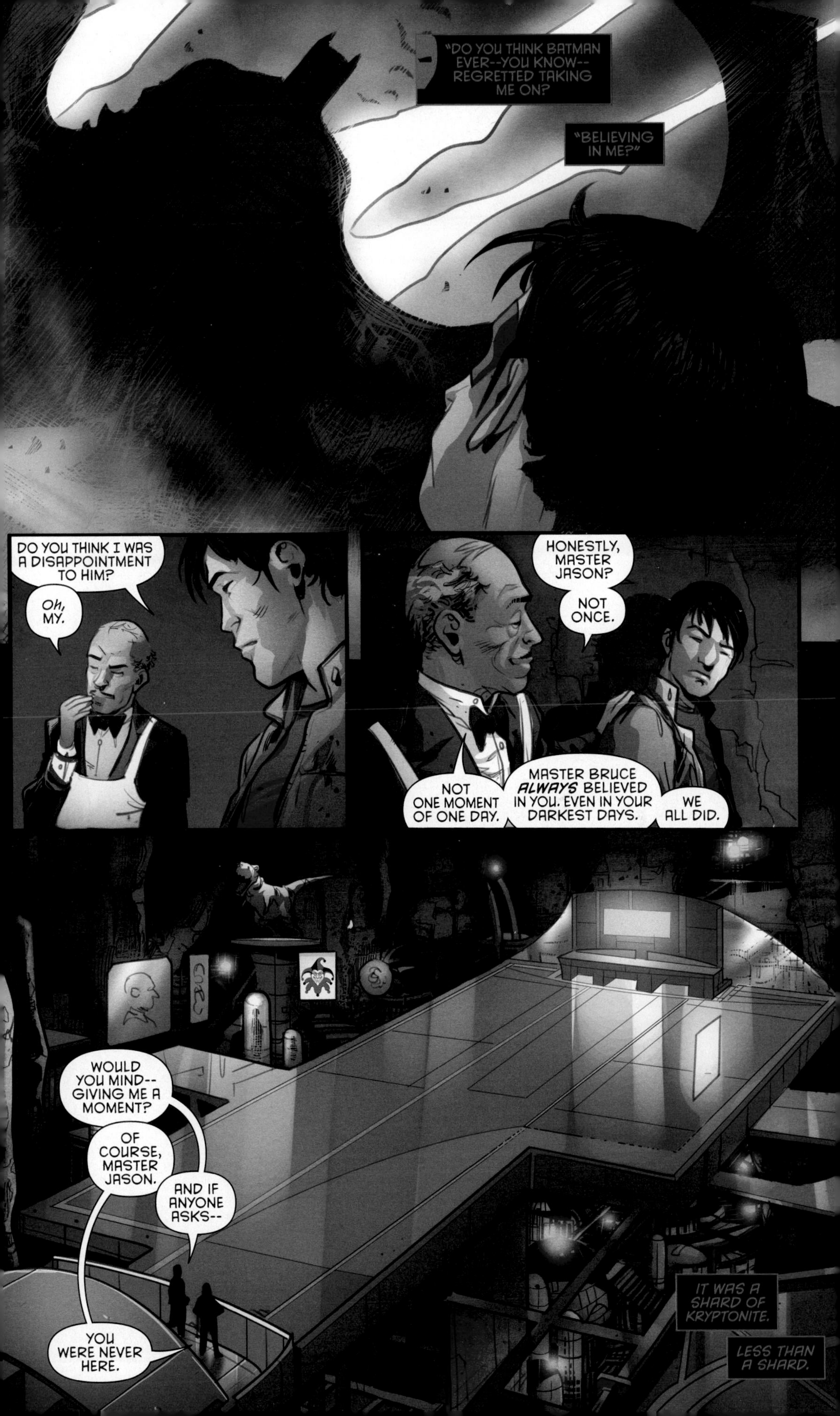
"DO YOU THINK BATMAN EVER--YOU KNOW--REGRETTED TAKING ME ON?
"BELIEVING IN ME?"
DO YOU THINK I WAS A DISAPPOINTMENT TO HIM?
Oh, MY.
HONESTLY, MASTER JASON?
NOT ONCE.
NOT ONE MOMENT OF ONE DAY.
MASTER BRUCE ALWAYS BELIEVED IN YOU. EVEN IN YOUR DARKEST DAYS.
WE ALL DID.
WOULD YOU MIND--GIVING ME A MOMENT?
OF COURSE, MASTER JASON.
AND IF ANYONE ASKS--
YOU WERE NEVER HERE.
IT WAS A SHARD OF KRYPTONITE.
LESS THAN A SHARD.

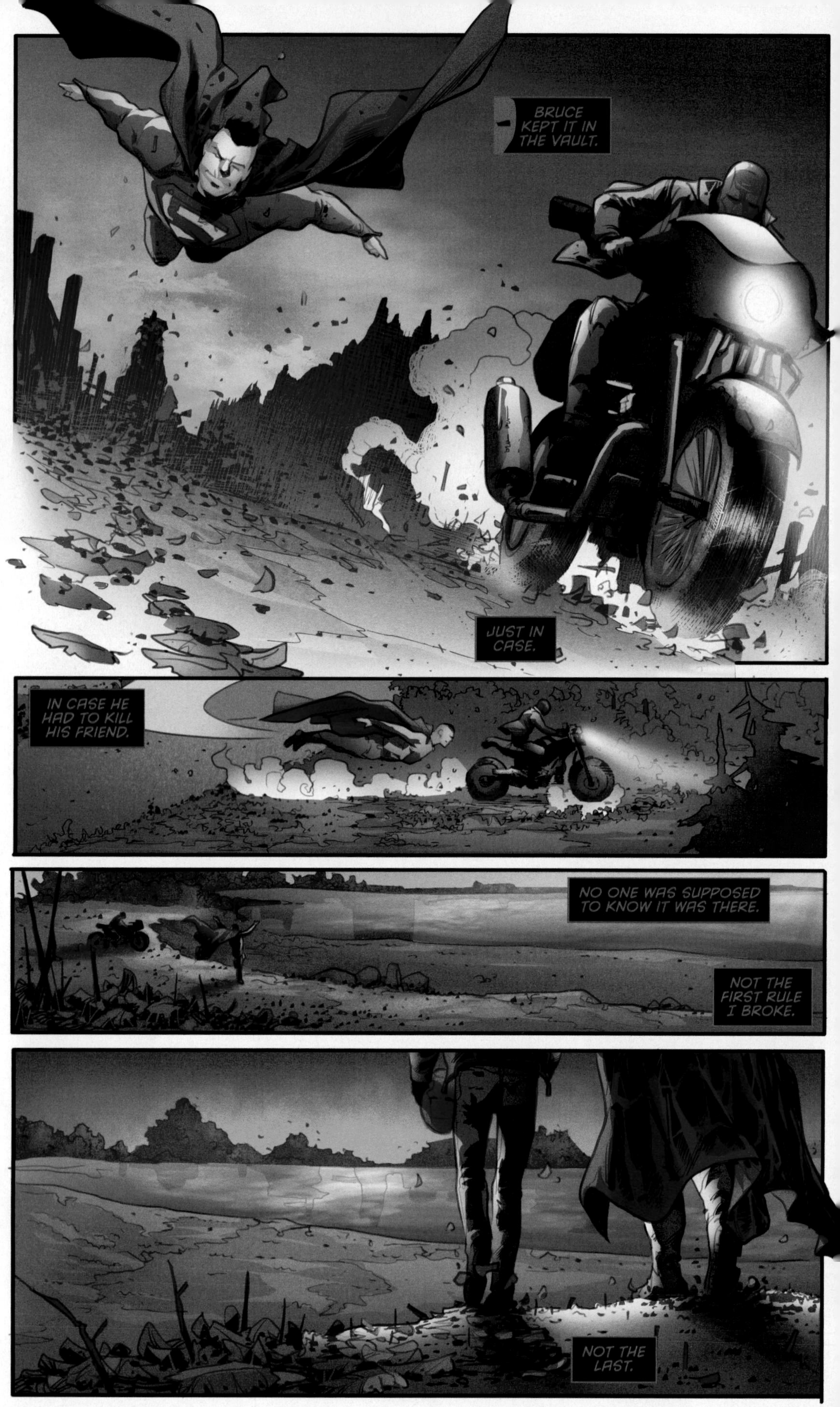
BRUCE KEPT IT IN THE VAULT.
JUST IN CASE.
IN CASE HE HAD TO KILL HIS FRIEND.
NO ONE WAS SUPPOSED TO KNOW IT WAS THERE.
NOT THE FIRST RULE I BROKE.
NOT THE LAST.

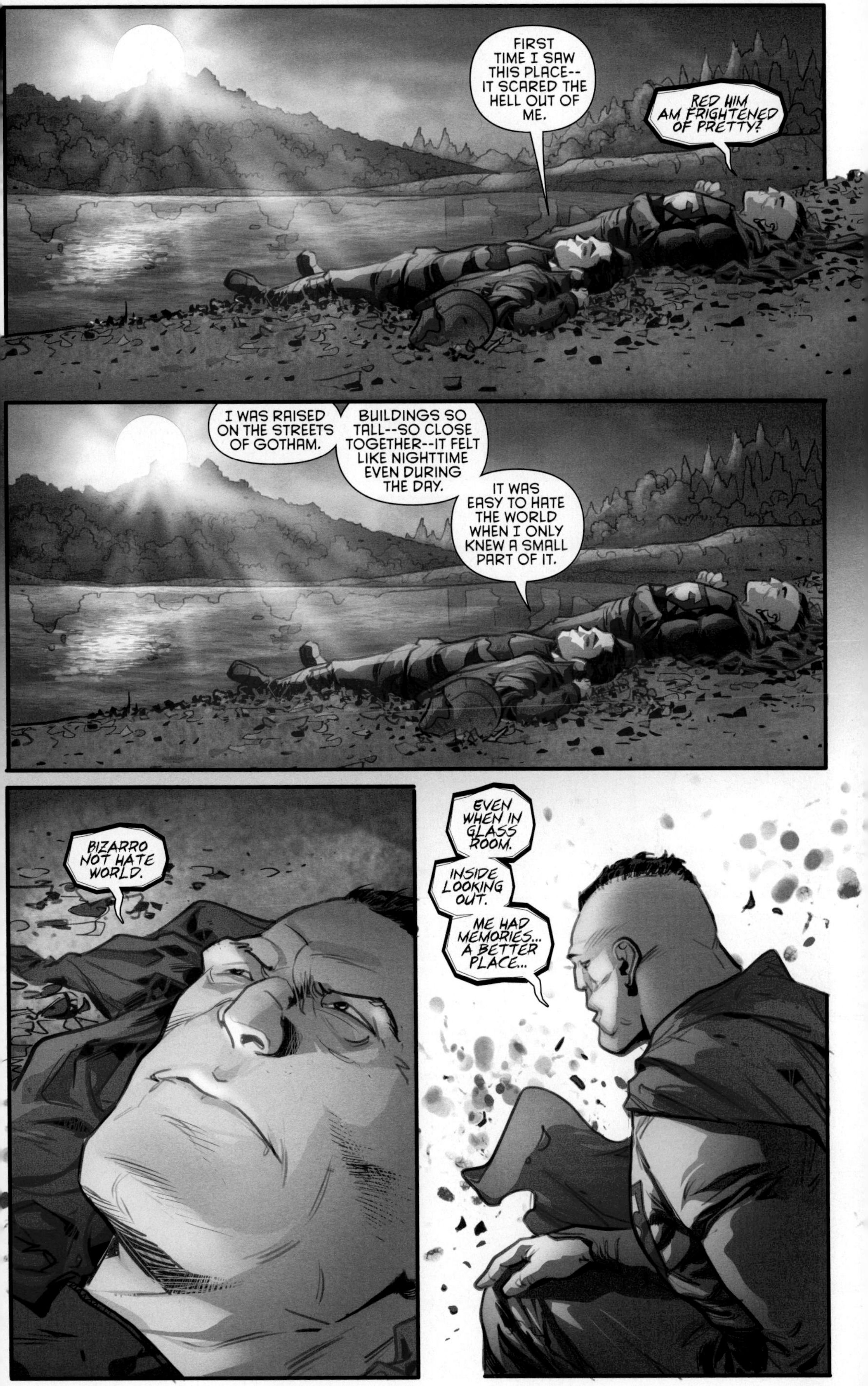
FIRST TIME I SAW THIS PLACE--IT SCARED THE HELL OUT OF ME.
RED HIM AM FRIGHTENED OF PRETTY?
I WAS RAISED ON THE STREETS OF GOTHAM.
BUILDINGS SO TALL--SO CLOSE TOGETHER--IT FELT LIKE NIGHTTIME EVEN DURING THE DAY.
IT WAS EASY TO HATE THE WORLD WHEN I ONLY KNEW A SMALL PART OF IT.
BIZARRO NOT HATE WORLD.
EVEN WHEN IN GLASS ROOM.
INSIDE LOOKING OUT.
ME HAD MEMORIES... A BETTER PLACE...

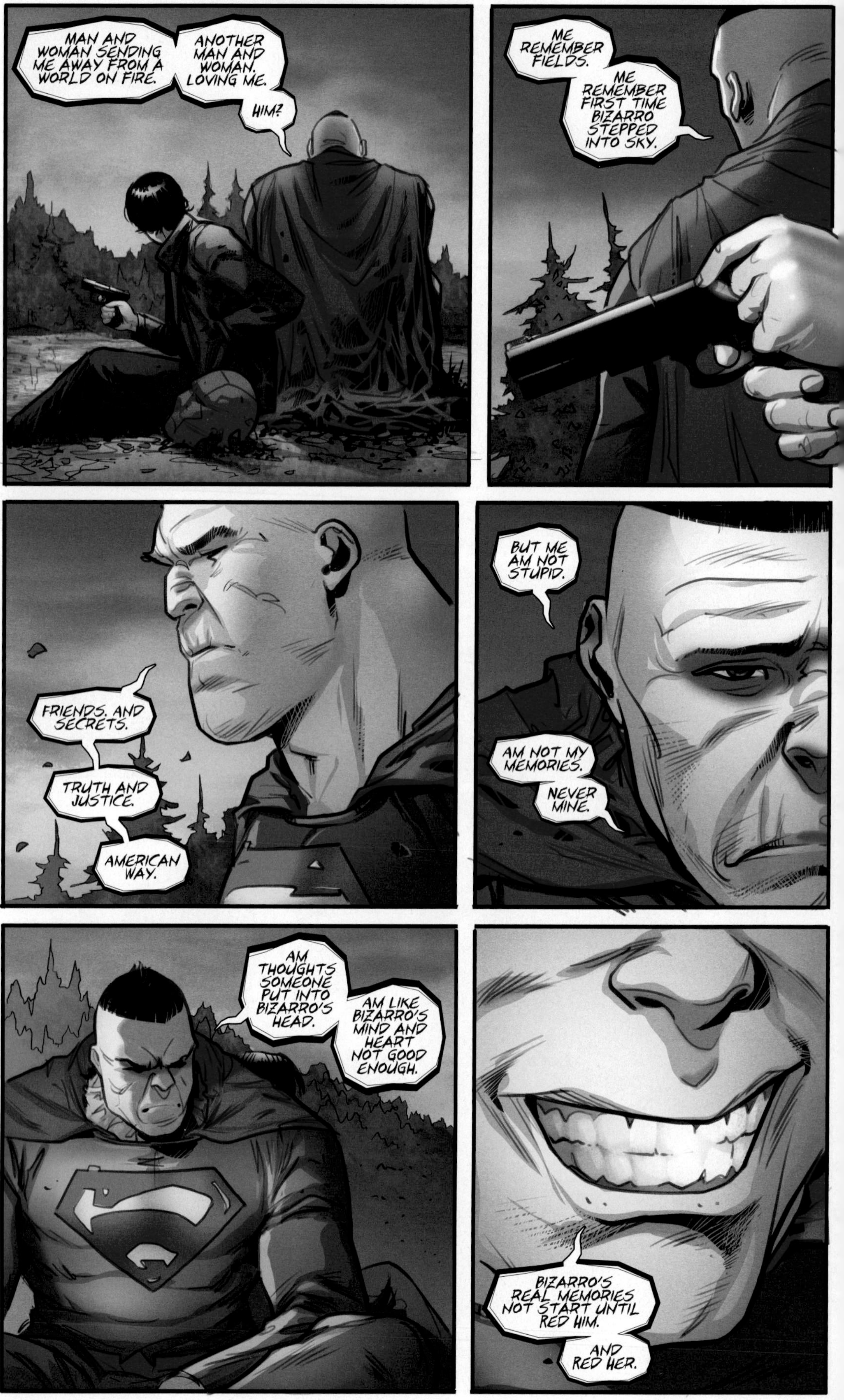
MAN AND WOMAN SENDING ME AWAY FROM A WORLD ON FIRE.
ANOTHER MAN AND WOMAN. LOVING ME.
HIM?
ME REMEMBER FIELDS.
ME REMEMBER FIRST TIME BIZARRO STEPPED INTO SKY.
FRIENDS. AND SECRETS.
TRUTH AND JUSTICE.
AMERICAN WAY.
BUT ME AM NOT STUPID.
AM NOT MY MEMORIES.
NEVER MINE.
AM THOUGHTS SOMEONE PUT INTO BIZARRO'S HEAD.
AM LIKE BIZARRO'S MIND AND HEART NOT GOOD ENOUGH.
BIZARRO'S REAL MEMORIES NOT START UNTIL RED HIM.
AND RED HER.

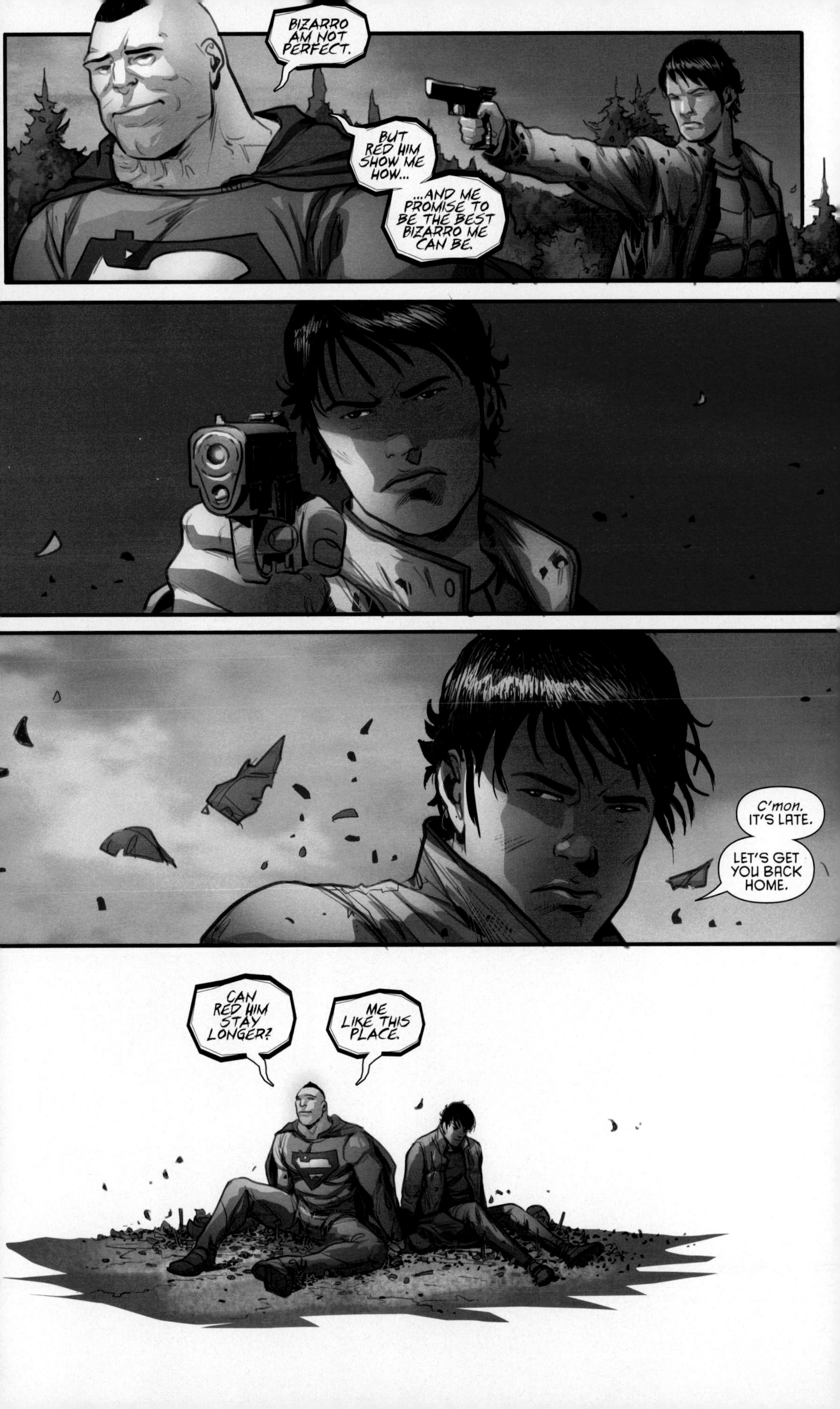
BIZARRO AM NOT PERFECT.
BUT RED HIM SHOW ME HOW...
...AND ME PROMISE TO BE THE BEST BIZARRO ME CAN BE.
C'mon. IT'S LATE.
LET'S GET YOU BACK HOME.
CAN RED HIM STAY LONGER?
ME LIKE THIS PLACE.

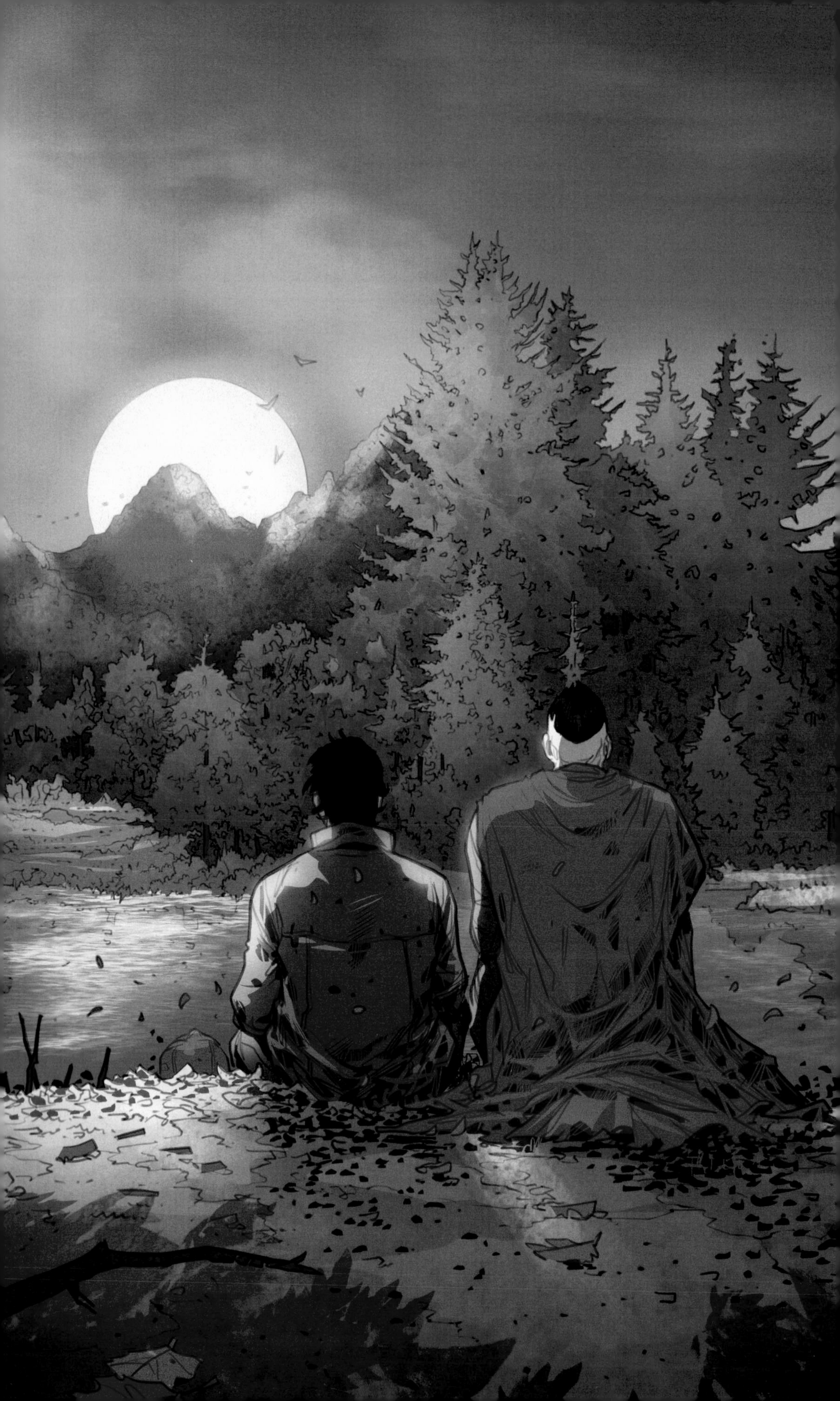

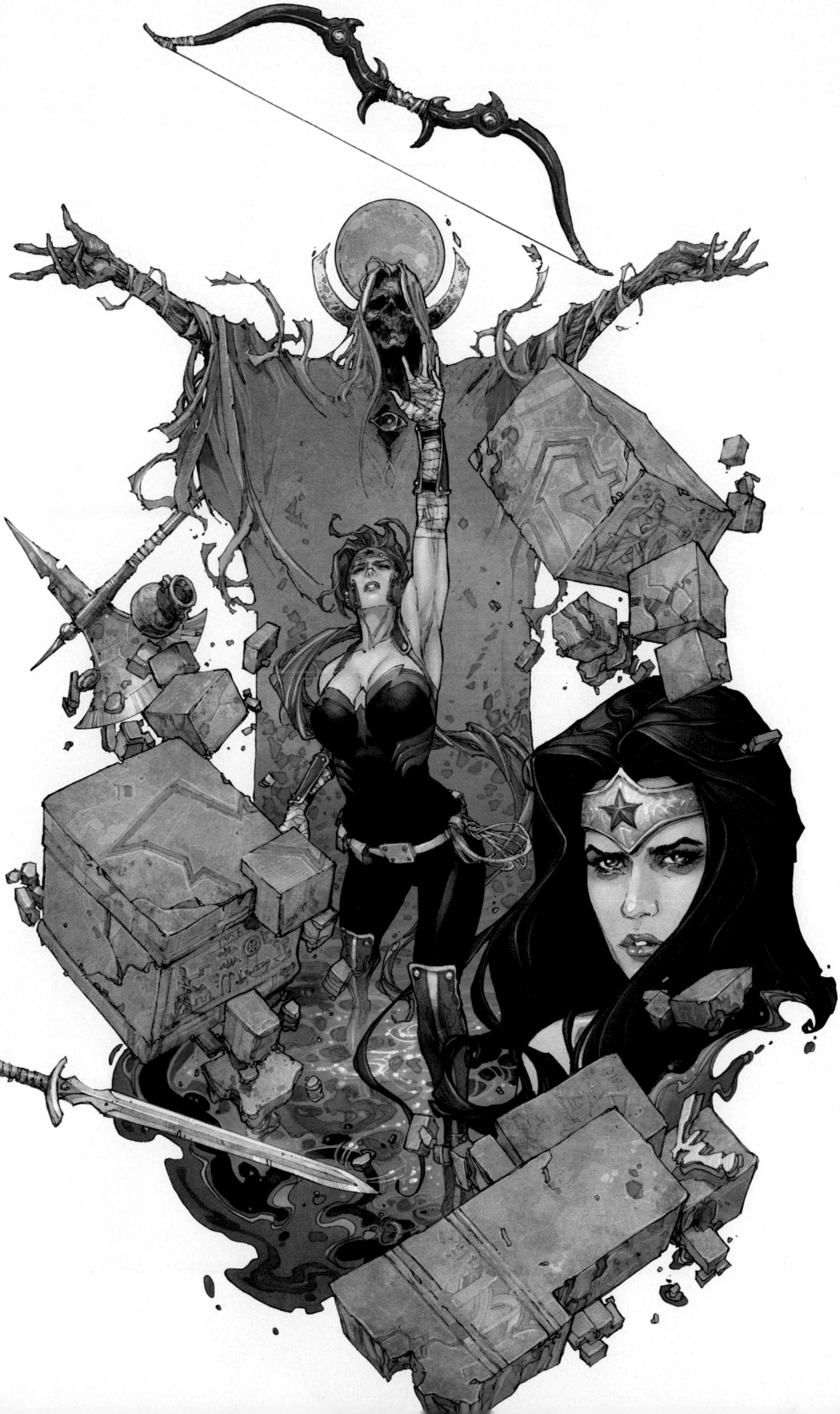

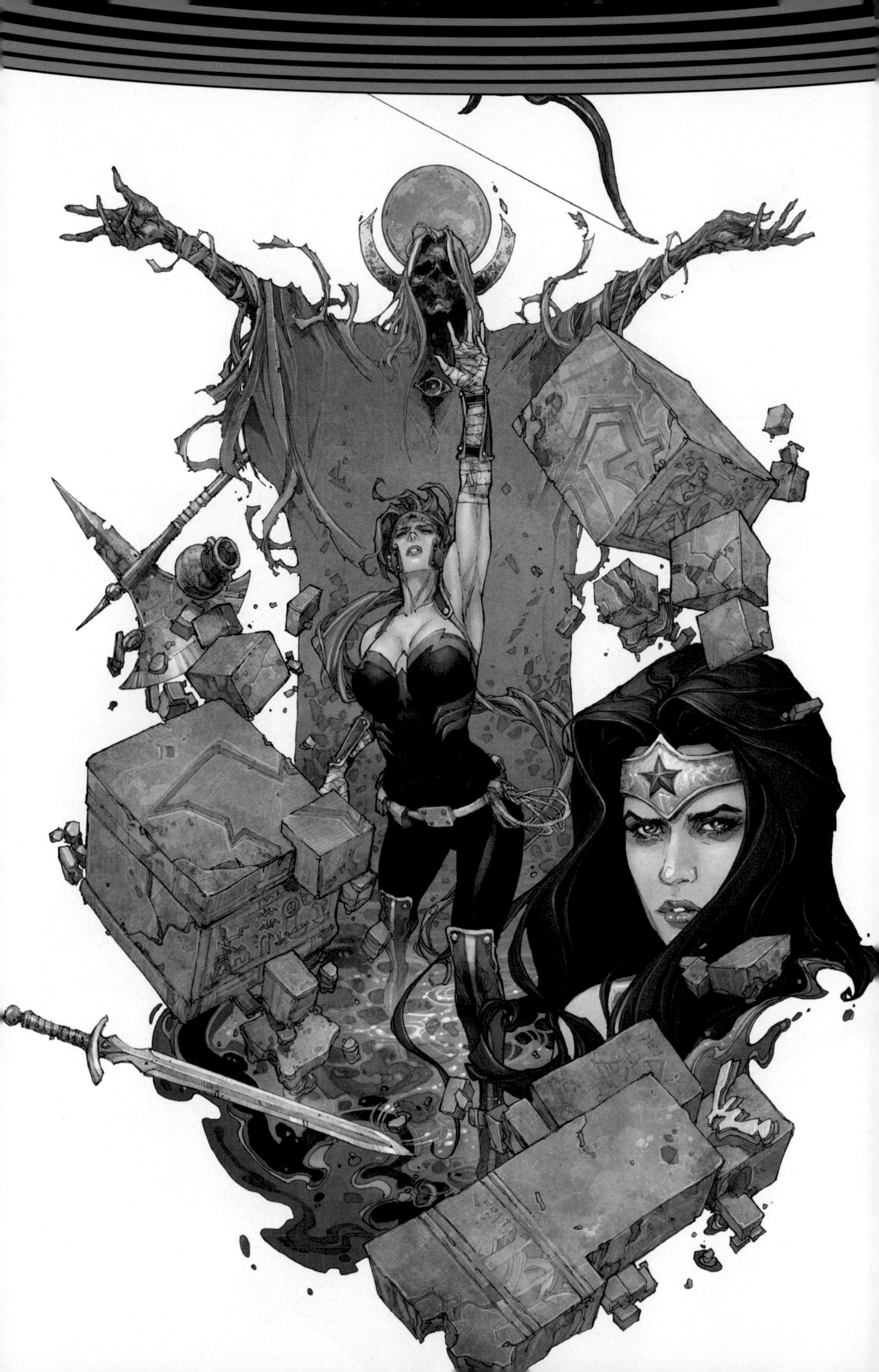

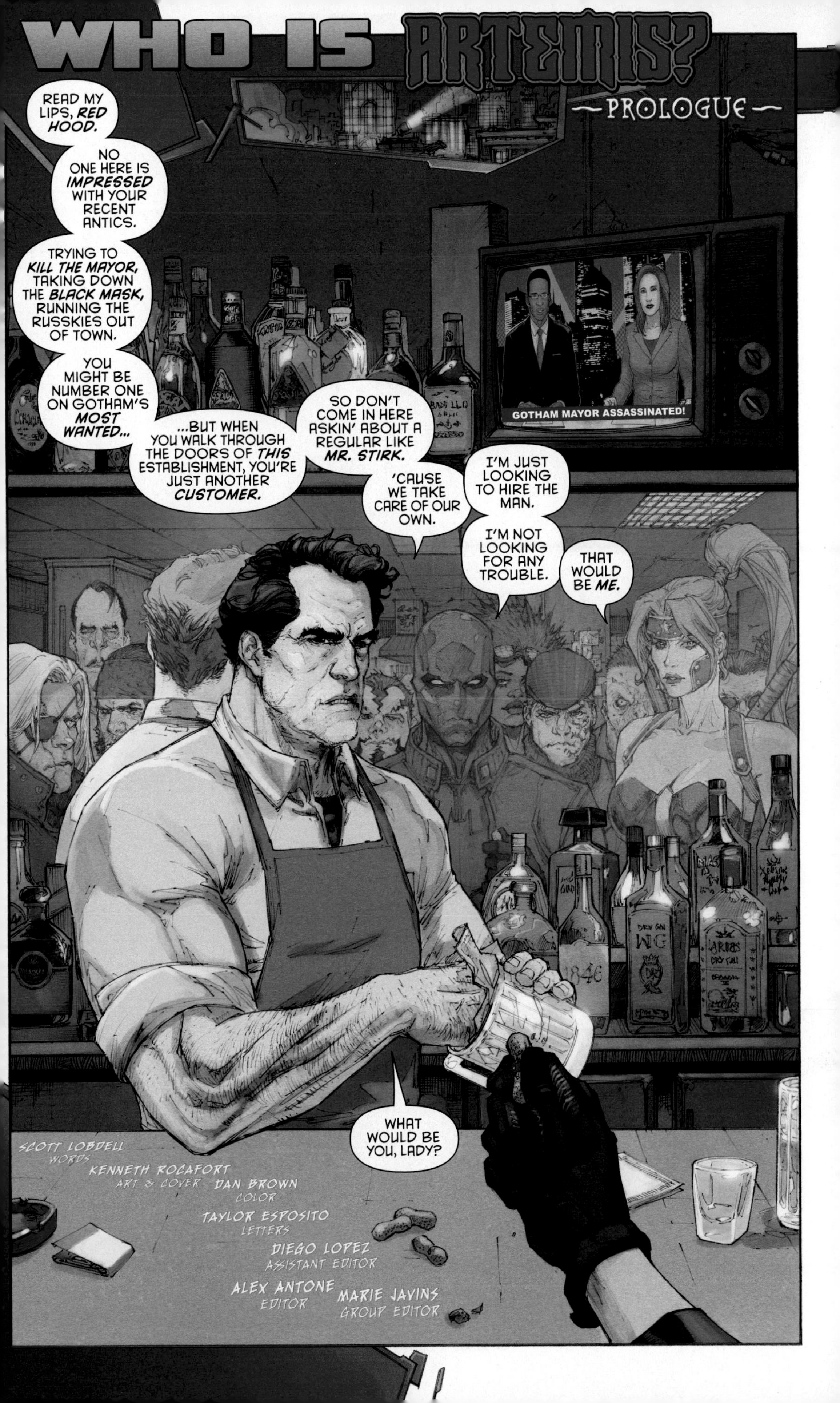

WHO IS ARTEMIS?
—PROLOGUE—
READ MY LIPS, RED HOOD.
NO ONE HERE IS IMPRESSED WITH YOUR RECENT ANTICS.
TRYING TO KILL THE MAYOR, TAKING DOWN THE BLACK MASK, RUNNING THE RUSSKIES OUT OF TOWN.
YOU MIGHT BE NUMBER ONE ON GOTHAM'S MOST WANTED...
...BUT WHEN YOU WALK THROUGH THE DOORS OF THIS ESTABLISHMENT, YOU'RE JUST ANOTHER CUSTOMER.
SO DON'T COME IN HERE ASKIN' ABOUT A REGULAR LIKE MR. STIRK.
'CAUSE WE TAKE CARE OF OUR OWN.
GOTHAM MAYOR ASSASSINATED!
I'M JUST LOOKING TO HIRE THE MAN.
I'M NOT LOOKING FOR ANY TROUBLE.
THAT WOULD BE ME.
WHAT WOULD BE YOU, LADY?
SCOTT LOBDELL WORDS
KENNETH ROCAFORT ART & COVER
DAN BROWN COLOR
TAYLOR ESPOSITO LETTERS
DIEGO LOPEZ ASSISTANT EDITOR
ALEX ANTONE EDITOR
MARIE JAVINS GROUP EDITOR

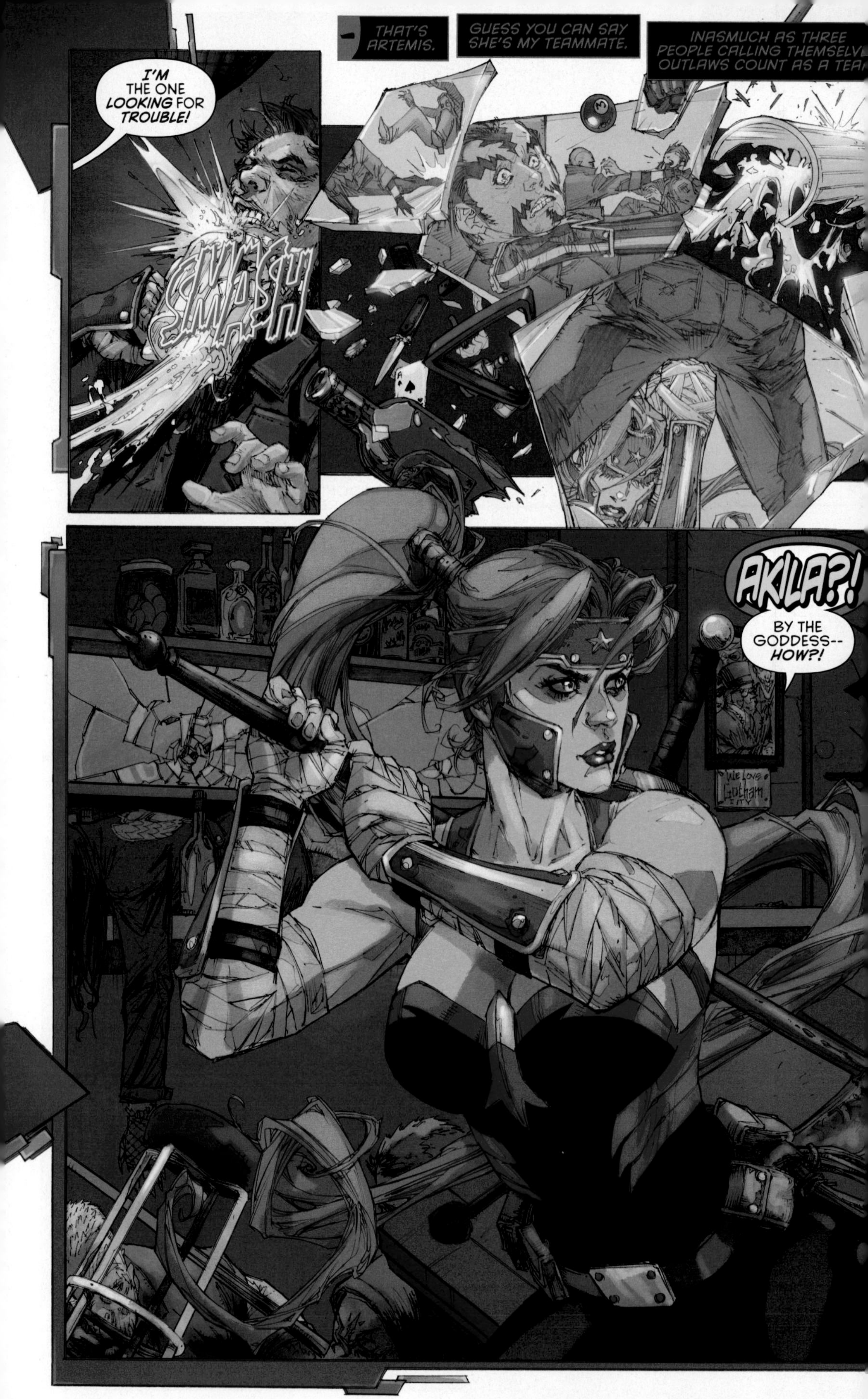
I'M THE ONE LOOKING FOR TROUBLE!
SMASH
THAT'S ARTEMIS.
GUESS YOU CAN SAY SHE'S MY TEAMMATE.
INASMUCH AS THREE PEOPLE CALLING THEMSELV OUTLAWS COUNT AS A TEA
AKILA?!
BY THE GODDESS-- HOW?!
WE LOVE Gotham CITY

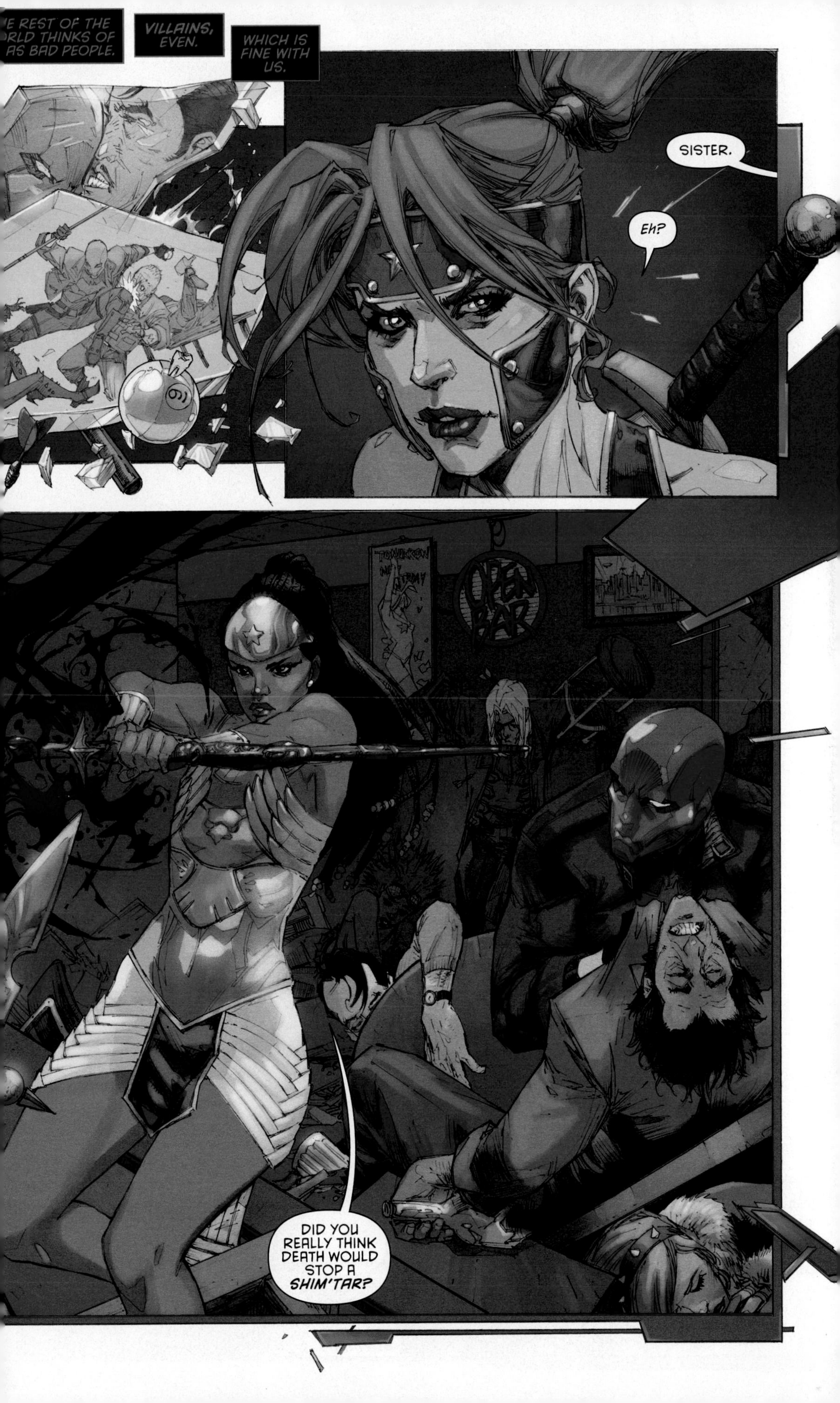
E REST OF THE
RLD THINKS OF
AS BAD PEOPLE.
VILLAINS, EVEN.
WHICH IS FINE WITH US.
SISTER.
Eh?
DID YOU REALLY THINK DEATH WOULD STOP A SHIM'TAR?

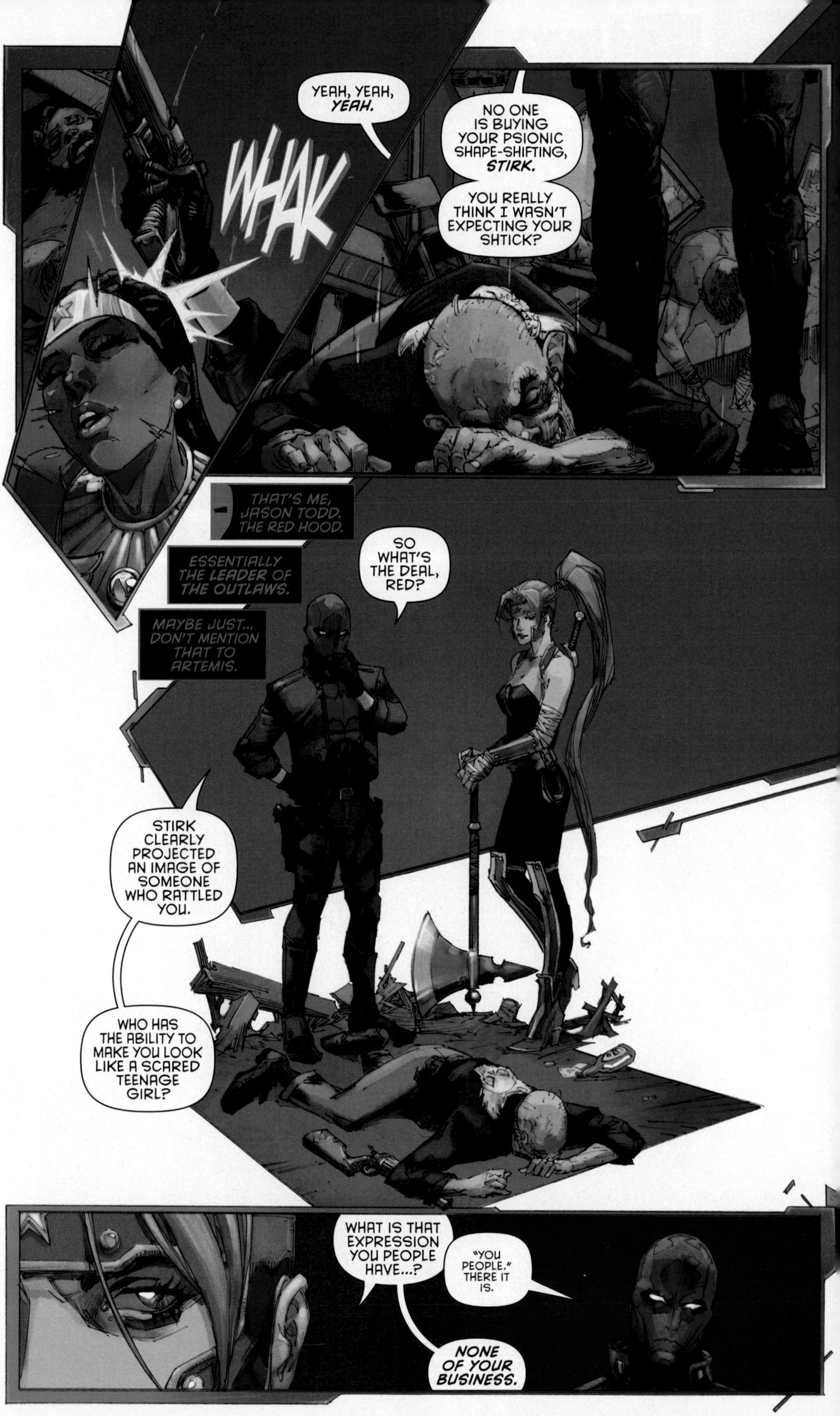
WHAK
YEAH, YEAH, YEAH.
NO ONE IS BUYING YOUR PSIONIC SHAPE-SHIFTING, STIRK.
YOU REALLY THINK I WASN'T EXPECTING YOUR SHTICK?
THAT'S ME, JASON TODD. THE RED HOOD.
ESSENTIALLY THE LEADER OF THE OUTLAWS.
MAYBE JUST... DON'T MENTION THAT TO ARTEMIS.
SO WHAT'S THE DEAL, RED?
STIRK CLEARLY PROJECTED AN IMAGE OF SOMEONE WHO RATTLED YOU.
WHO HAS THE ABILITY TO MAKE YOU LOOK LIKE A SCARED TEENAGE GIRL?
WHAT IS THAT EXPRESSION YOU PEOPLE HAVE...?
"YOU PEOPLE." THERE IT IS.
NONE OF YOUR BUSINESS.

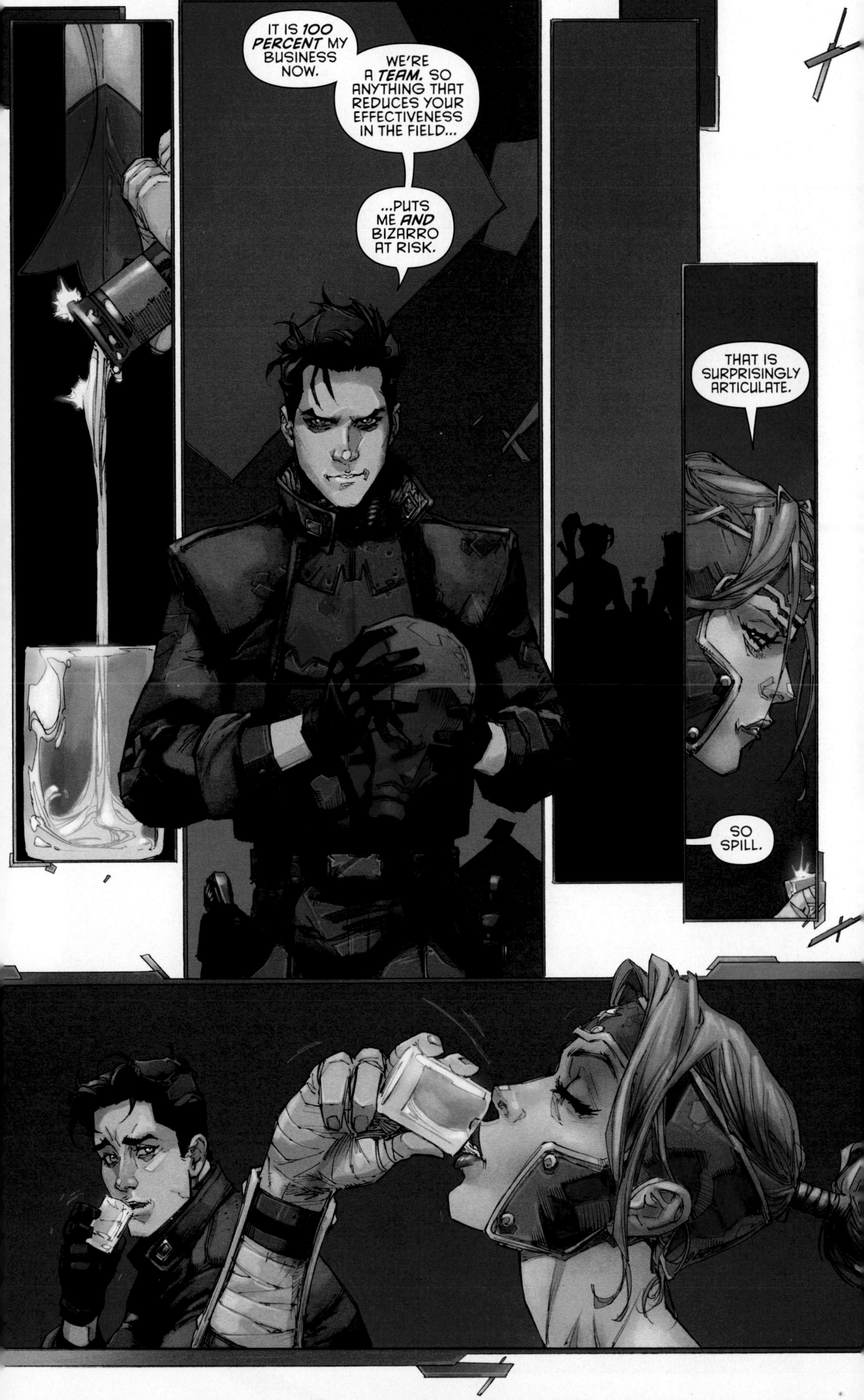
IT IS 100 PERCENT MY BUSINESS NOW.
WE'RE A TEAM. SO ANYTHING THAT REDUCES YOUR EFFECTIVENESS IN THE FIELD...
...PUTS ME AND BIZARRO AT RISK.
THAT IS SURPRISINGLY ARTICULATE.
SO SPILL.

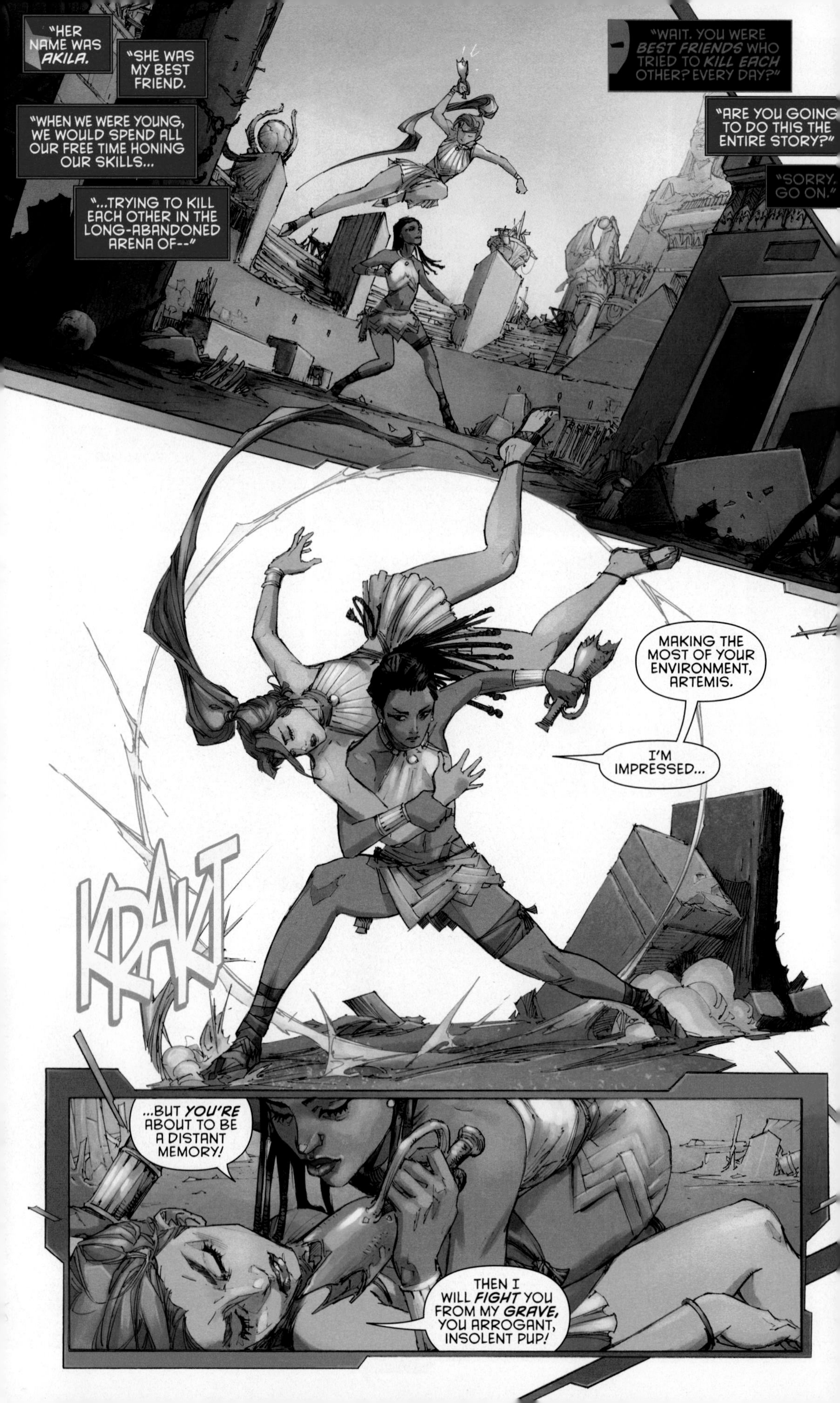
"HER NAME WAS AKILA.
"SHE WAS MY BEST FRIEND.
"WHEN WE WERE YOUNG, WE WOULD SPEND ALL OUR FREE TIME HONING OUR SKILLS...
"...TRYING TO KILL EACH OTHER IN THE LONG-ABANDONED ARENA OF--"
"WAIT. YOU WERE BEST FRIENDS WHO TRIED TO KILL EACH OTHER? EVERY DAY?"
"ARE YOU GOING TO DO THIS THE ENTIRE STORY?"
"SORRY. GO ON."
MAKING THE MOST OF YOUR ENVIRONMENT, ARTEMIS.
I'M IMPRESSED...
KRAKT
...BUT YOU'RE ABOUT TO BE A DISTANT MEMORY!
THEN I WILL FIGHT YOU FROM MY GRAVE, YOU ARROGANT, INSOLENT PUP!

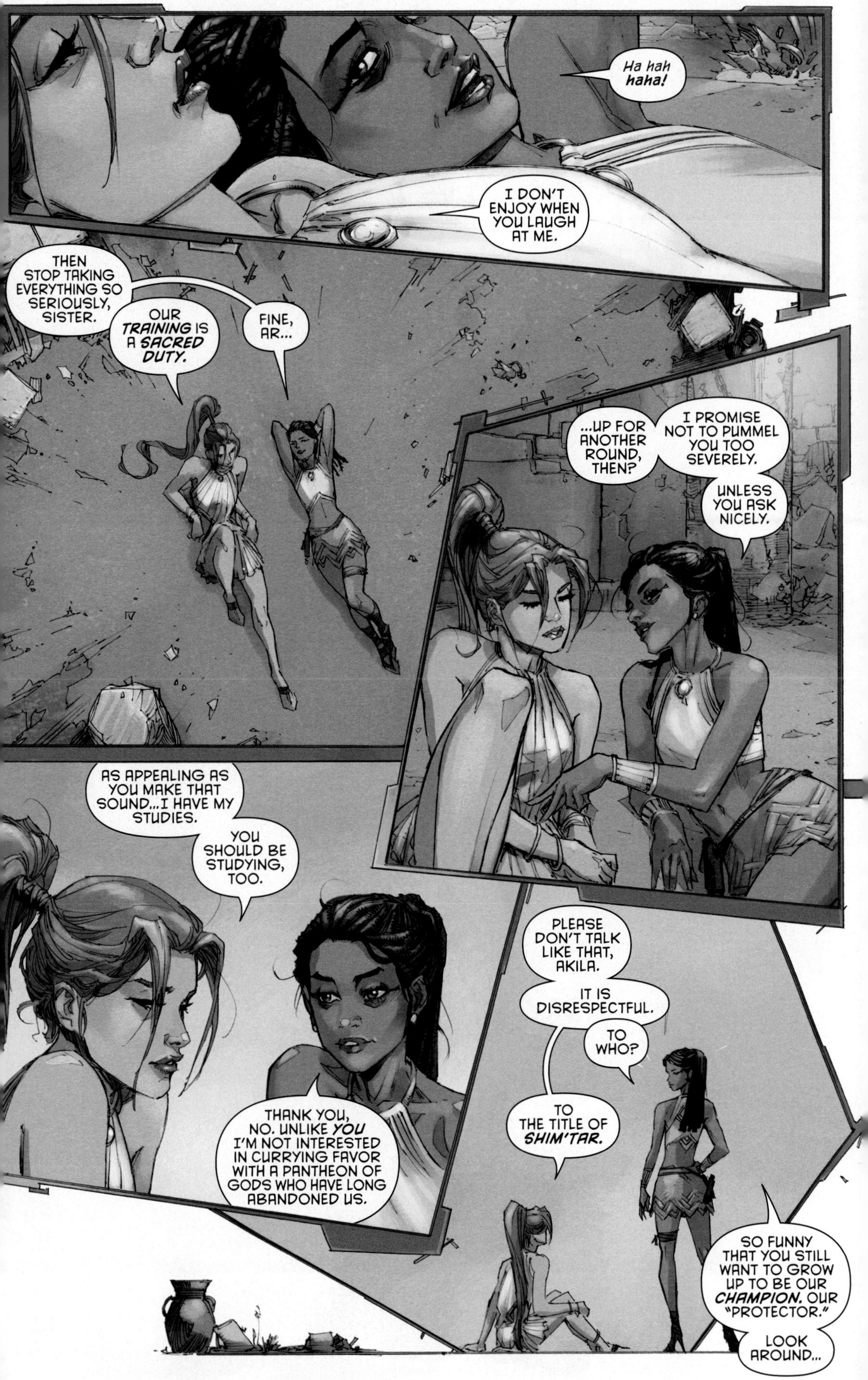

Ha hah haha!
I DON'T ENJOY WHEN YOU LAUGH AT ME.
THEN STOP TAKING EVERYTHING SO SERIOUSLY, SISTER.
OUR *TRAINING* IS A *SACRED DUTY.*
FINE, AR...
...UP FOR ANOTHER ROUND, THEN?
I PROMISE NOT TO PUMMEL YOU TOO SEVERELY.
UNLESS YOU ASK NICELY.
AS APPEALING AS YOU MAKE THAT SOUND...I HAVE MY STUDIES.
YOU SHOULD BE STUDYING, TOO.
THANK YOU, NO. UNLIKE *YOU* I'M NOT INTERESTED IN CURRYING FAVOR WITH A PANTHEON OF GODS WHO HAVE LONG ABANDONED US.
PLEASE DON'T TALK LIKE THAT, AKILA.
IT IS DISRESPECTFUL.
TO WHO?
TO THE TITLE OF *SHIM'TAR.*
SO FUNNY THAT YOU STILL WANT TO GROW UP TO BE OUR *CHAMPION.* OUR "PROTECTOR."
LOOK AROUND...

...WHAT EXACTLY DO YOU THINK YOU'RE GOING TO PROTECT?
A FAILED COLONY OF WARRIOR WOMEN ENSCONCED BEHIND A MYSTICAL SANDSTORM?
THAT'S SOMETHING YOU PLAN TO DEDICATE YOUR LIFE TO PRESERVING?
BANA-MIGHDALL WILL RISE AGAIN, AKILA.
THE SHIM'TAR NEEDS TO BE READY.
AND YES, WHILE THERE IS NOTHING I WANT MORE...
...I KNOW IN MY HEART THE GODS WILL CHOOSE YOU, SISTER--THE BEST AMONG US.
I DON'T WANT THE THINGS YOU WANT, AR.
IF I HAVE TO DO THIS--I DON'T WANT TO DO IT ALONE...
...I DON'T WANT TO DO ANYTHING WITHOUT YOU.

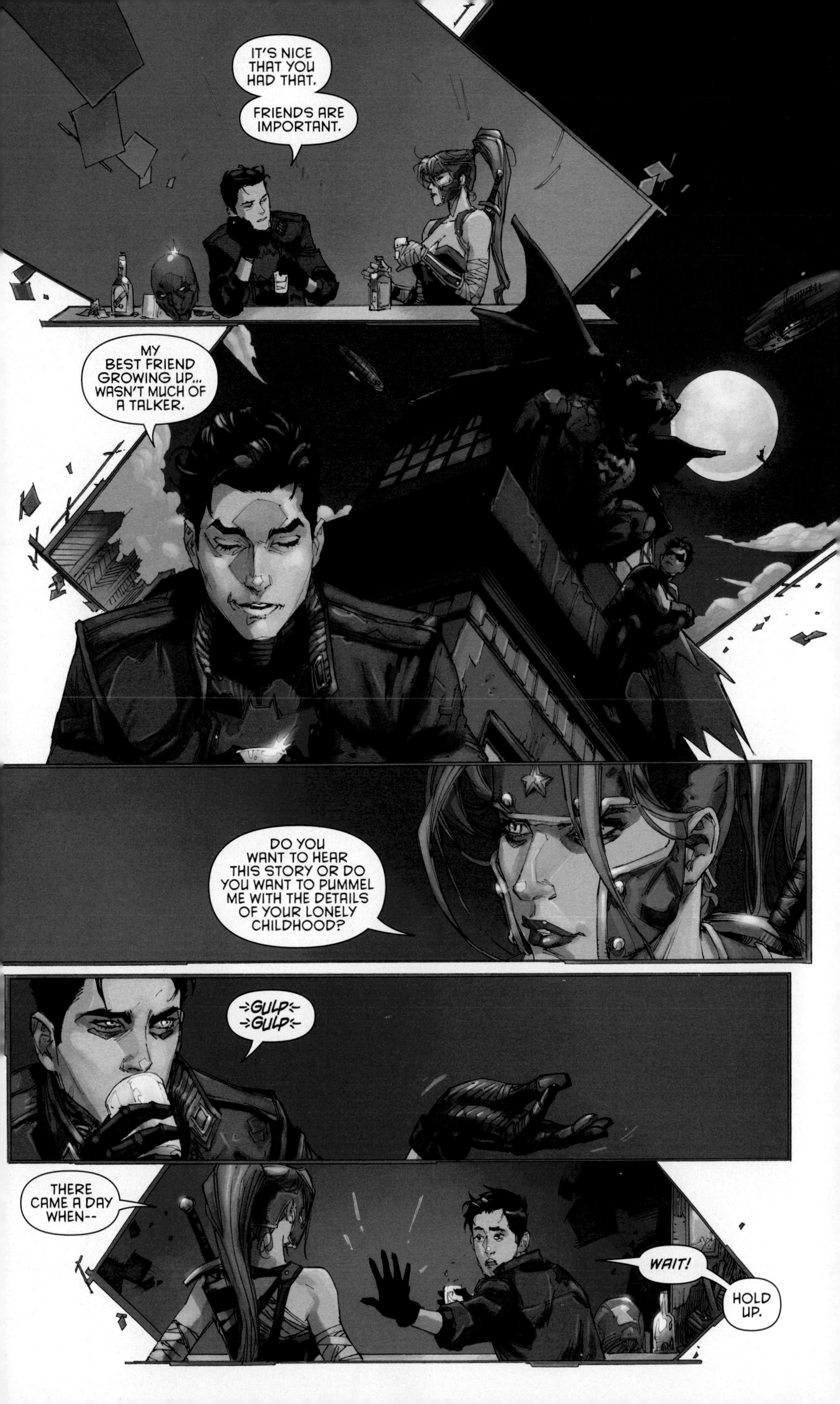
IT'S NICE THAT YOU HAD THAT.
FRIENDS ARE IMPORTANT.
MY BEST FRIEND GROWING UP... WASN'T MUCH OF A TALKER.
DO YOU WANT TO HEAR THIS STORY OR DO YOU WANT TO PUMMEL ME WITH THE DETAILS OF YOUR LONELY CHILDHOOD?
GULP GULP
THERE CAME A DAY WHEN--
WAIT!
HOLD UP.

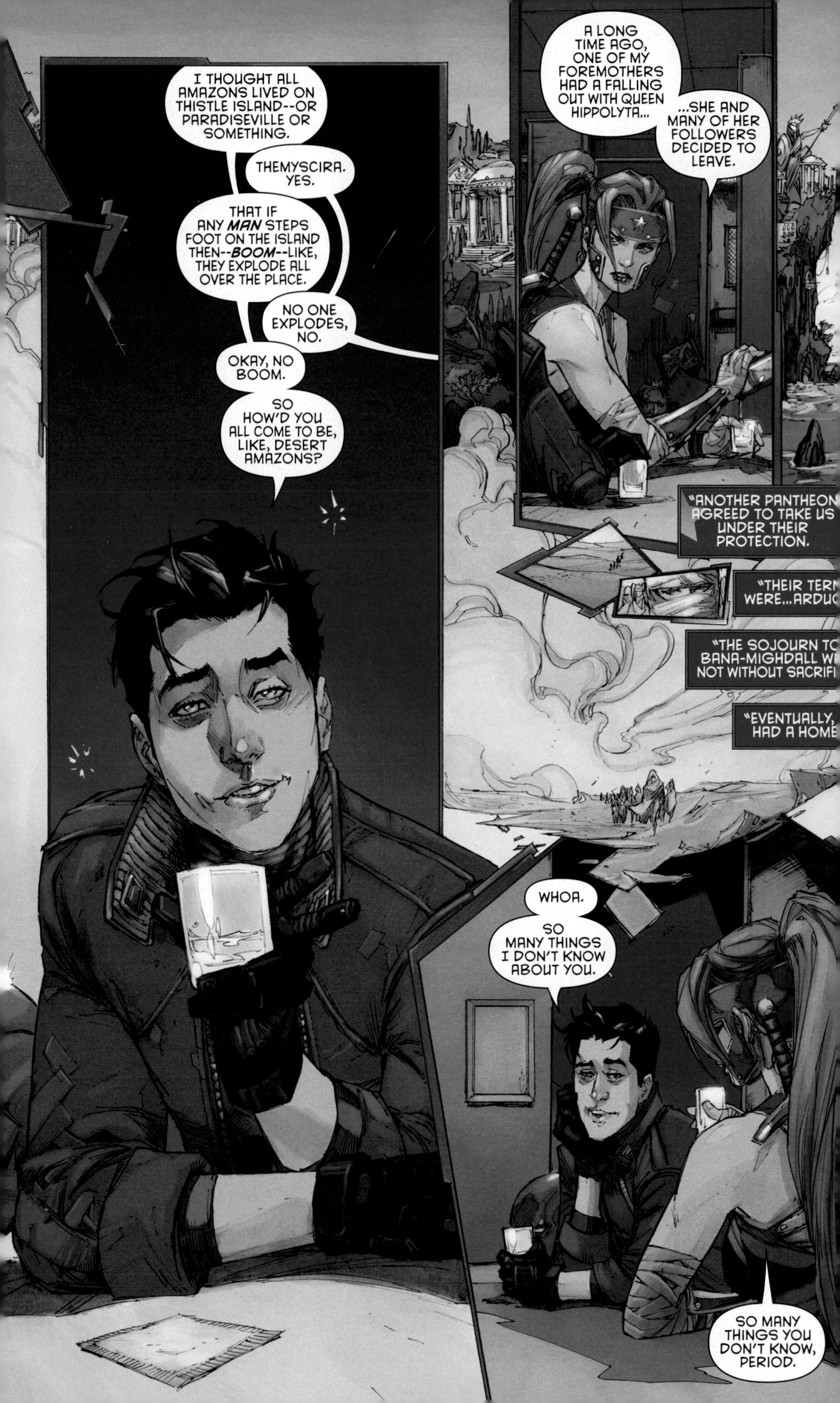

I THOUGHT ALL AMAZONS LIVED ON THISTLE ISLAND--OR PARADISEVILLE OR SOMETHING.
THEMYSCIRA. YES.
THAT IF ANY *MAN* STEPS FOOT ON THE ISLAND THEN--*BOOM*--LIKE, THEY EXPLODE ALL OVER THE PLACE.
NO ONE EXPLODES, NO.
OKAY, NO BOOM.
SO HOW'D YOU ALL COME TO BE, LIKE, DESERT AMAZONS?
A LONG TIME AGO, ONE OF MY FOREMOTHERS HAD A FALLING OUT WITH QUEEN HIPPOLYTA...
...SHE AND MANY OF HER FOLLOWERS DECIDED TO LEAVE.
"ANOTHER PANTHEON AGREED TO TAKE US UNDER THEIR PROTECTION.
"THEIR TERM WERE...ARDUO
"THE SOJOURN TO BANA-MIGHDALL W NOT WITHOUT SACRIFI
"EVENTUALLY, HAD A HOME
WHOA.
SO MANY THINGS I DON'T KNOW ABOUT YOU.
SO MANY THINGS YOU DON'T KNOW, PERIOD.

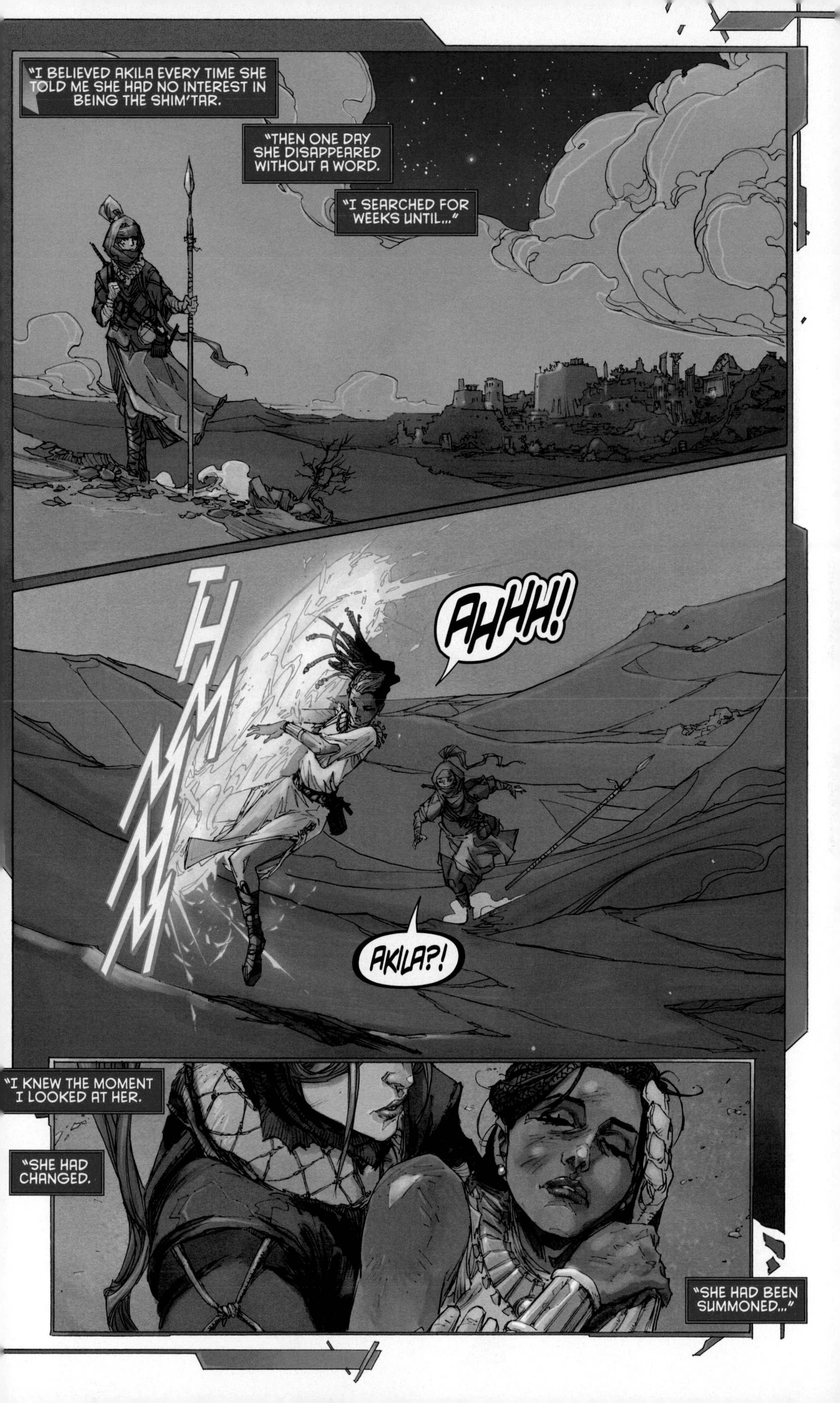
"I BELIEVED AKILA EVERY TIME SHE TOLD ME SHE HAD NO INTEREST IN BEING THE SHIM'TAR.
"THEN ONE DAY SHE DISAPPEARED WITHOUT A WORD.
"I SEARCHED FOR WEEKS UNTIL..."
THMMMM
AHHH!
AKILA?!
"I KNEW THE MOMENT I LOOKED AT HER.
"SHE HAD CHANGED.
"SHE HAD BEEN SUMMONED..."

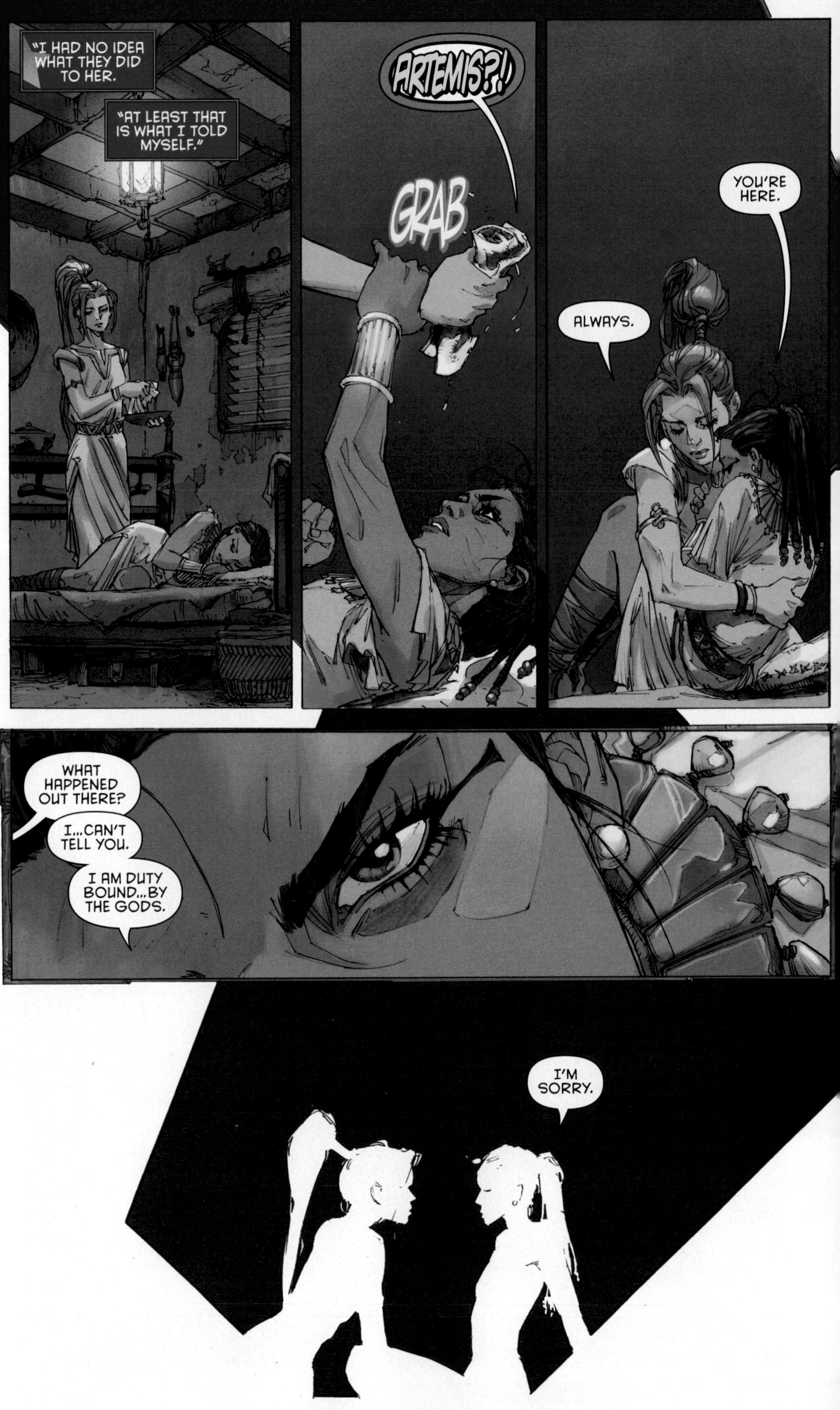

"I HAD NO IDEA WHAT THEY DID TO HER.
"AT LEAST THAT IS WHAT I TOLD MYSELF."
ARTEMIS?!
GRAB
YOU'RE HERE.
ALWAYS.
WHAT HAPPENED OUT THERE?
I...CAN'T TELL YOU.
I AM DUTY BOUND...BY THE GODS.
I'M SORRY.

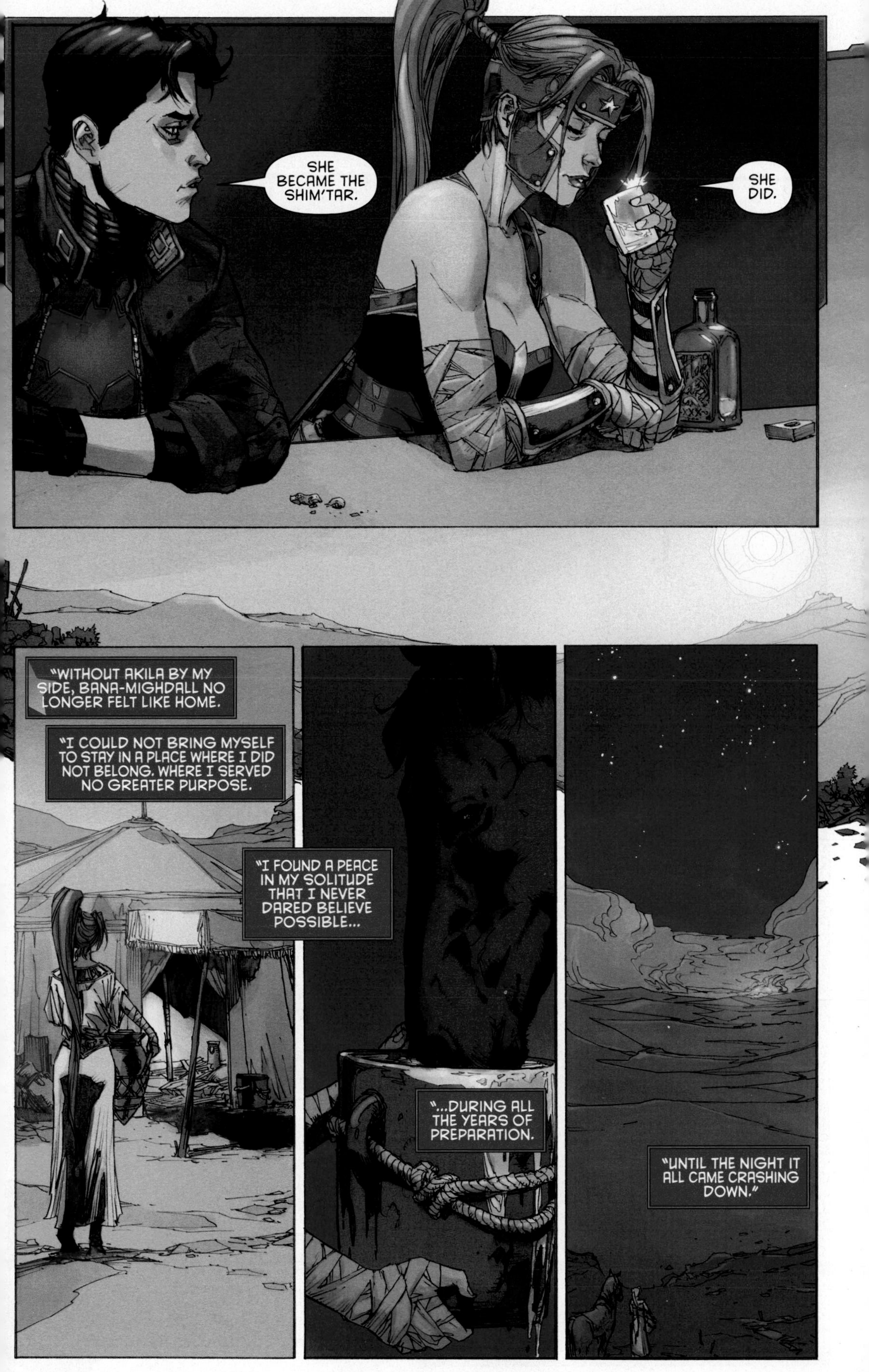

SHE BECAME THE SHIM'TAR.
SHE DID.
"WITHOUT AKILA BY MY SIDE, BANA-MIGHDALL NO LONGER FELT LIKE HOME.
"I COULD NOT BRING MYSELF TO STAY IN A PLACE WHERE I DID NOT BELONG. WHERE I SERVED NO GREATER PURPOSE.
"I FOUND A PEACE IN MY SOLITUDE THAT I NEVER DARED BELIEVE POSSIBLE...
"...DURING ALL THE YEARS OF PREPARATION.
"UNTIL THE NIGHT IT ALL CAME CRASHING DOWN."

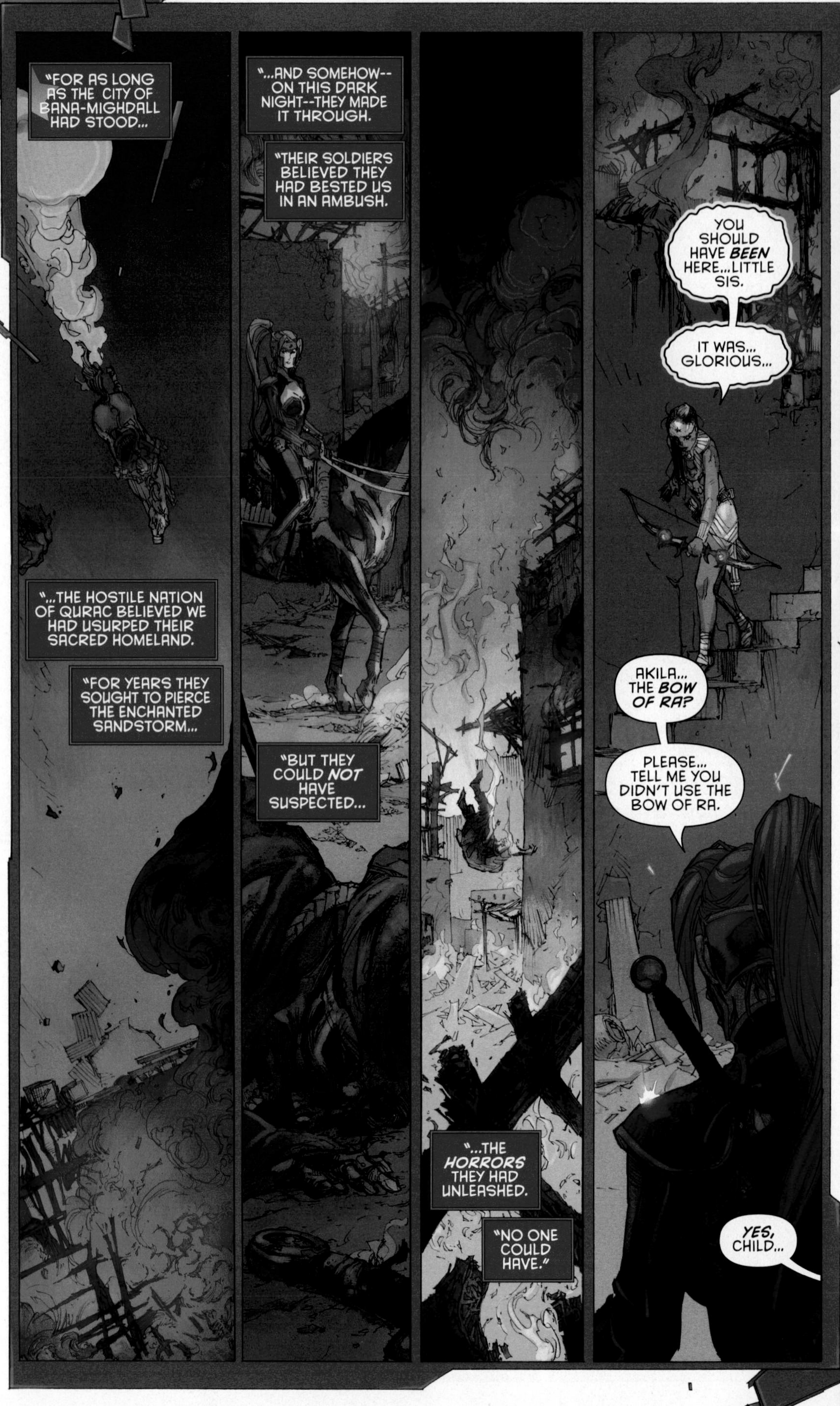

"FOR AS LONG AS THE CITY OF BANA-MIGHDALL HAD STOOD...
"...THE HOSTILE NATION OF QURAC BELIEVED WE HAD USURPED THEIR SACRED HOMELAND.
"FOR YEARS THEY SOUGHT TO PIERCE THE ENCHANTED SANDSTORM...
"...AND SOMEHOW--ON THIS DARK NIGHT--THEY MADE IT THROUGH.
"THEIR SOLDIERS BELIEVED THEY HAD BESTED US IN AN AMBUSH.
"BUT THEY COULD *NOT* HAVE SUSPECTED...
"...THE *HORRORS* THEY HAD UNLEASHED.
"NO ONE COULD HAVE."
YOU SHOULD HAVE *BEEN* HERE...LITTLE SIS.
IT WAS... GLORIOUS...
AKILA... THE *BOW OF RA?*
PLEASE... TELL ME YOU DIDN'T USE THE BOW OF RA.
YES, CHILD...

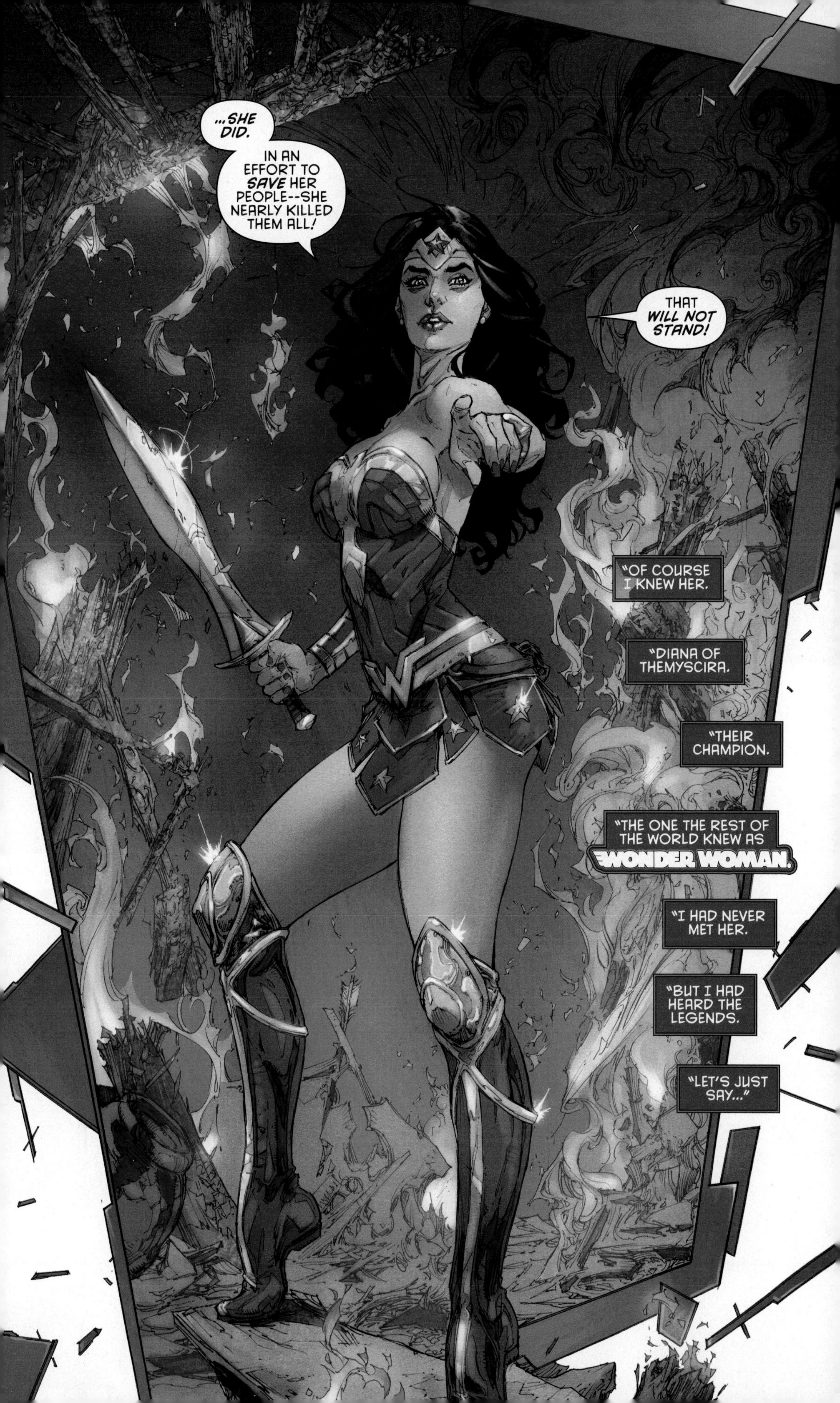
...SHE DID.
IN AN EFFORT TO SAVE HER PEOPLE--SHE NEARLY KILLED THEM ALL!
THAT WILL NOT STAND!
"OF COURSE I KNEW HER.
"DIANA OF THEMYSCIRA.
"THEIR CHAMPION.
"THE ONE THE REST OF THE WORLD KNEW AS
WONDER WOMAN.
"I HAD NEVER MET HER.
"BUT I HAD HEARD THE LEGENDS.
"LET'S JUST SAY..."

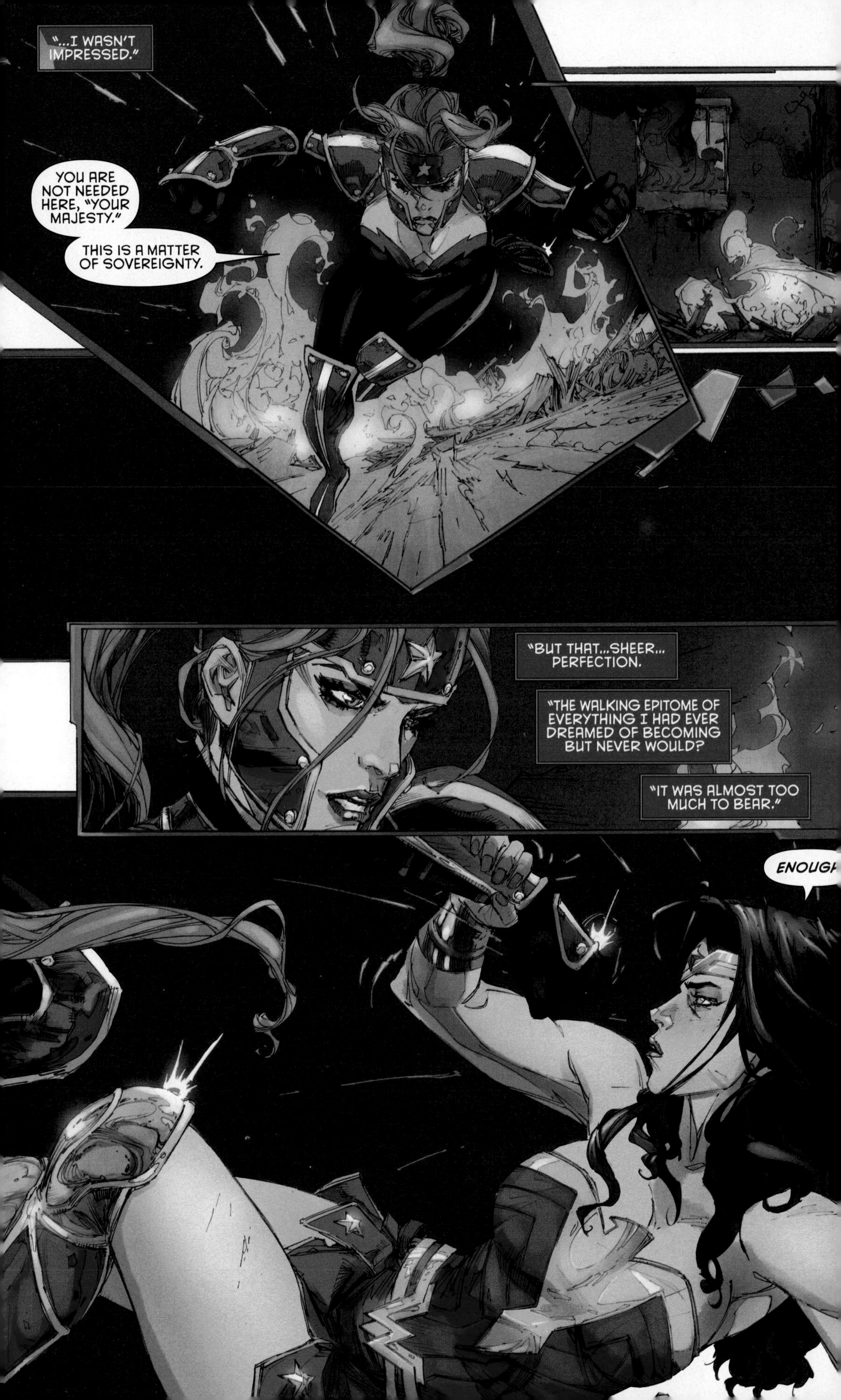

"...I WASN'T IMPRESSED."
YOU ARE NOT NEEDED HERE, "YOUR MAJESTY."
THIS IS A MATTER OF SOVEREIGNTY.
"BUT THAT...SHEER... PERFECTION.
"THE WALKING EPITOME OF EVERYTHING I HAD EVER DREAMED OF BECOMING BUT NEVER WOULD?
"IT WAS ALMOST TOO MUCH TO BEAR."
ENOUGH

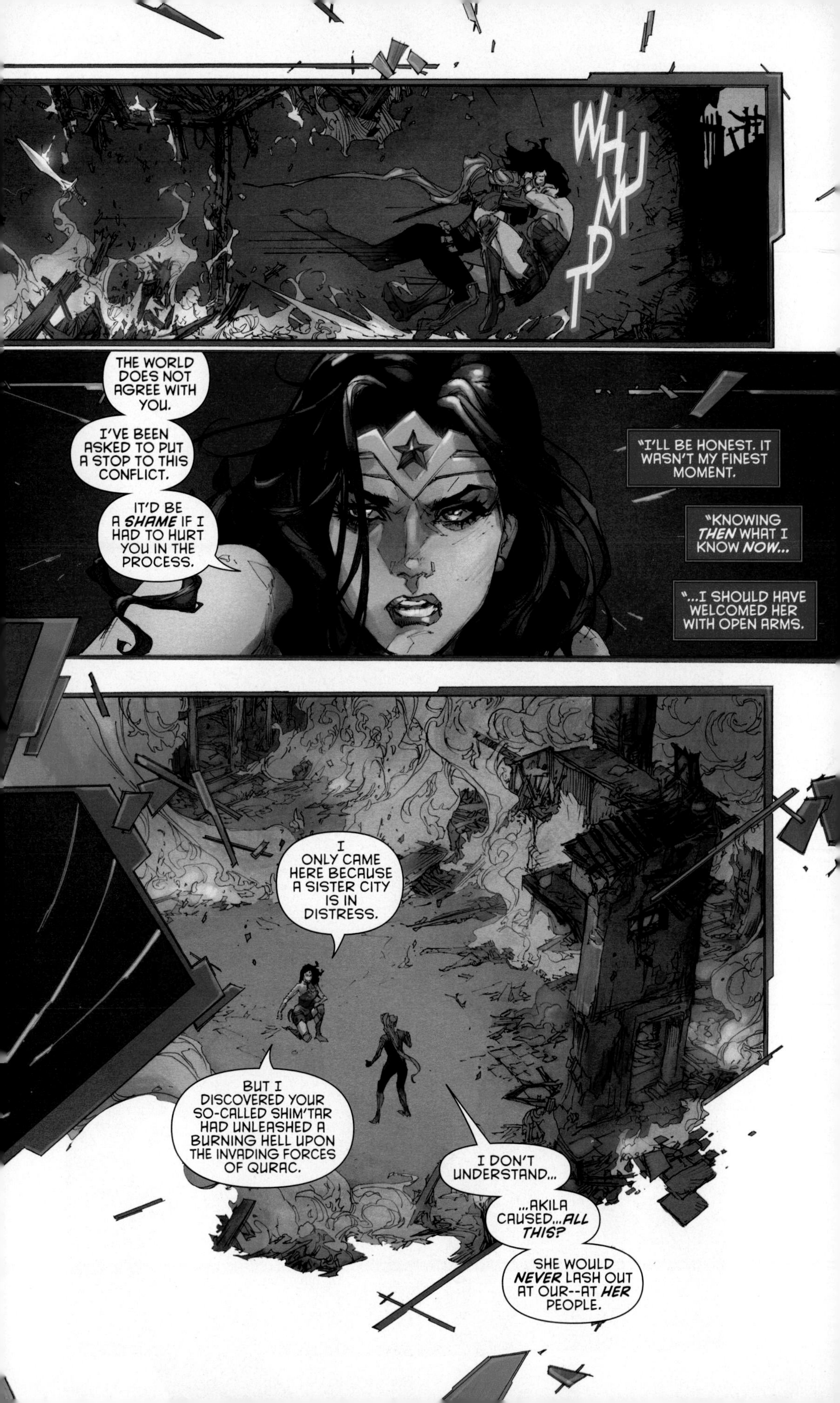
WHUMPT
THE WORLD DOES NOT AGREE WITH YOU.
I'VE BEEN ASKED TO PUT A STOP TO THIS CONFLICT.
IT'D BE A SHAME IF I HAD TO HURT YOU IN THE PROCESS.
"I'LL BE HONEST. IT WASN'T MY FINEST MOMENT.
"KNOWING THEN WHAT I KNOW NOW...
"...I SHOULD HAVE WELCOMED HER WITH OPEN ARMS.
I ONLY CAME HERE BECAUSE A SISTER CITY IS IN DISTRESS.
BUT I DISCOVERED YOUR SO-CALLED SHIM'TAR HAD UNLEASHED A BURNING HELL UPON THE INVADING FORCES OF QURAC.
I DON'T UNDERSTAND...
...AKILA CAUSED...ALL THIS?
SHE WOULD NEVER LASH OUT AT OUR--AT HER PEOPLE.

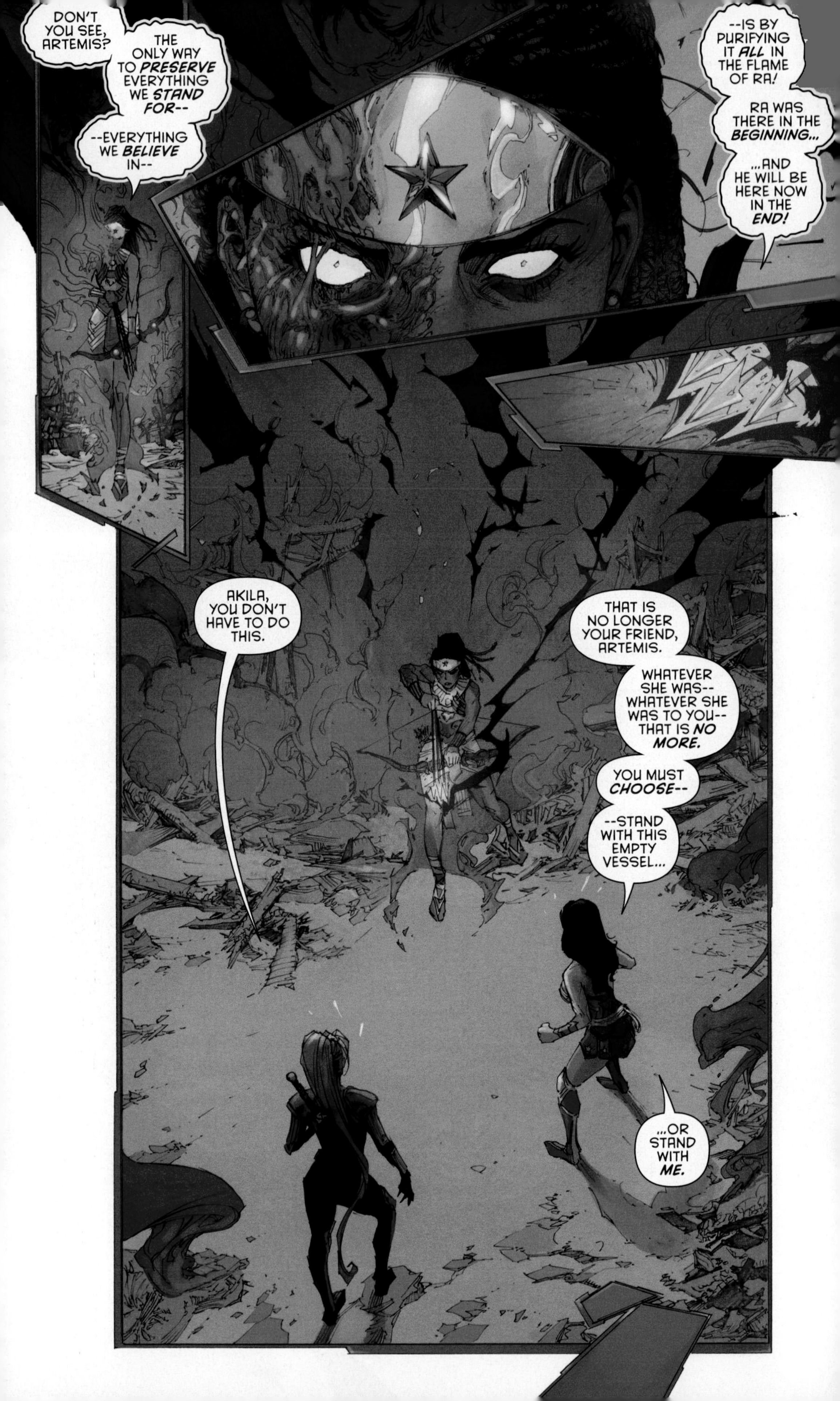
DON'T YOU SEE, ARTEMIS?
THE ONLY WAY TO PRESERVE EVERYTHING WE STAND FOR--
--EVERYTHING WE BELIEVE IN--
--IS BY PURIFYING IT ALL IN THE FLAME OF RA!
RA WAS THERE IN THE BEGINNING...
...AND HE WILL BE HERE NOW IN THE END!
AKILA, YOU DON'T HAVE TO DO THIS.
THAT IS NO LONGER YOUR FRIEND, ARTEMIS.
WHATEVER SHE WAS--WHATEVER SHE WAS TO YOU--THAT IS NO MORE.
YOU MUST CHOOSE--
--STAND WITH THIS EMPTY VESSEL...
...OR STAND WITH ME.

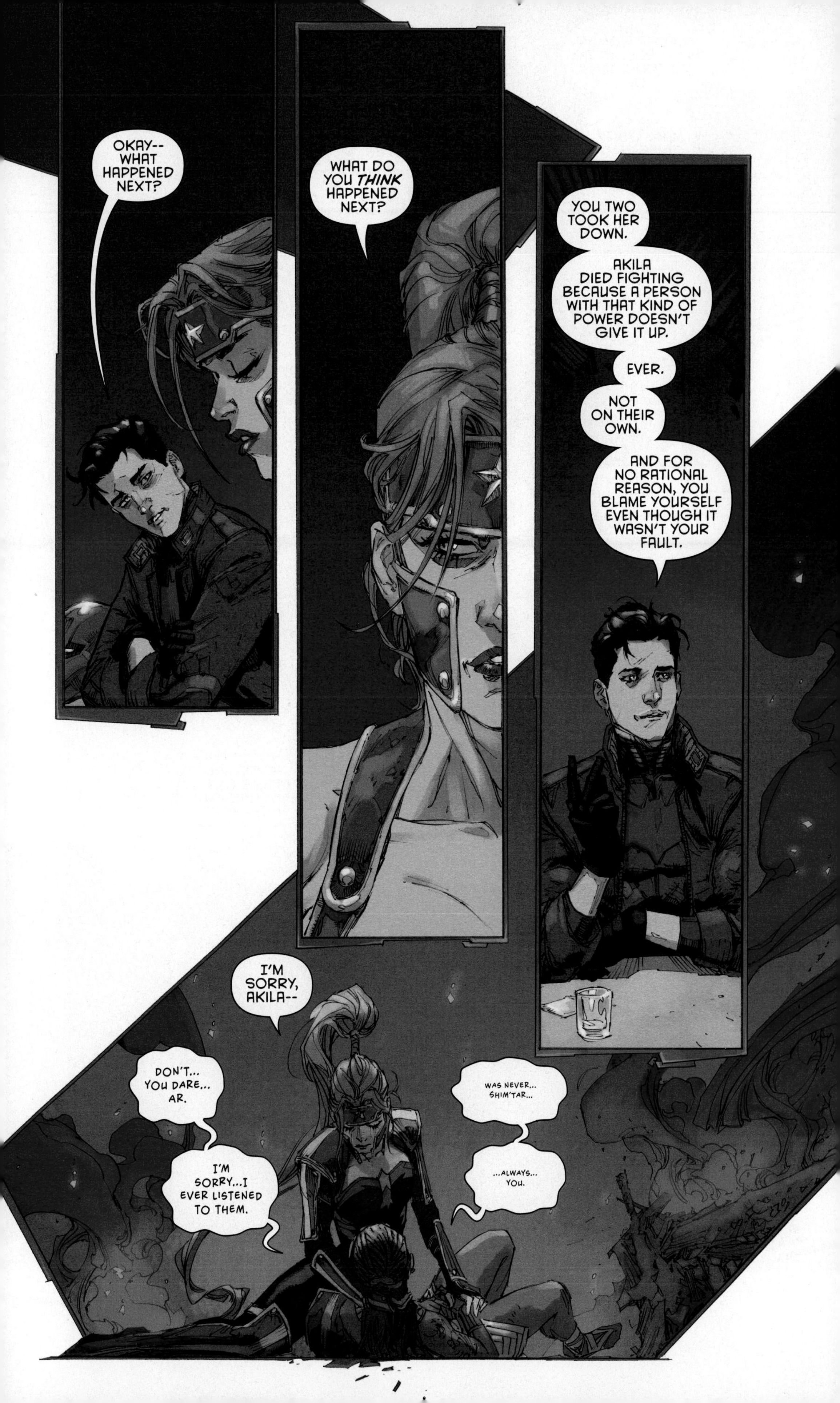
OKAY-- WHAT HAPPENED NEXT?
WHAT DO YOU *THINK* HAPPENED NEXT?
YOU TWO TOOK HER DOWN.
AKILA DIED FIGHTING BECAUSE A PERSON WITH THAT KIND OF POWER DOESN'T GIVE IT UP.
EVER.
NOT ON THEIR OWN.
AND FOR NO RATIONAL REASON, YOU BLAME YOURSELF EVEN THOUGH IT WASN'T YOUR FAULT.
I'M SORRY, AKILA--
DON'T... YOU DARE... AR.
I'M SORRY...I EVER LISTENED TO THEM.
WAS NEVER... SHIM'TAR...
...ALWAYS... YOU.

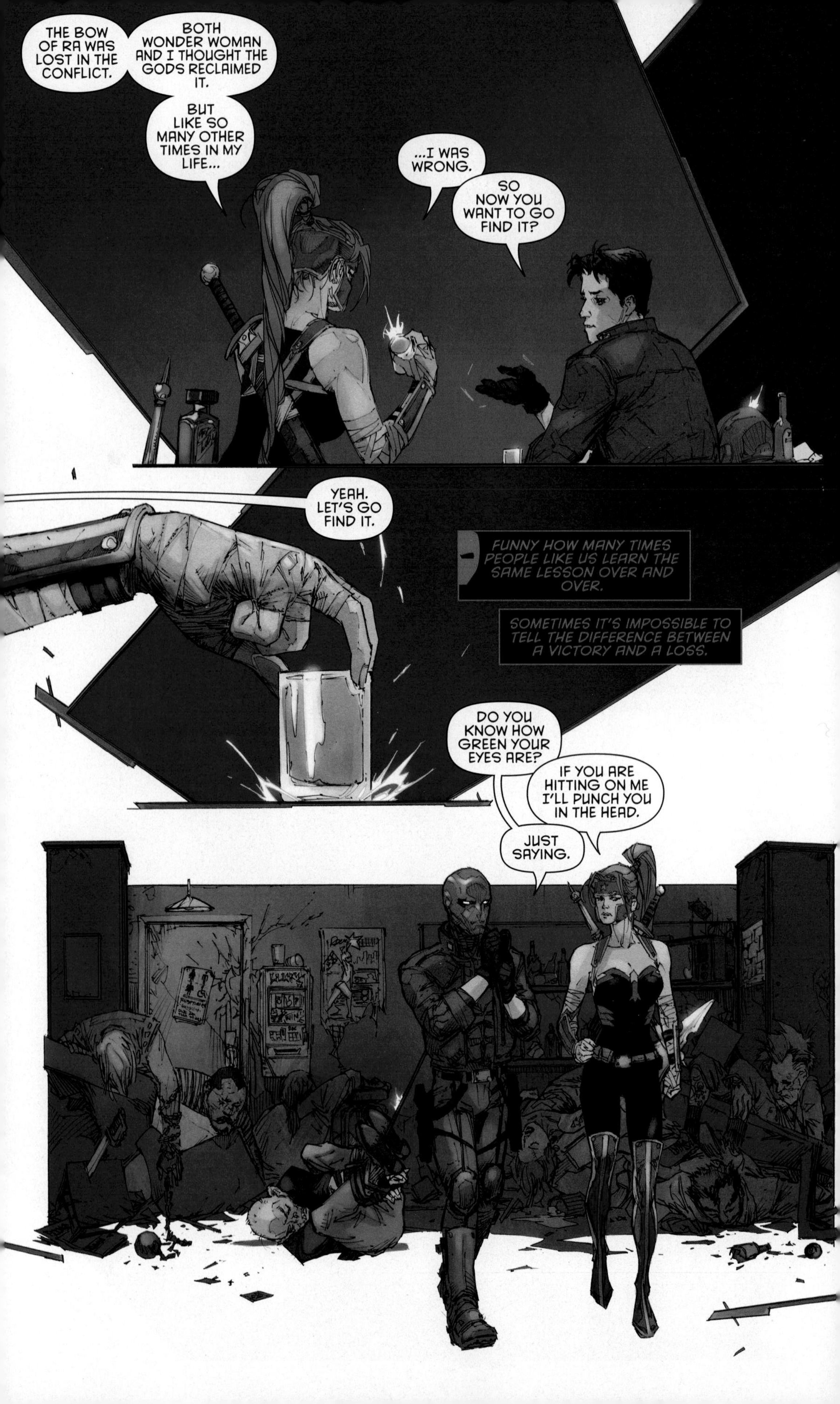
THE BOW OF RA WAS LOST IN THE CONFLICT.
BOTH WONDER WOMAN AND I THOUGHT THE GODS RECLAIMED IT.
BUT LIKE SO MANY OTHER TIMES IN MY LIFE...
...I WAS WRONG.
SO NOW YOU WANT TO GO FIND IT?
YEAH. LET'S GO FIND IT.
FUNNY HOW MANY TIMES PEOPLE LIKE US LEARN THE SAME LESSON OVER AND OVER.
SOMETIMES IT'S IMPOSSIBLE TO TELL THE DIFFERENCE BETWEEN A VICTORY AND A LOSS.
DO YOU KNOW HOW GREEN YOUR EYES ARE?
IF YOU ARE HITTING ON ME I'LL PUNCH YOU IN THE HEAD.
JUST SAYING.

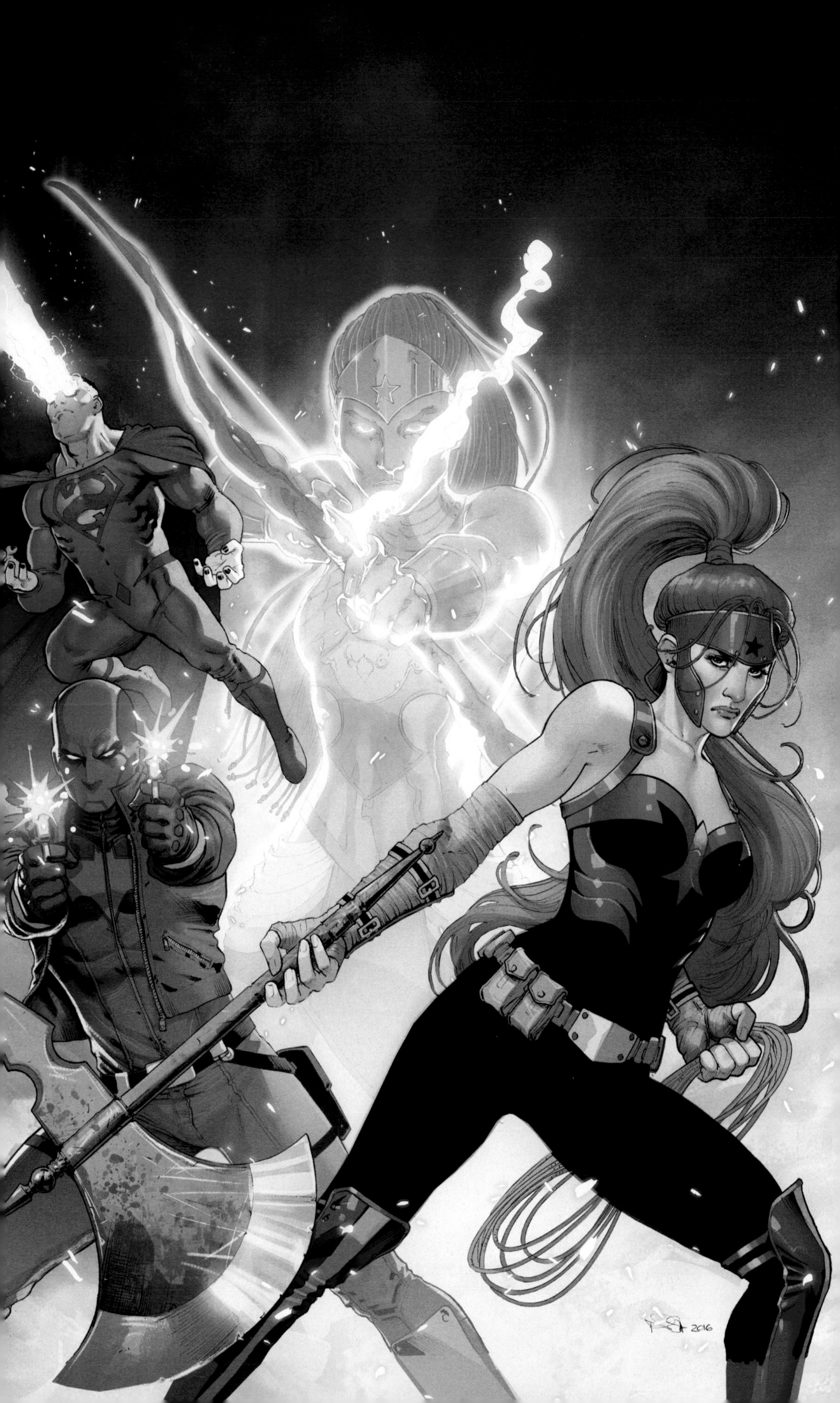

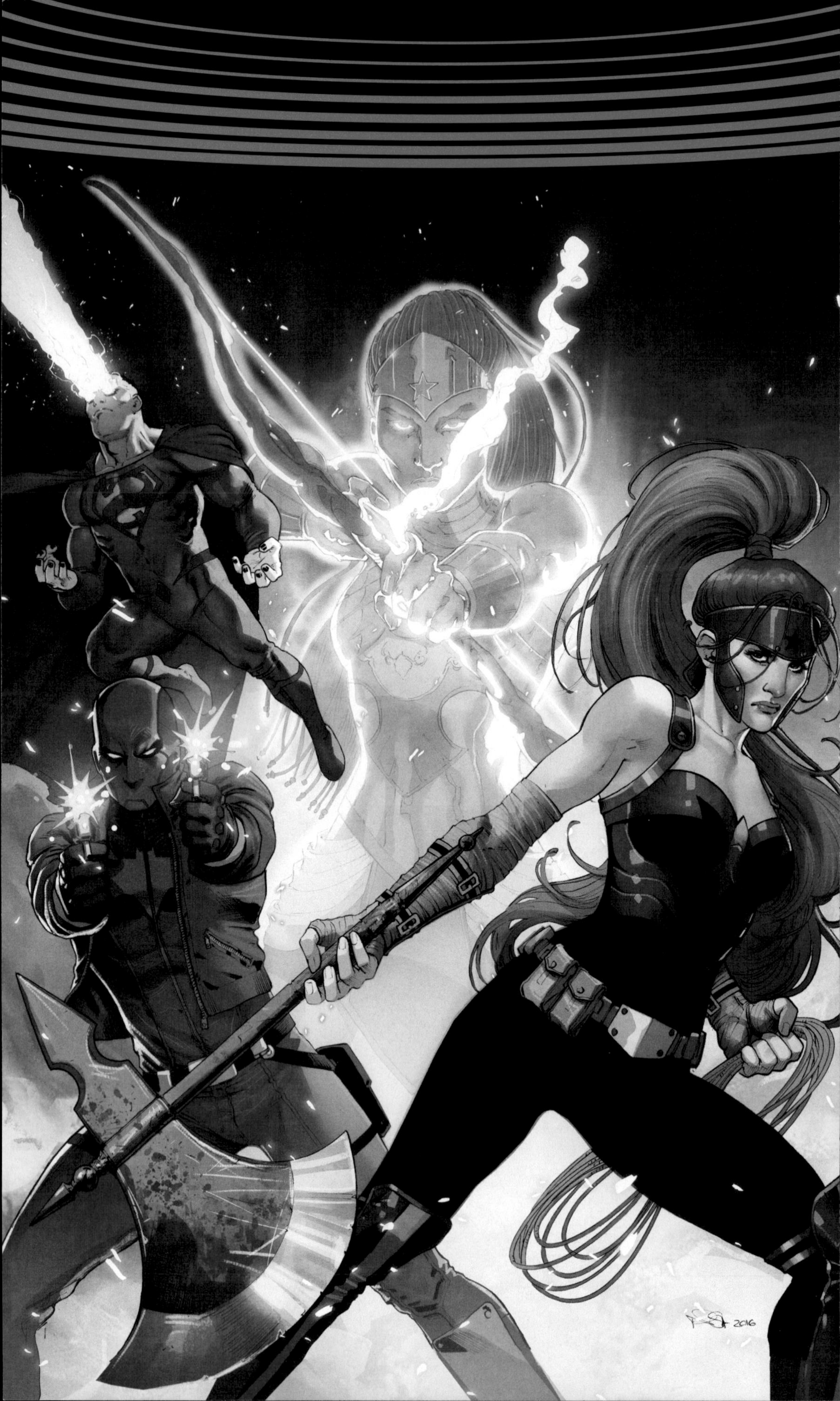
2016

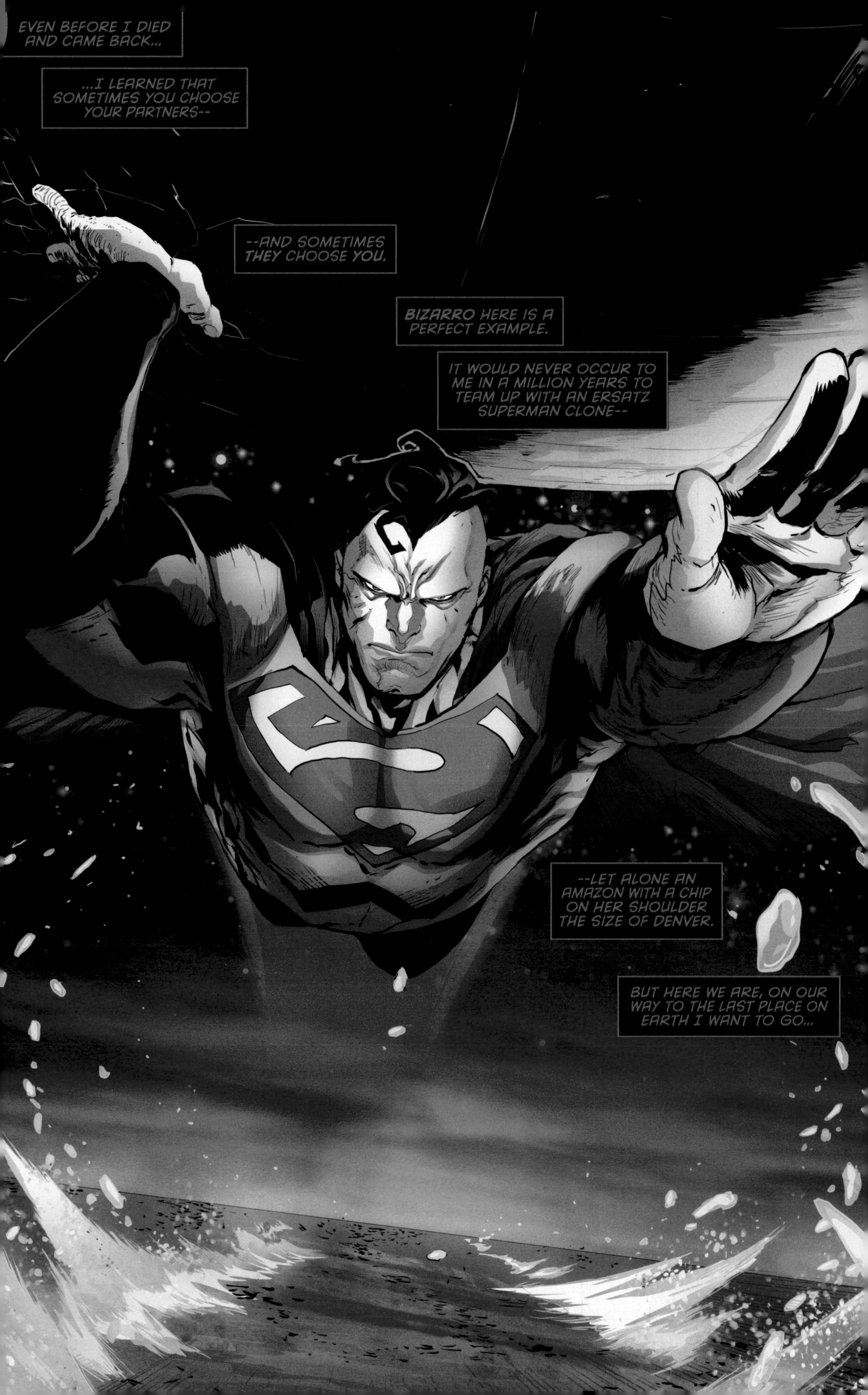
EVEN BEFORE I DIED AND CAME BACK...
...I LEARNED THAT SOMETIMES YOU CHOOSE YOUR PARTNERS--
--AND SOMETIMES THEY CHOOSE YOU.
BIZARRO HERE IS A PERFECT EXAMPLE.
IT WOULD NEVER OCCUR TO ME IN A MILLION YEARS TO TEAM UP WITH AN ERSATZ SUPERMAN CLONE--
--LET ALONE AN AMAZON WITH A CHIP ON HER SHOULDER THE SIZE OF DENVER.
BUT HERE WE ARE, ON OUR WAY TO THE LAST PLACE ON EARTH I WANT TO GO...

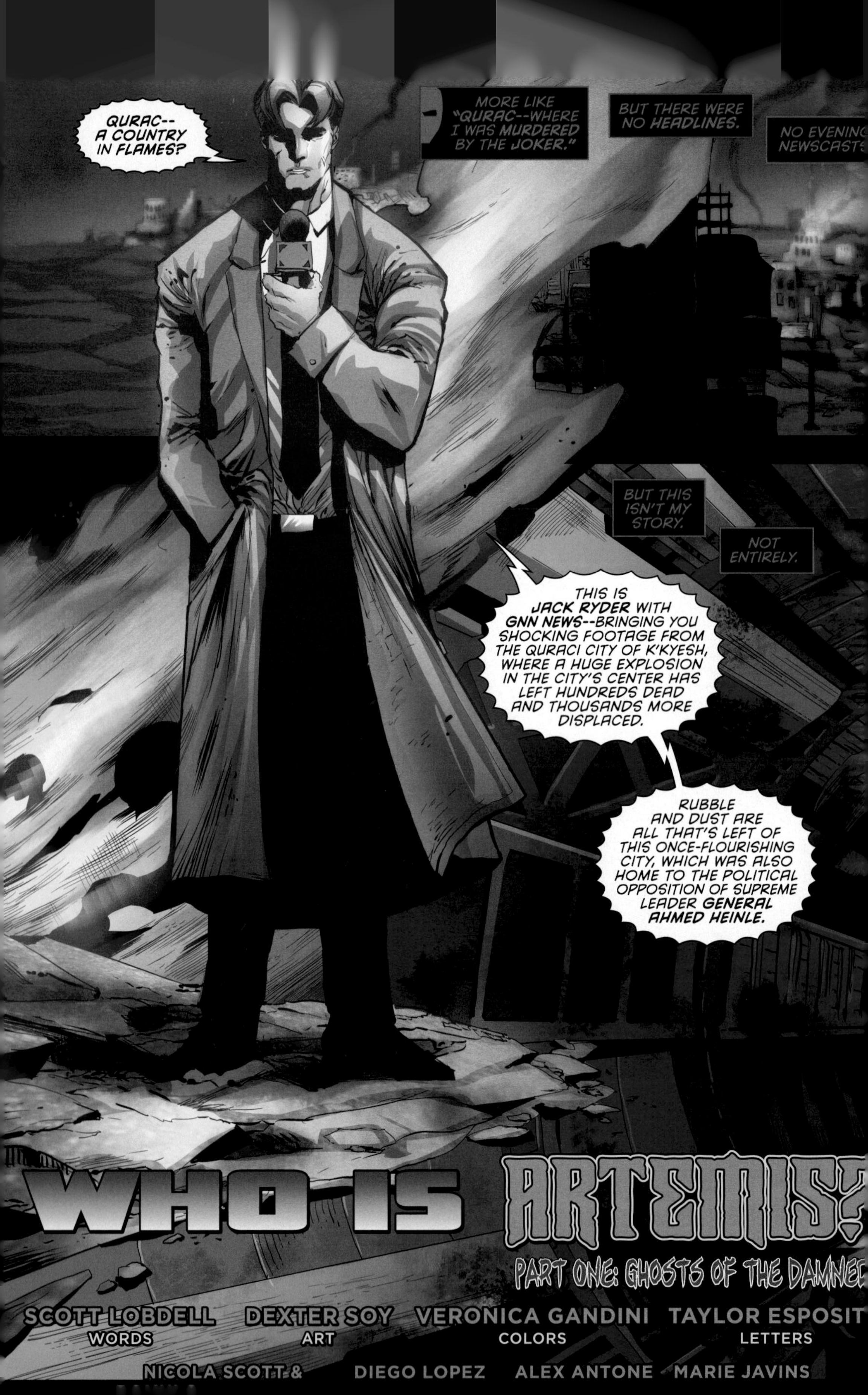
QURAC-- A COUNTRY IN FLAMES?
MORE LIKE "QURAC--WHERE I WAS MURDERED BY THE JOKER."
BUT THERE WERE NO HEADLINES.
NO EVENING NEWSCASTS
BUT THIS ISN'T MY STORY.
NOT ENTIRELY.
THIS IS JACK RYDER WITH GNN NEWS--BRINGING YOU SHOCKING FOOTAGE FROM THE QURACI CITY OF K'KYESH, WHERE A HUGE EXPLOSION IN THE CITY'S CENTER HAS LEFT HUNDREDS DEAD AND THOUSANDS MORE DISPLACED.
RUBBLE AND DUST ARE ALL THAT'S LEFT OF THIS ONCE-FLOURISHING CITY, WHICH WAS ALSO HOME TO THE POLITICAL OPPOSITION OF SUPREME LEADER GENERAL AHMED HEINLE.
WHO IS ARTEMIS?
PART ONE: GHOSTS OF THE DAMNED
SCOTT LOBDELL WORDS
DEXTER SOY ART
VERONICA GANDINI COLORS
TAYLOR ESPOSIT LETTERS
NICOLA SCOTT &
DIEGO LOPEZ
ALEX ANTONE
MARIE JAVINS

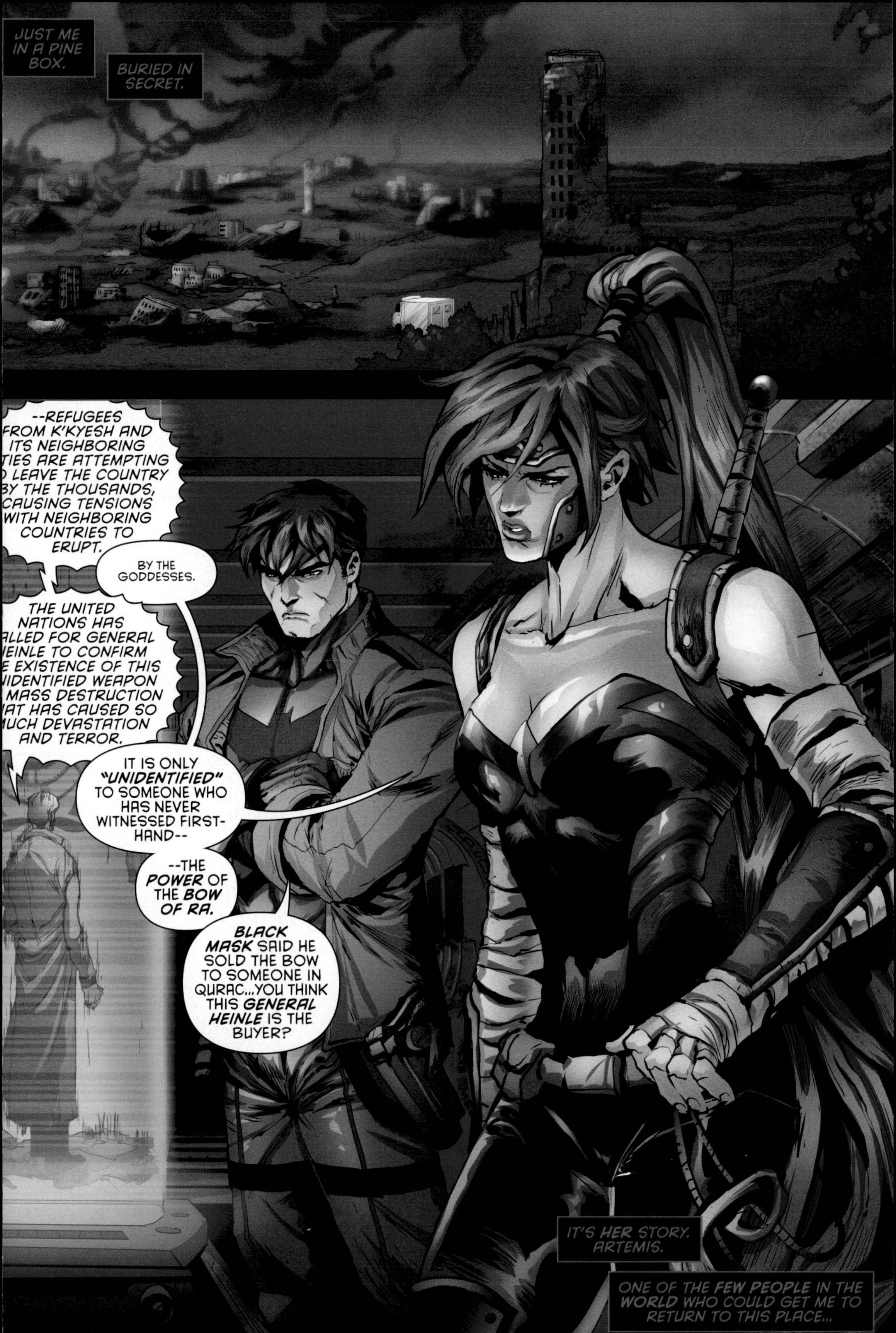

JUST ME IN A PINE BOX.
BURIED IN SECRET.
--REFUGEES FROM K'KYESH AND ITS NEIGHBORING TIES ARE ATTEMPTING D LEAVE THE COUNTRY BY THE THOUSANDS, CAUSING TENSIONS WITH NEIGHBORING COUNTRIES TO ERUPT.
BY THE GODDESSES.
THE UNITED NATIONS HAS ALLED FOR GENERAL HEINLE TO CONFIRM E EXISTENCE OF THIS UNIDENTIFIED WEAPON MASS DESTRUCTION AT HAS CAUSED SO MUCH DEVASTATION AND TERROR.
IT IS ONLY "UNIDENTIFIED" TO SOMEONE WHO HAS NEVER WITNESSED FIRST-HAND--
--THE POWER OF THE BOW OF RA.
BLACK MASK SAID HE SOLD THE BOW TO SOMEONE IN QURAC...YOU THINK THIS GENERAL HEINLE IS THE BUYER?
IT'S HER STORY. ARTEMIS.
ONE OF THE FEW PEOPLE IN THE WORLD WHO COULD GET ME TO RETURN TO THIS PLACE...

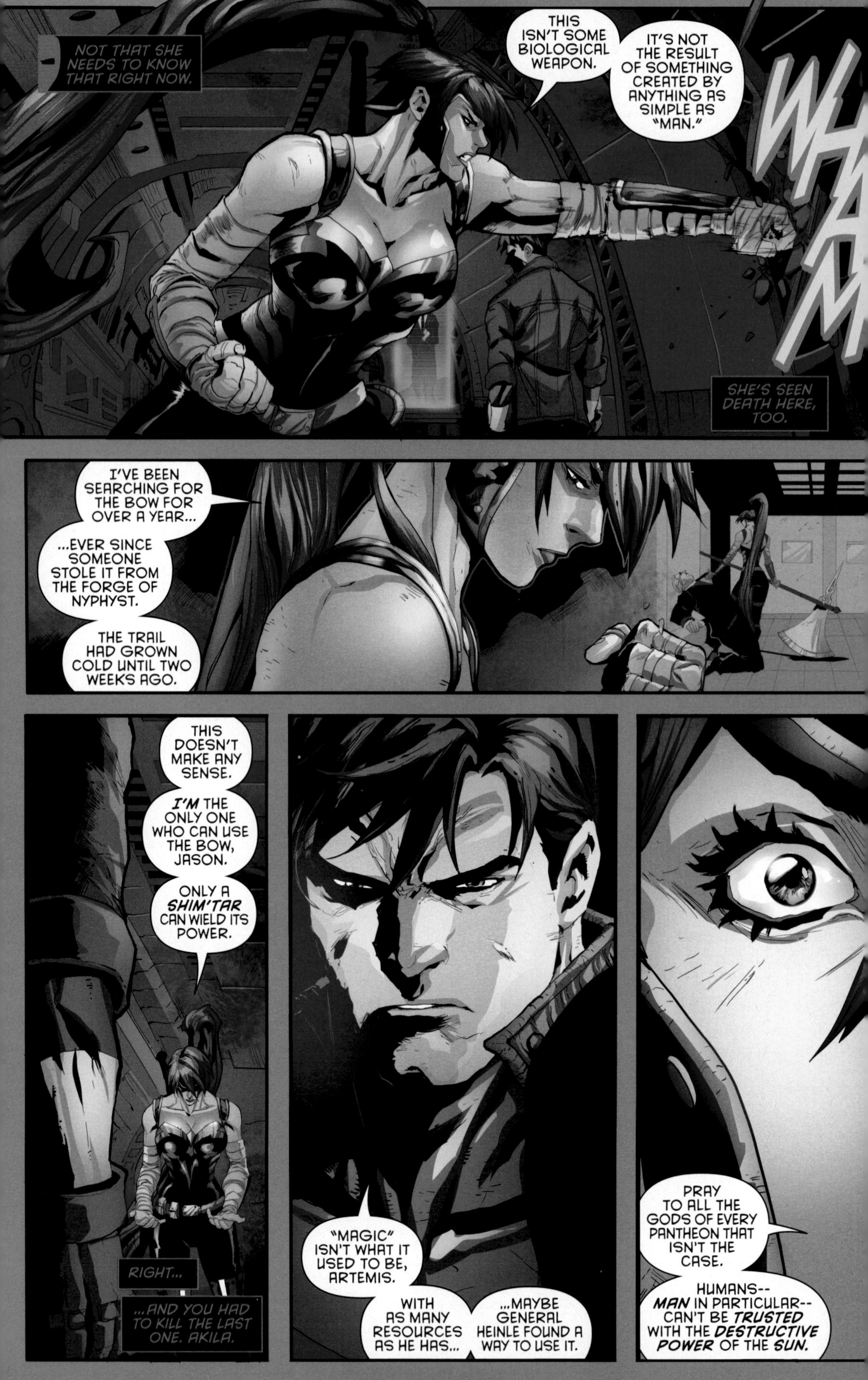

NOT THAT SHE NEEDS TO KNOW THAT RIGHT NOW.
THIS ISN'T SOME BIOLOGICAL WEAPON.
IT'S NOT THE RESULT OF SOMETHING CREATED BY ANYTHING AS SIMPLE AS "MAN."
WHAM
SHE'S SEEN DEATH HERE, TOO.
I'VE BEEN SEARCHING FOR THE BOW FOR OVER A YEAR...
...EVER SINCE SOMEONE STOLE IT FROM THE FORGE OF NYPHYST.
THE TRAIL HAD GROWN COLD UNTIL TWO WEEKS AGO.
THIS DOESN'T MAKE ANY SENSE.
I'M THE ONLY ONE WHO CAN USE THE BOW, JASON.
ONLY A SHIM'TAR CAN WIELD ITS POWER.
RIGHT...
...AND YOU HAD TO KILL THE LAST ONE. AKILA.
"MAGIC" ISN'T WHAT IT USED TO BE, ARTEMIS.
WITH AS MANY RESOURCES AS HE HAS...
...MAYBE GENERAL HEINLE FOUND A WAY TO USE IT.
PRAY TO ALL THE GODS OF EVERY PANTHEON THAT ISN'T THE CASE.
HUMANS--MAN IN PARTICULAR--CAN'T BE TRUSTED WITH THE DESTRUCTIVE POWER OF THE SUN.

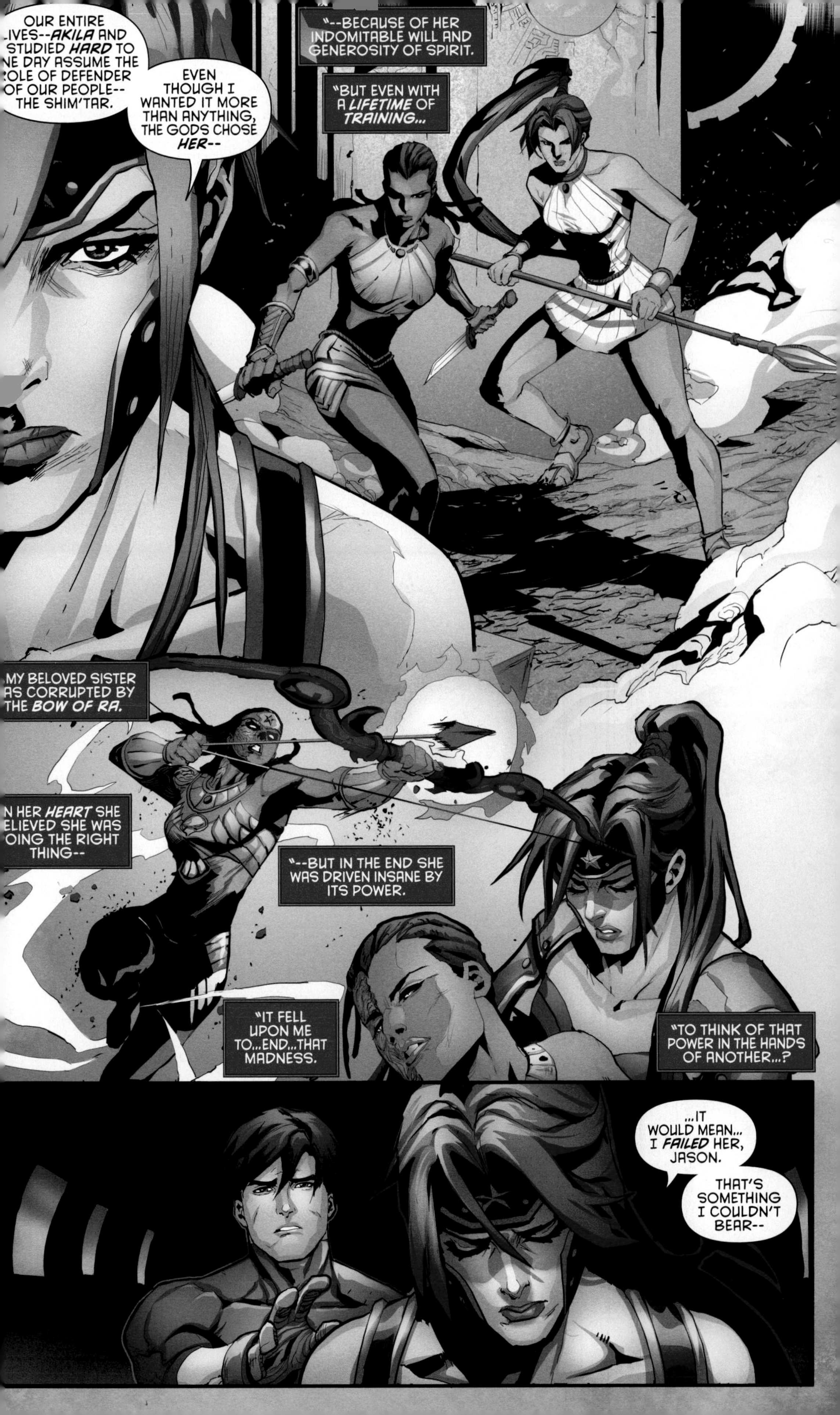
OUR ENTIRE LIVES--AKILA AND STUDIED HARD TO NE DAY ASSUME THE ROLE OF DEFENDER OF OUR PEOPLE-- THE SHIM'TAR.
EVEN THOUGH I WANTED IT MORE THAN ANYTHING, THE GODS CHOSE HER--
"--BECAUSE OF HER INDOMITABLE WILL AND GENEROSITY OF SPIRIT.
"BUT EVEN WITH A LIFETIME OF TRAINING...
MY BELOVED SISTER AS CORRUPTED BY THE BOW OF RA.
N HER HEART SHE ELIEVED SHE WAS OING THE RIGHT THING--
"--BUT IN THE END SHE WAS DRIVEN INSANE BY ITS POWER.
"IT FELL UPON ME TO...END...THAT MADNESS.
"TO THINK OF THAT POWER IN THE HANDS OF ANOTHER...?
...IT WOULD MEAN... I FAILED HER, JASON.
THAT'S SOMETHING I COULDN'T BEAR--

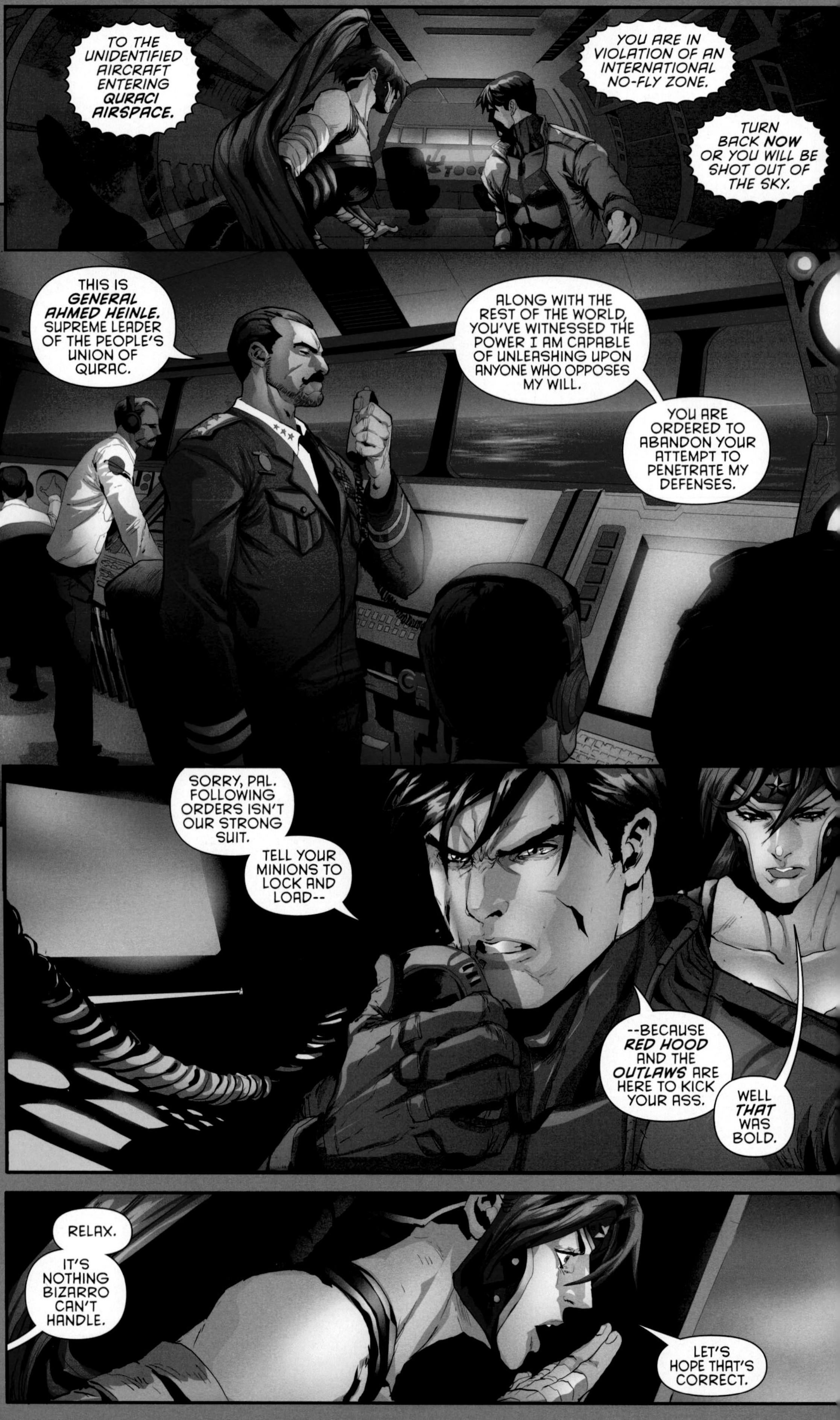
TO THE UNIDENTIFIED AIRCRAFT ENTERING QURACI AIRSPACE.
YOU ARE IN VIOLATION OF AN INTERNATIONAL NO-FLY ZONE.
TURN BACK NOW OR YOU WILL BE SHOT OUT OF THE SKY.
THIS IS GENERAL AHMED HEINLE. SUPREME LEADER OF THE PEOPLE'S UNION OF QURAC.
ALONG WITH THE REST OF THE WORLD, YOU'VE WITNESSED THE POWER I AM CAPABLE OF UNLEASHING UPON ANYONE WHO OPPOSES MY WILL.
YOU ARE ORDERED TO ABANDON YOUR ATTEMPT TO PENETRATE MY DEFENSES.
SORRY, PAL. FOLLOWING ORDERS ISN'T OUR STRONG SUIT.
TELL YOUR MINIONS TO LOCK AND LOAD--
--BECAUSE RED HOOD AND THE OUTLAWS ARE HERE TO KICK YOUR ASS.
WELL THAT WAS BOLD.
RELAX.
IT'S NOTHING BIZARRO CAN'T HANDLE.
LET'S HOPE THAT'S CORRECT.

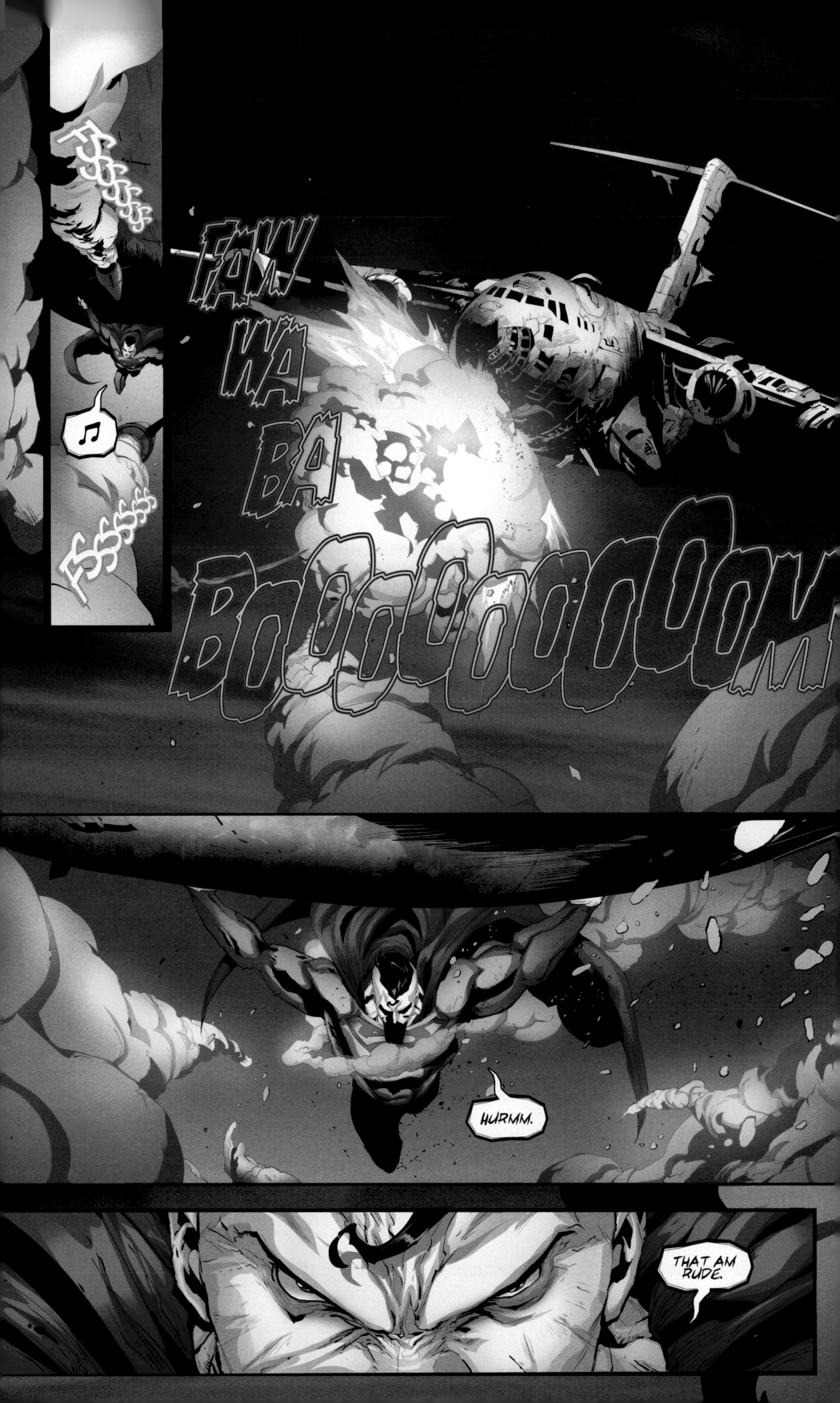

FSSSSSSS
♫
FSSSSSS
FAW
WA
BA
BOOOOOOOOOM
HURMM.
THAT AM RUDE.

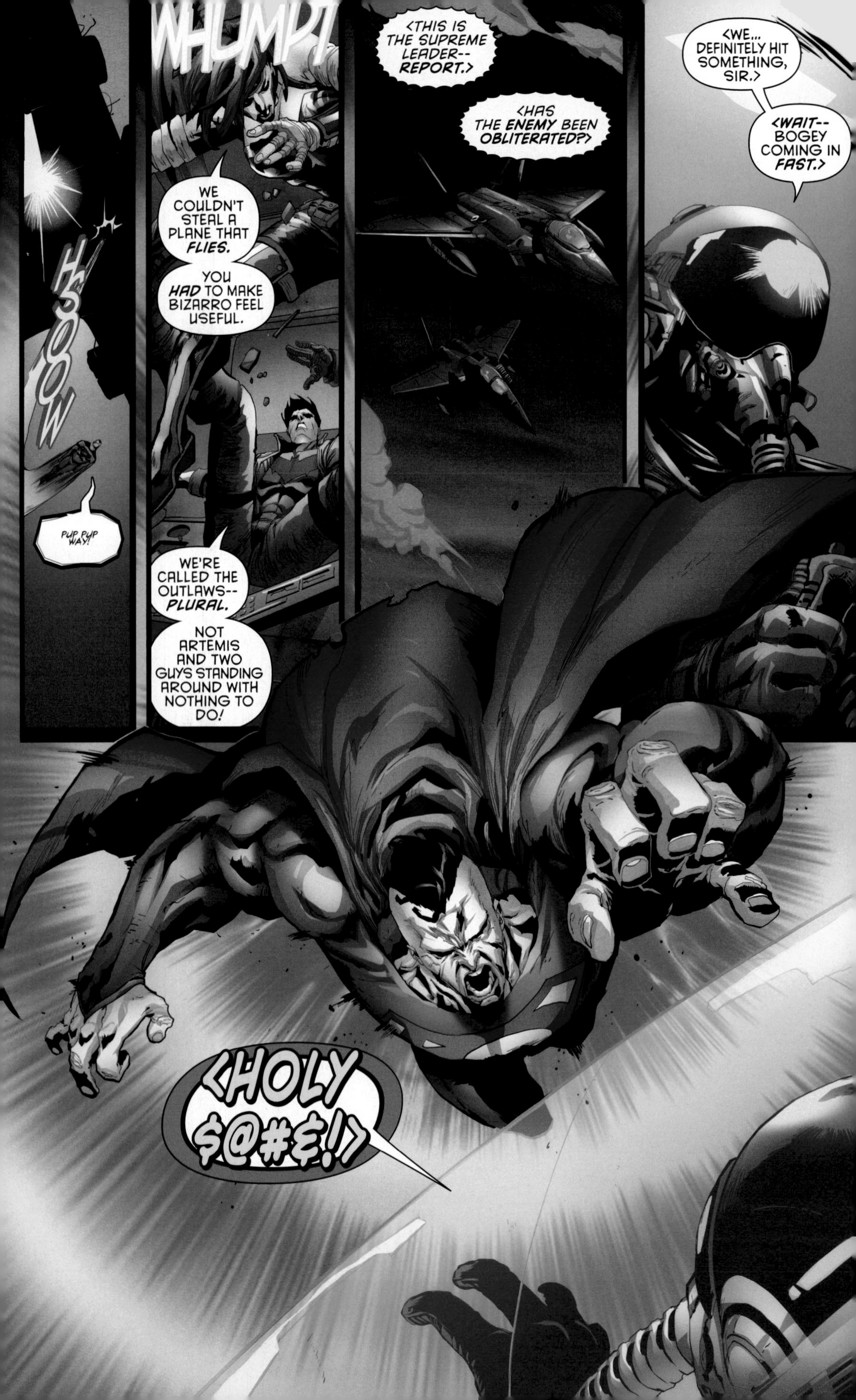
HSOOOW
PUP PUP WAY!
WHUMP!
WE COULDN'T STEAL A PLANE THAT FLIES.
YOU HAD TO MAKE BIZARRO FEEL USEFUL.
WE'RE CALLED THE OUTLAWS-- PLURAL.
NOT ARTEMIS AND TWO GUYS STANDING AROUND WITH NOTHING TO DO!
<THIS IS THE SUPREME LEADER-- REPORT.>
<HAS THE ENEMY BEEN OBLITERATED?>
<WE... DEFINITELY HIT SOMETHING, SIR.>
<WAIT-- BOGEY COMING IN FAST.>
<HOLY $@#&!>

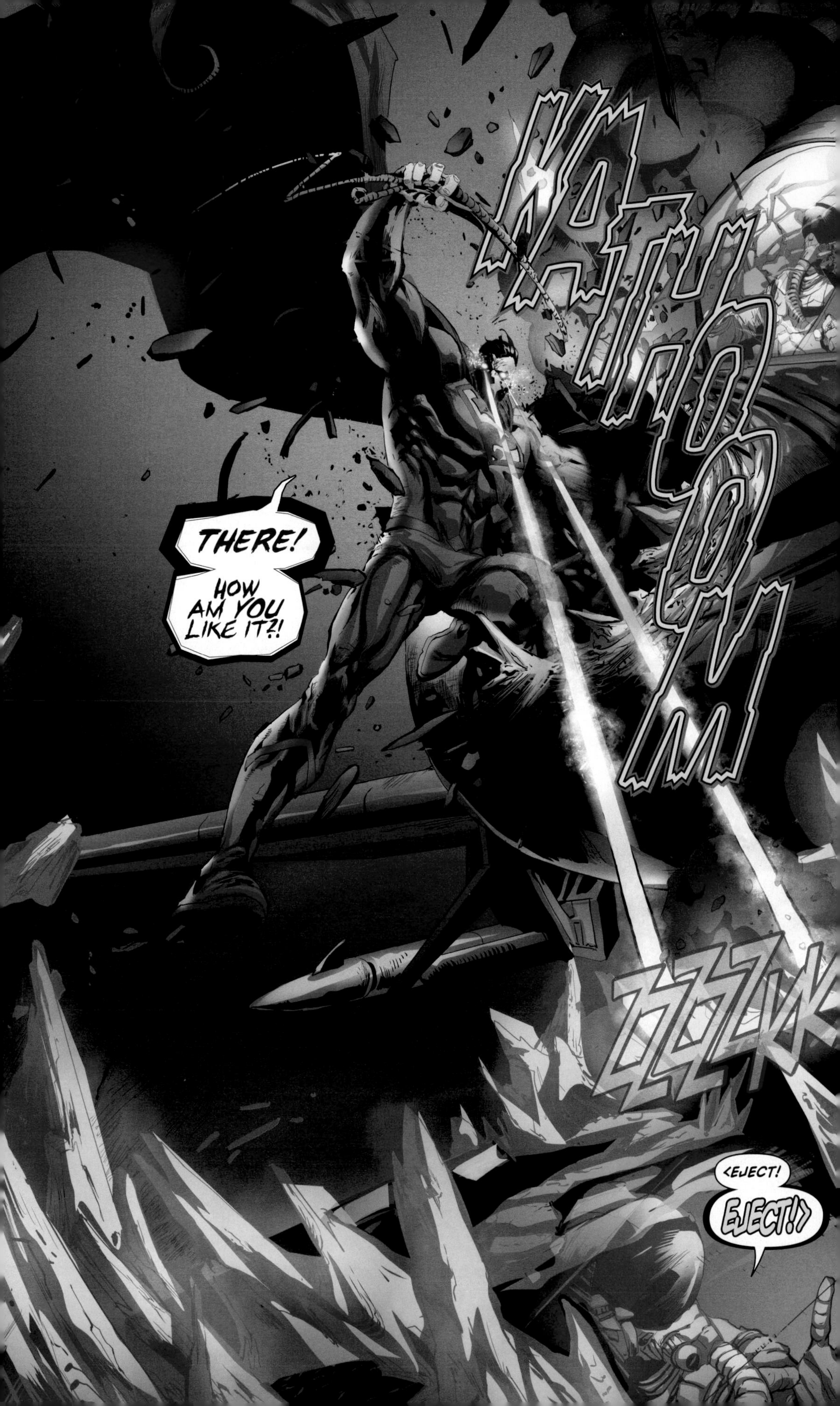
KATHOOM
THERE!
HOW AM YOU LIKE IT?!
ZZZZVVK
<EJECT! EJECT!>

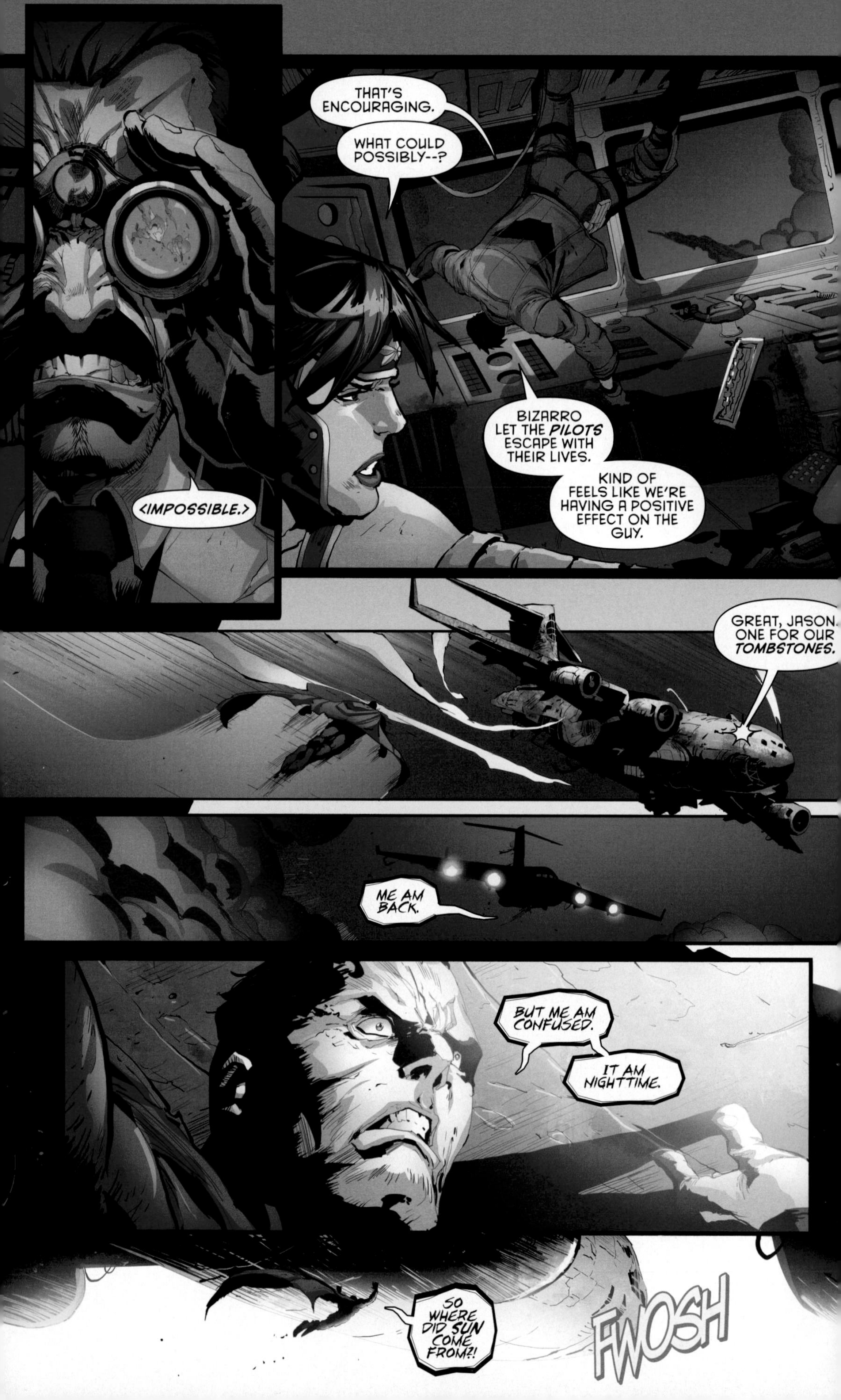
THAT'S ENCOURAGING.
WHAT COULD POSSIBLY--?
<IMPOSSIBLE.>
BIZARRO LET THE *PILOTS* ESCAPE WITH THEIR LIVES.
KIND OF FEELS LIKE WE'RE HAVING A POSITIVE EFFECT ON THE GUY.
GREAT, JASON. ONE FOR OUR *TOMBSTONES.*
ME AM BACK.
BUT ME AM CONFUSED.
IT AM NIGHTTIME.
SO WHERE DID *SUN* COME FROM?!
FWOSH

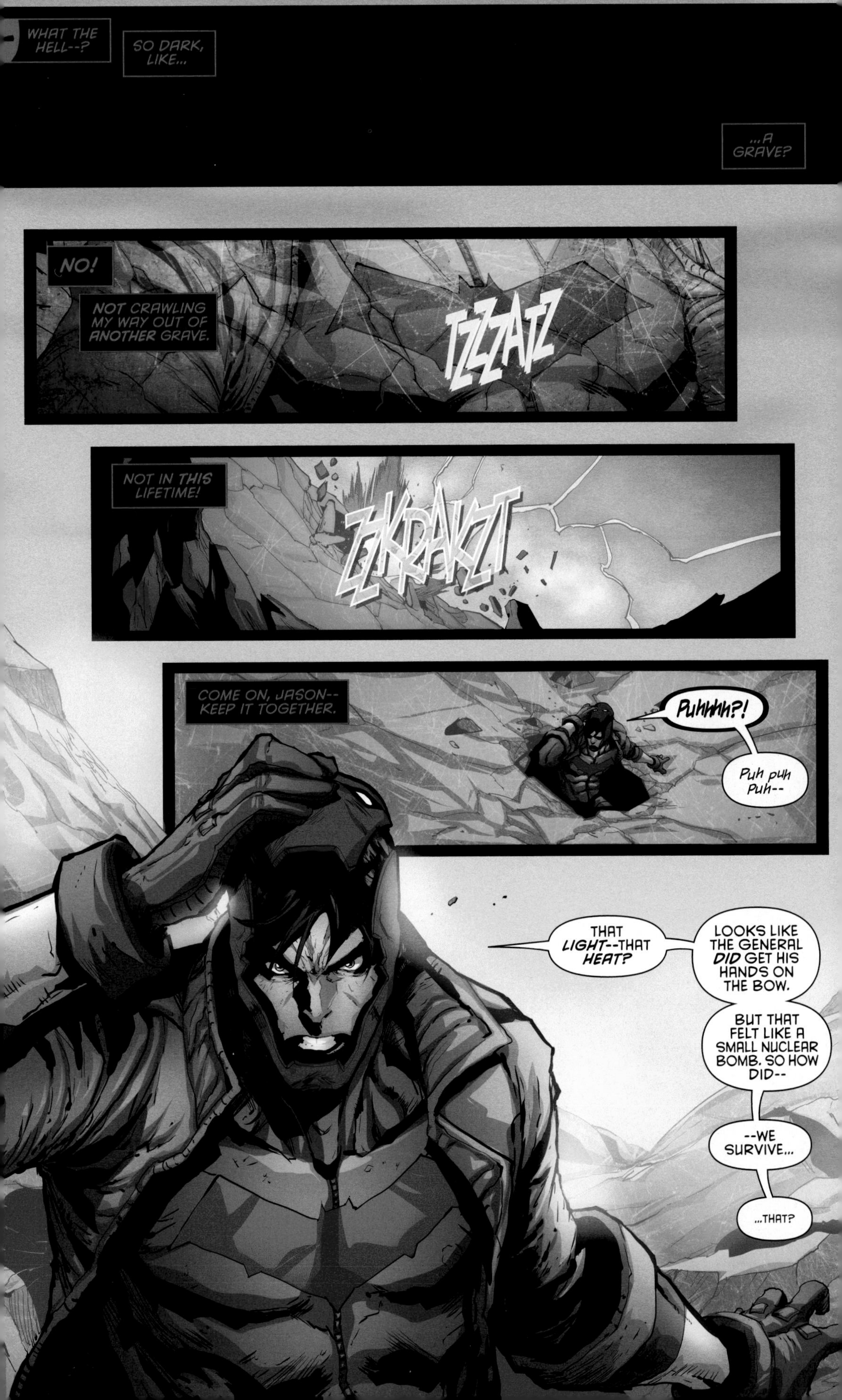
WHAT THE HELL--?
SO DARK, LIKE...
...A GRAVE?
NO!
NOT CRAWLING MY WAY OUT OF ANOTHER GRAVE.
TZZZATZ
NOT IN THIS LIFETIME!
ZZKRAKZT
COME ON, JASON-- KEEP IT TOGETHER.
Puhhhh?!
Puh puh Puh--
THAT LIGHT--THAT HEAT?
LOOKS LIKE THE GENERAL DID GET HIS HANDS ON THE BOW.
BUT THAT FELT LIKE A SMALL NUCLEAR BOMB. SO HOW DID--
--WE SURVIVE...
...THAT?

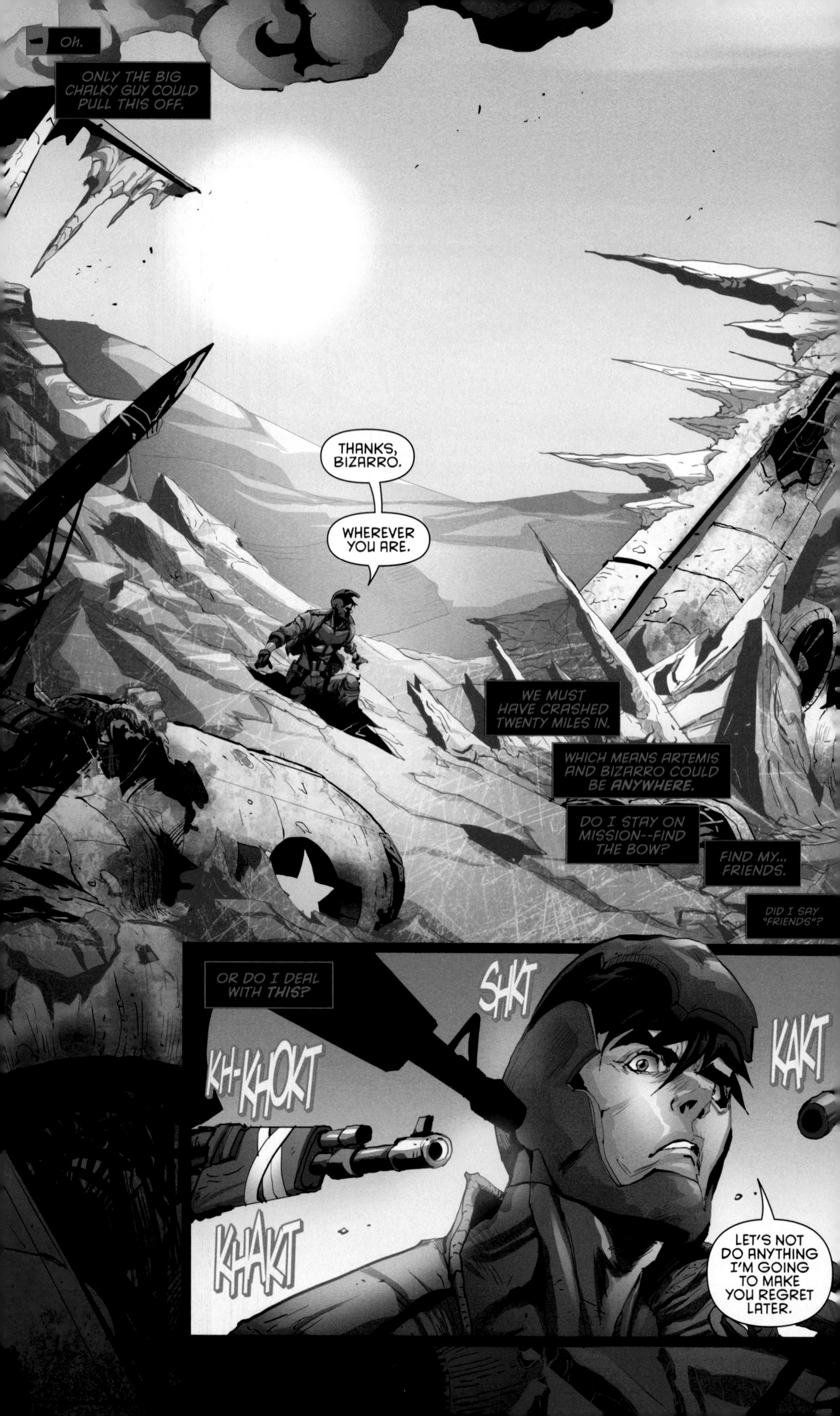
Oh.
ONLY THE BIG CHALKY GUY COULD PULL THIS OFF.
THANKS, BIZARRO.
WHEREVER YOU ARE.
WE MUST HAVE CRASHED TWENTY MILES IN.
WHICH MEANS ARTEMIS AND BIZARRO COULD BE ANYWHERE.
DO I STAY ON MISSION--FIND THE BOW?
FIND MY... FRIENDS.
DID I SAY "FRIENDS"?
OR DO I DEAL WITH THIS?
SHKT
KH-KHOKT
KAKT
KHAKT
LET'S NOT DO ANYTHING I'M GOING TO MAKE YOU REGRET LATER.

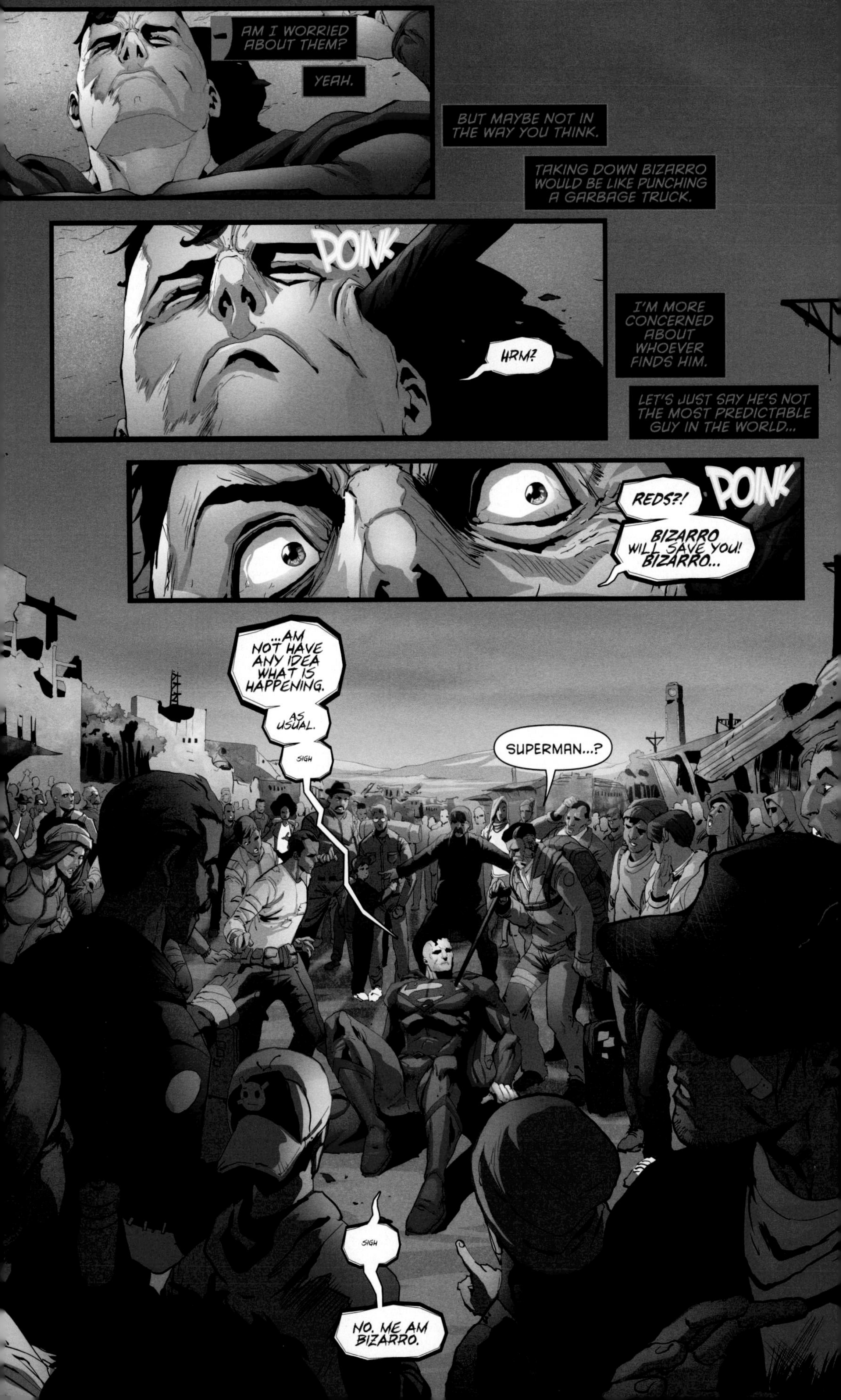
AM I WORRIED ABOUT THEM?
YEAH.
BUT MAYBE NOT IN THE WAY YOU THINK.
TAKING DOWN BIZARRO WOULD BE LIKE PUNCHING A GARBAGE TRUCK.
POINK
HRM?
I'M MORE CONCERNED ABOUT WHOEVER FINDS HIM.
LET'S JUST SAY HE'S NOT THE MOST PREDICTABLE GUY IN THE WORLD...
REDS?!
BIZARRO WILL SAVE YOU! BIZARRO...
POINK
...AM NOT HAVE ANY IDEA WHAT IS HAPPENING.
AS USUAL.
SIGH
SUPERMAN...?
SIGH
NO. ME AM BIZARRO.

WELL, CONSIDERING YOU FELL OUT OF THE *SKY* AND, YOU KNOW, *LIVED*...

...PERHAPS YOU CAN ASSIST US ANYWAY?

MAYBE LATER.

ME NEED TO FIND RED HIM.

PLEASE, MISTER!

OLAN, NO!

PLEASE, YOU *HAVE* TO *HELP* US!

HELP HOW, SMALL MAN?

THE GENERAL DESTROYED OUR *HOMES*.

WE HAVE NOWHERE TO *LIVE*.

PLEASE.

WE HAVE TO GET SOMEPLACE *SAFE*.

WE NEED TO GET *AWAY* FROM HERE.

AWAY...?

HRM.

ME SUPPOSE YOU CAN COME WITH BIZARRO.

RED HIM AND RED HER WILL KNOW WHAT TO DO.

AND YOU WON'T LET THE GENERAL'S MEN HURT US?

PROMISE.

WHO KNOWS WHAT TROUBLE HE'S GETTING HIMSELF INTO

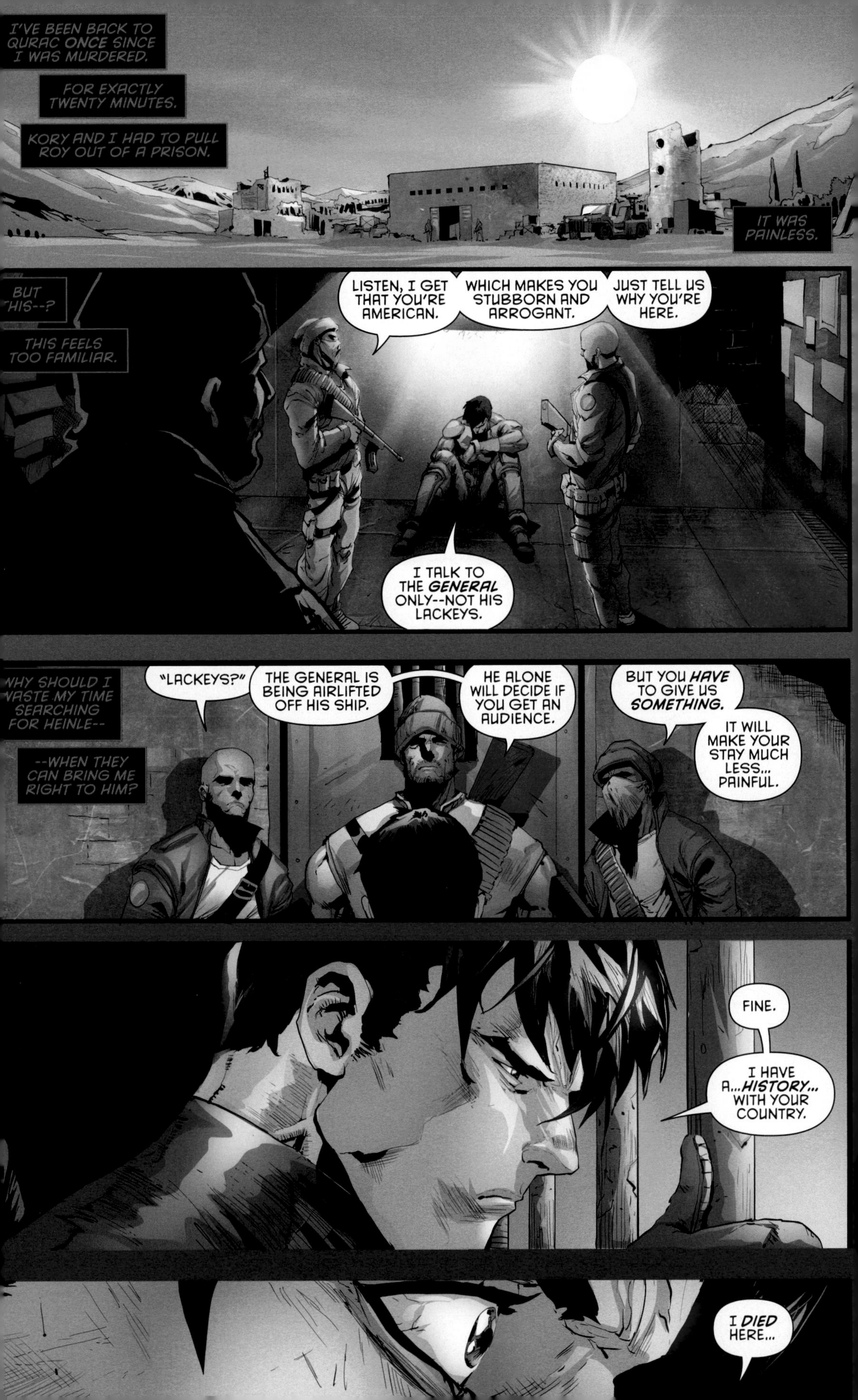
I'VE BEEN BACK TO QURAC ONCE SINCE I WAS MURDERED.
FOR EXACTLY TWENTY MINUTES.
KORY AND I HAD TO PULL ROY OUT OF A PRISON.
IT WAS PAINLESS.
BUT THIS--?
THIS FEELS TOO FAMILIAR.
LISTEN, I GET THAT YOU'RE AMERICAN.
WHICH MAKES YOU STUBBORN AND ARROGANT.
JUST TELL US WHY YOU'RE HERE.
I TALK TO THE GENERAL ONLY--NOT HIS LACKEYS.
WHY SHOULD I WASTE MY TIME SEARCHING FOR HEINLE--
--WHEN THEY CAN BRING ME RIGHT TO HIM?
"LACKEYS?"
THE GENERAL IS BEING AIRLIFTED OFF HIS SHIP.
HE ALONE WILL DECIDE IF YOU GET AN AUDIENCE.
BUT YOU HAVE TO GIVE US SOMETHING.
IT WILL MAKE YOUR STAY MUCH LESS... PAINFUL.
FINE.
I HAVE A...HISTORY... WITH YOUR COUNTRY.
I DIED HERE...

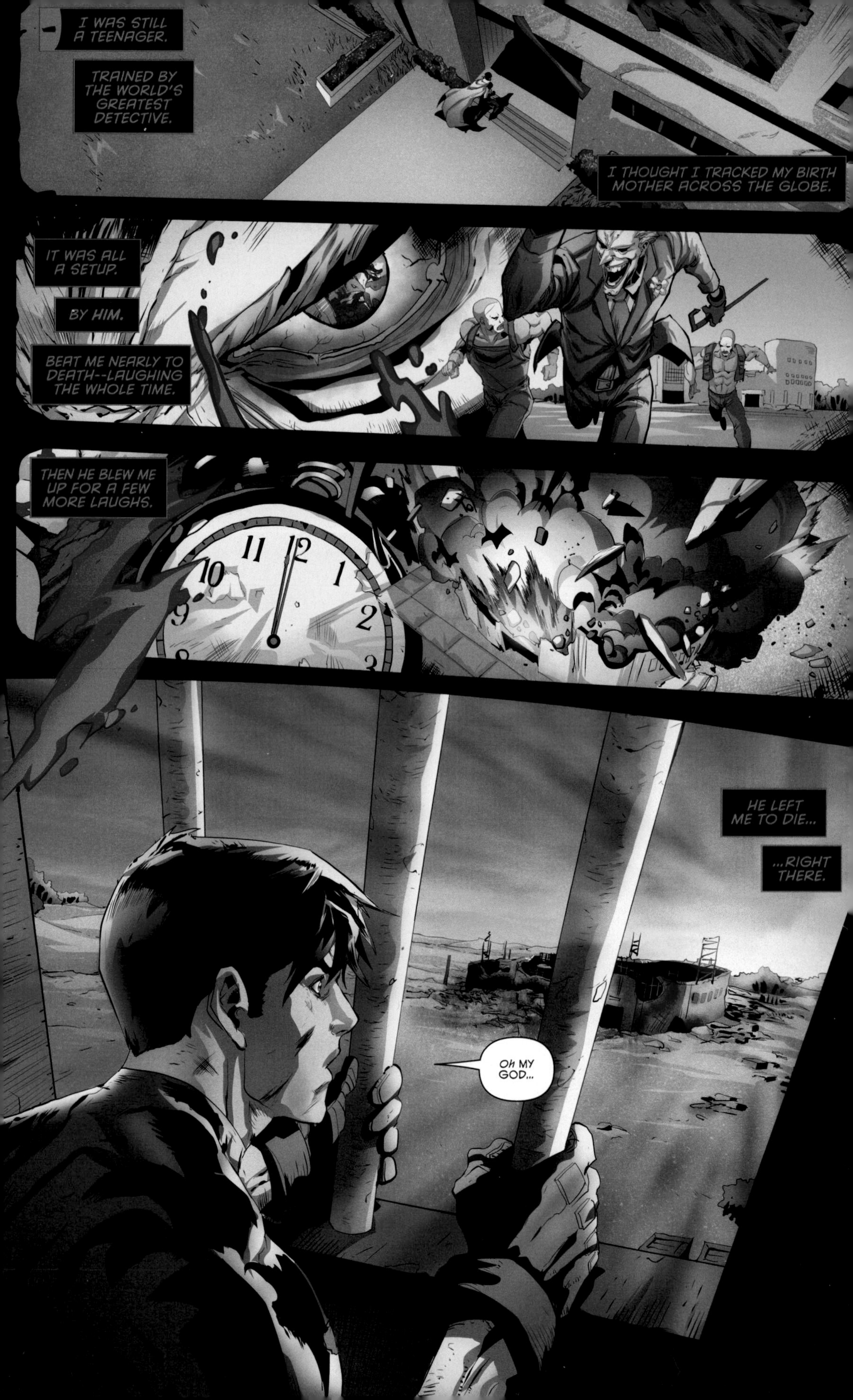

I WAS STILL A TEENAGER.
TRAINED BY THE WORLD'S GREATEST DETECTIVE.
I THOUGHT I TRACKED MY BIRTH MOTHER ACROSS THE GLOBE.
IT WAS ALL A SETUP.
BY HIM.
BEAT ME NEARLY TO DEATH--LAUGHING THE WHOLE TIME.
THEN HE BLEW ME UP FOR A FEW MORE LAUGHS.
HE LEFT ME TO DIE...
...RIGHT THERE.
Oh MY GOD...

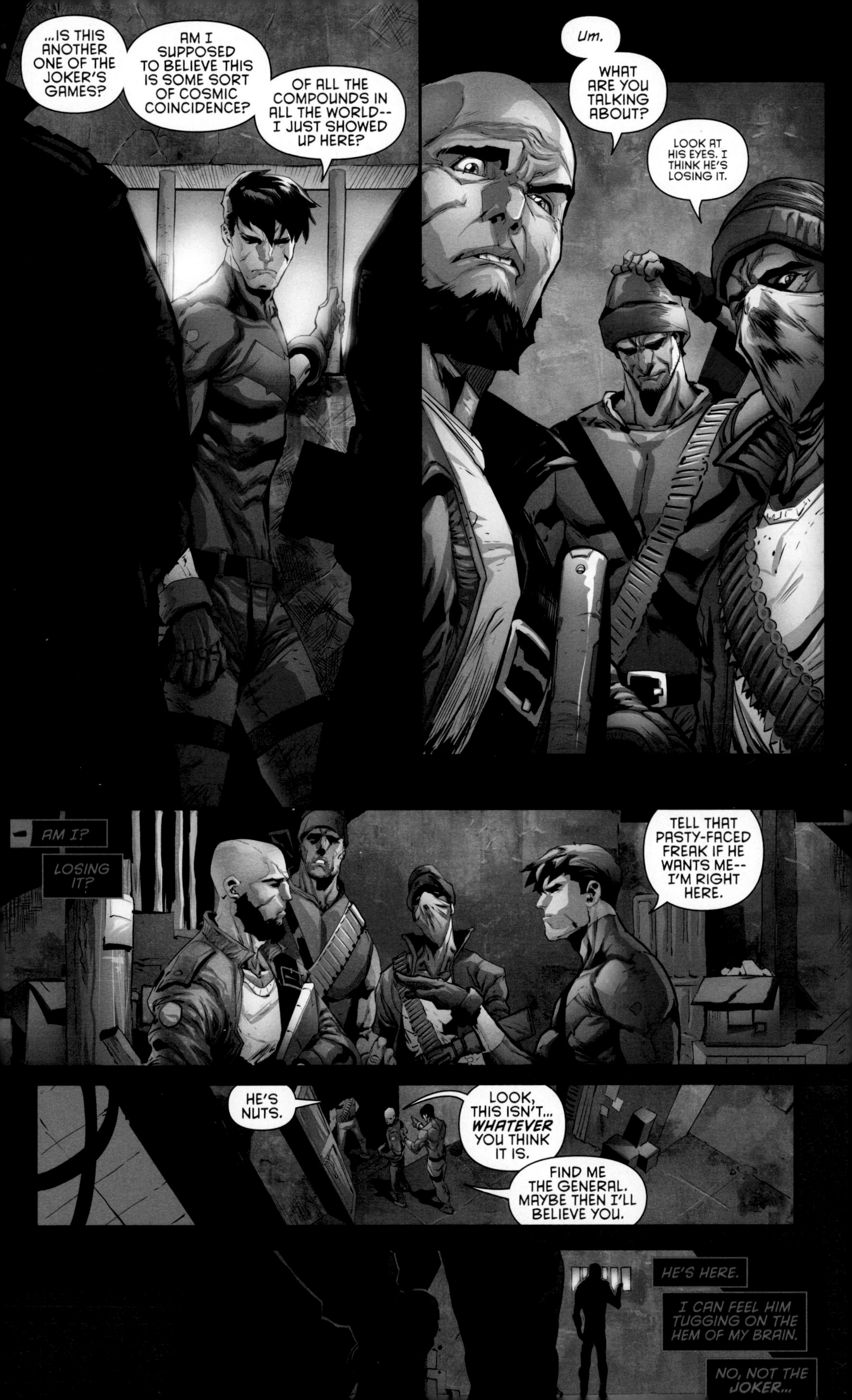
...IS THIS ANOTHER ONE OF THE JOKER'S GAMES?
AM I SUPPOSED TO BELIEVE THIS IS SOME SORT OF COSMIC COINCIDENCE?
OF ALL THE COMPOUNDS IN ALL THE WORLD-- I JUST SHOWED UP HERE?
Um.
WHAT ARE YOU TALKING ABOUT?
LOOK AT HIS EYES. I THINK HE'S LOSING IT.
AM I?
LOSING IT?
TELL THAT PASTY-FACED FREAK IF HE WANTS ME-- I'M RIGHT HERE.
HE'S NUTS.
LOOK, THIS ISN'T... WHATEVER YOU THINK IT IS.
FIND ME THE GENERAL. MAYBE THEN I'LL BELIEVE YOU.
HE'S HERE.
I CAN FEEL HIM TUGGING ON THE HEM OF MY BRAIN.
NO, NOT THE JOKER...

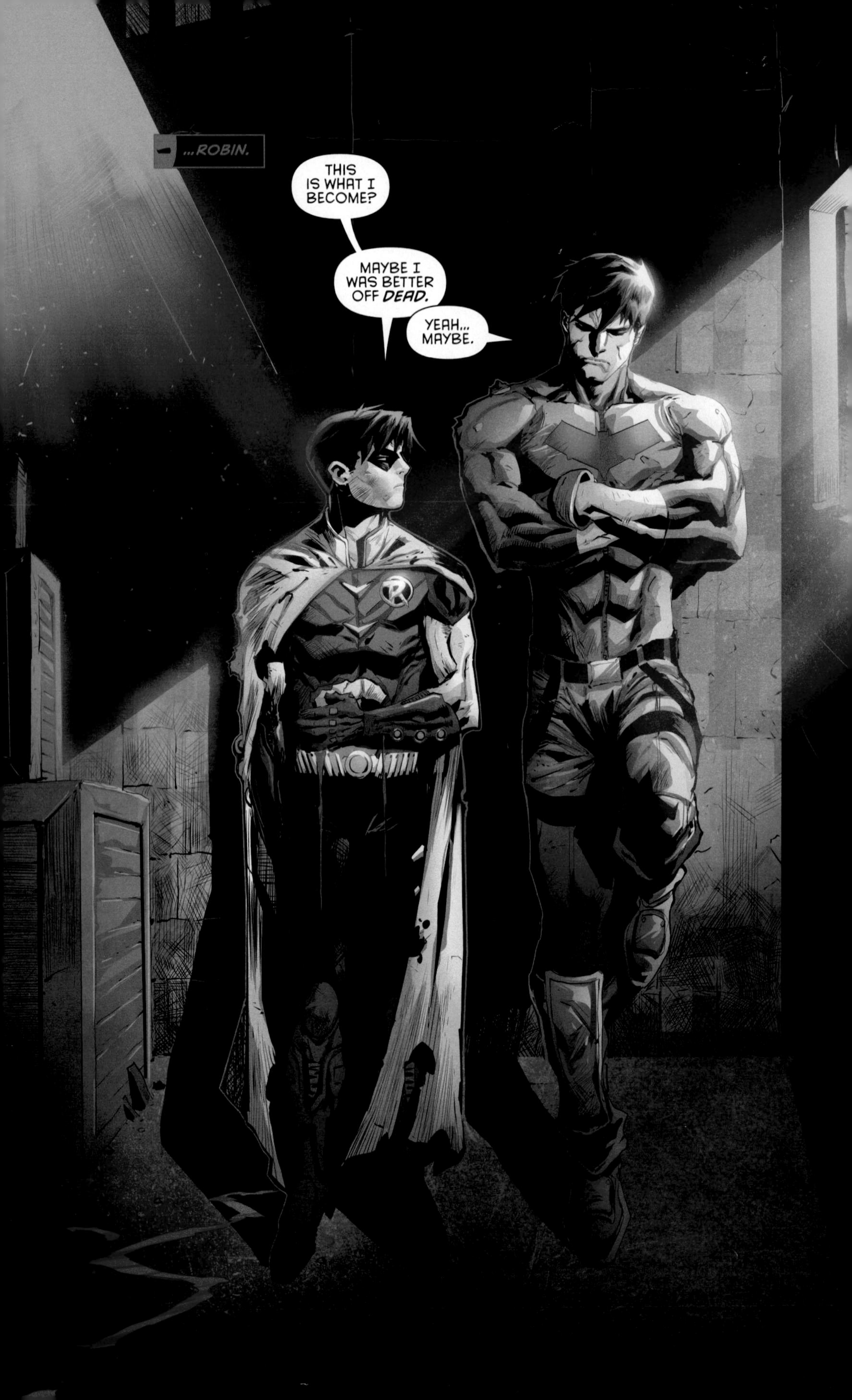
...ROBIN.
THIS IS WHAT I BECOME?
MAYBE I WAS BETTER OFF DEAD.
YEAH... MAYBE.

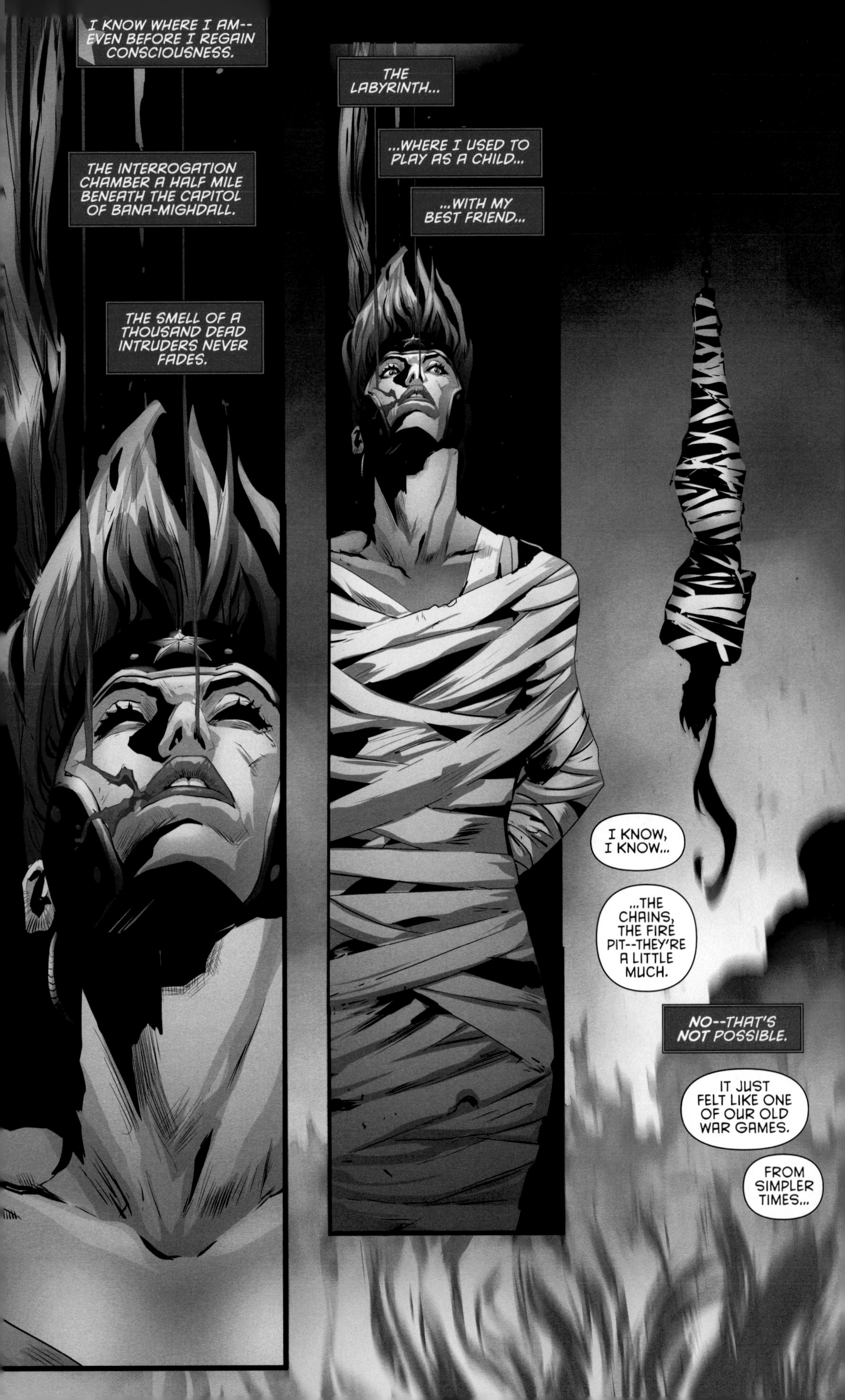

I KNOW WHERE I AM--EVEN BEFORE I REGAIN CONSCIOUSNESS.
THE INTERROGATION CHAMBER A HALF MILE BENEATH THE CAPITOL OF BANA-MIGHDALL.
THE SMELL OF A THOUSAND DEAD INTRUDERS NEVER FADES.
THE LABYRINTH...
...WHERE I USED TO PLAY AS A CHILD...
...WITH MY BEST FRIEND...
I KNOW, I KNOW...
...THE CHAINS, THE FIRE PIT--THEY'RE A LITTLE MUCH.
NO--THAT'S NOT POSSIBLE.
IT JUST FELT LIKE ONE OF OUR OLD WAR GAMES.
FROM SIMPLER TIMES...

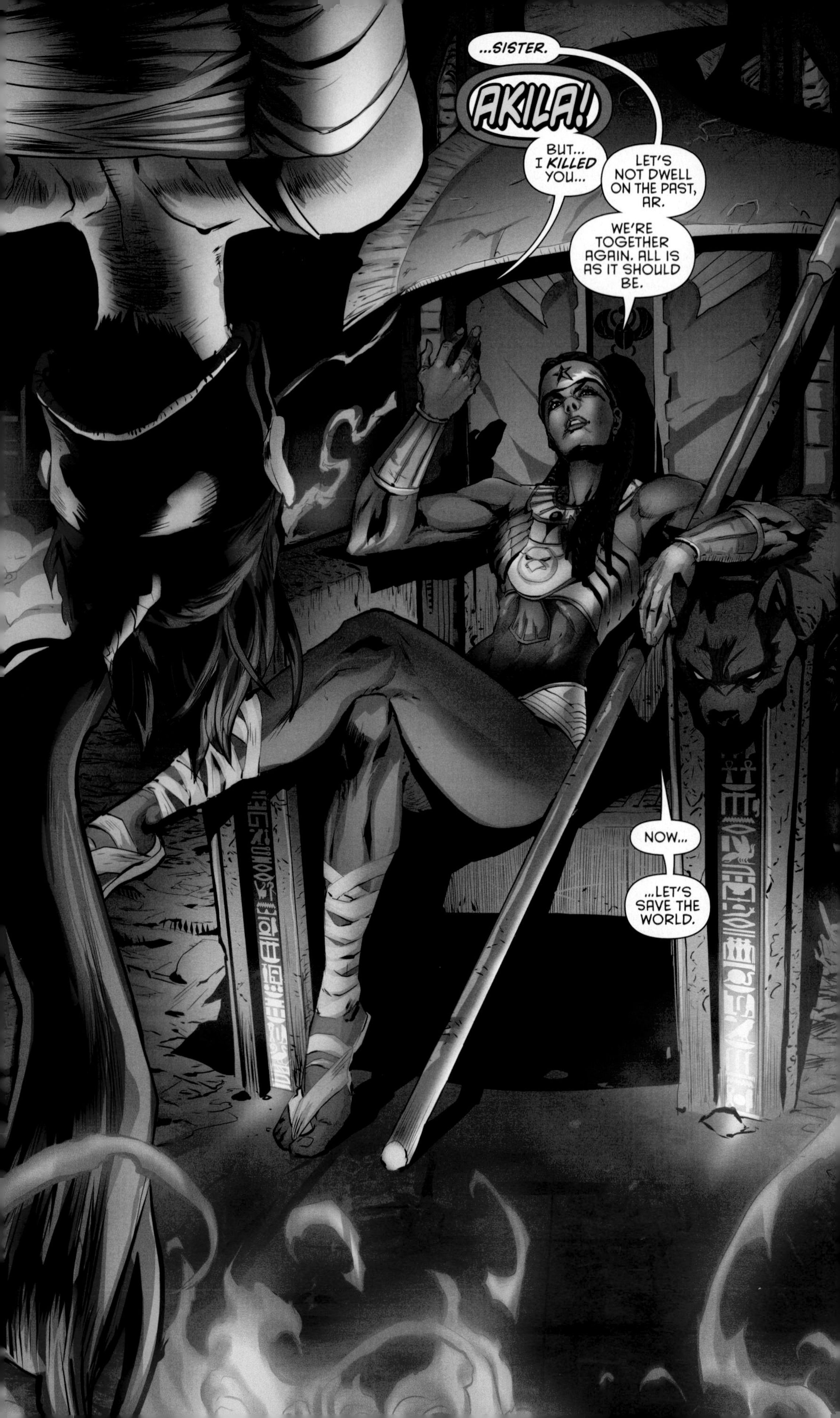

AKILA!
BUT... I KILLED YOU...
...SISTER.
LET'S NOT DWELL ON THE PAST, AR.
WE'RE TOGETHER AGAIN. ALL IS AS IT SHOULD BE.
NOW...
...LET'S SAVE THE WORLD.

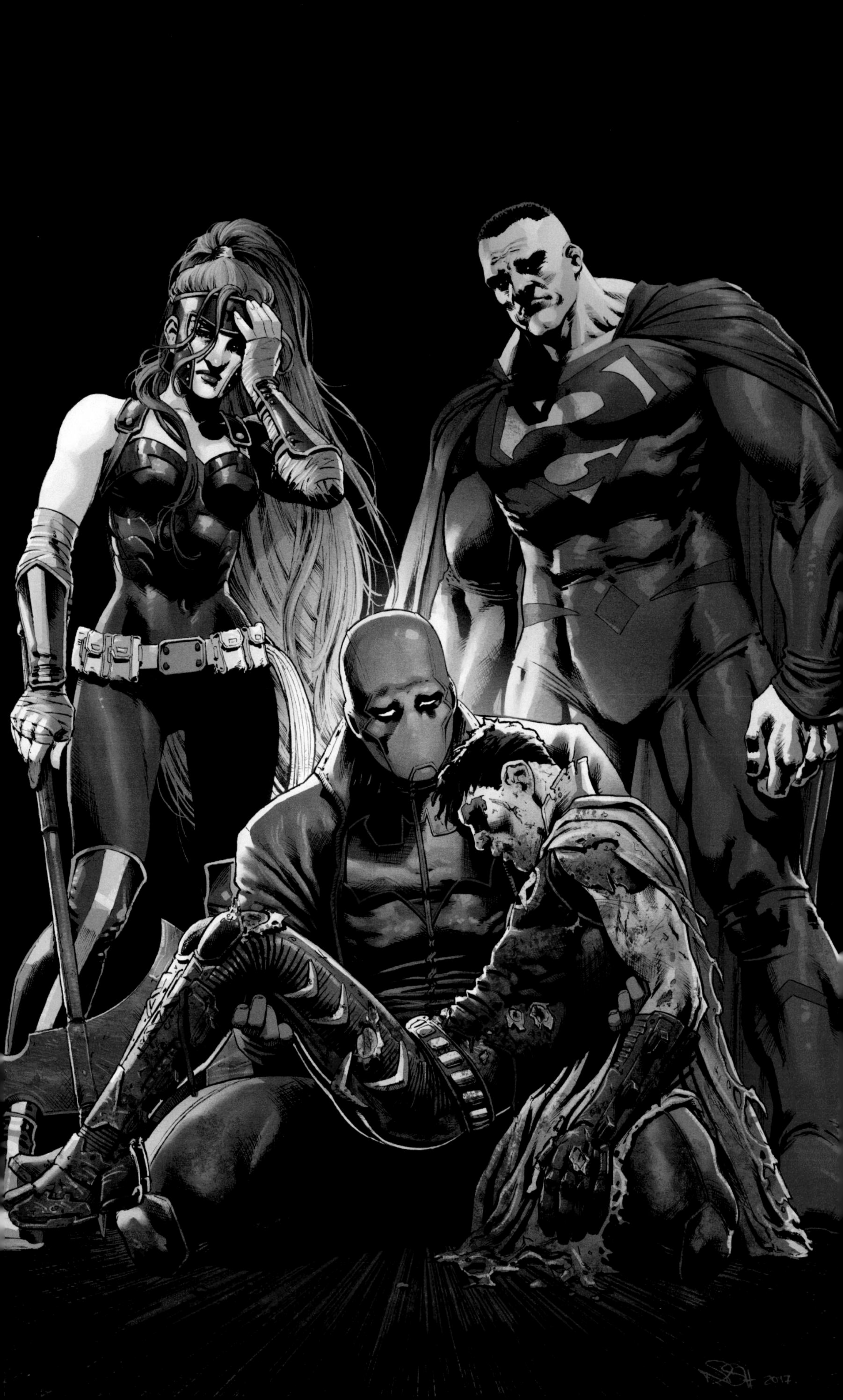

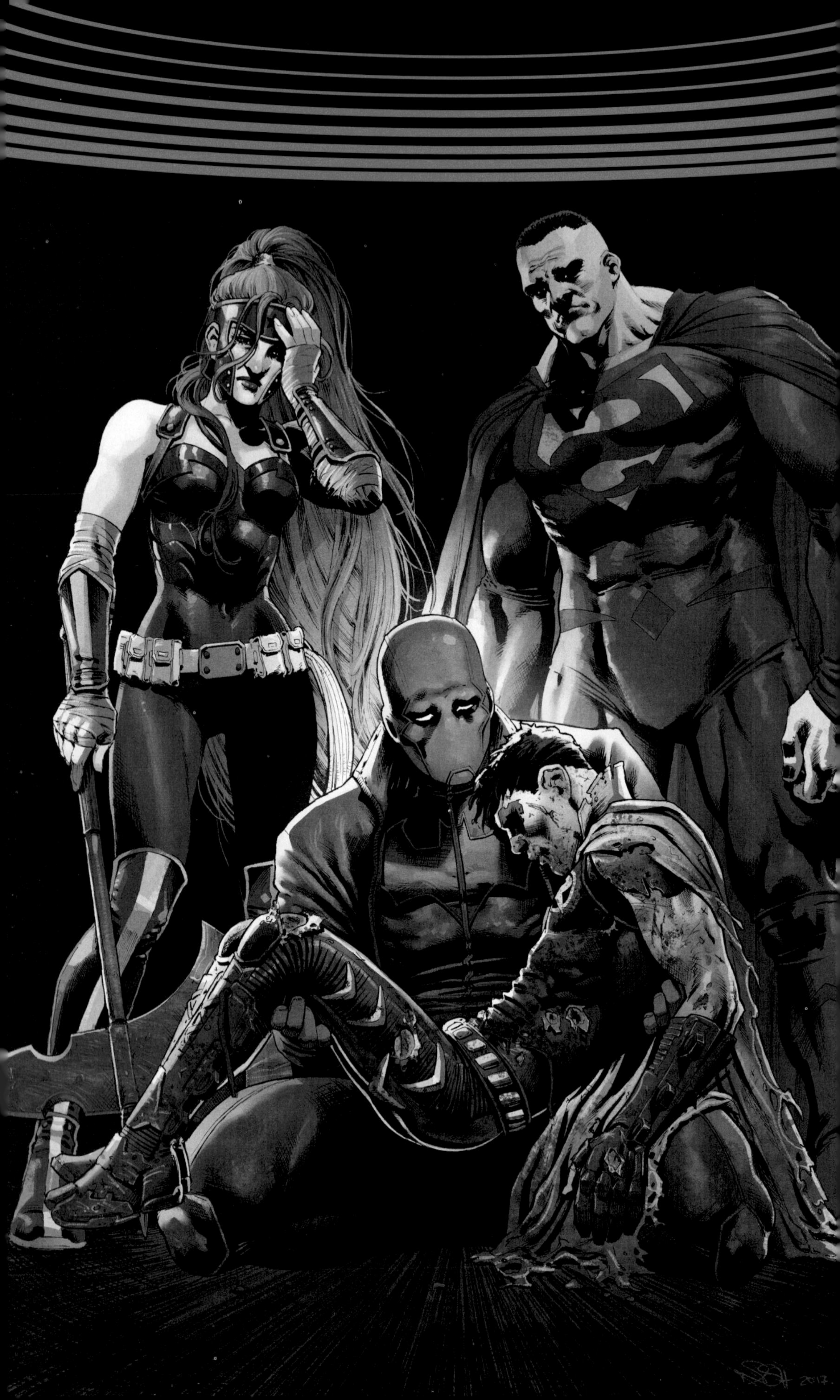

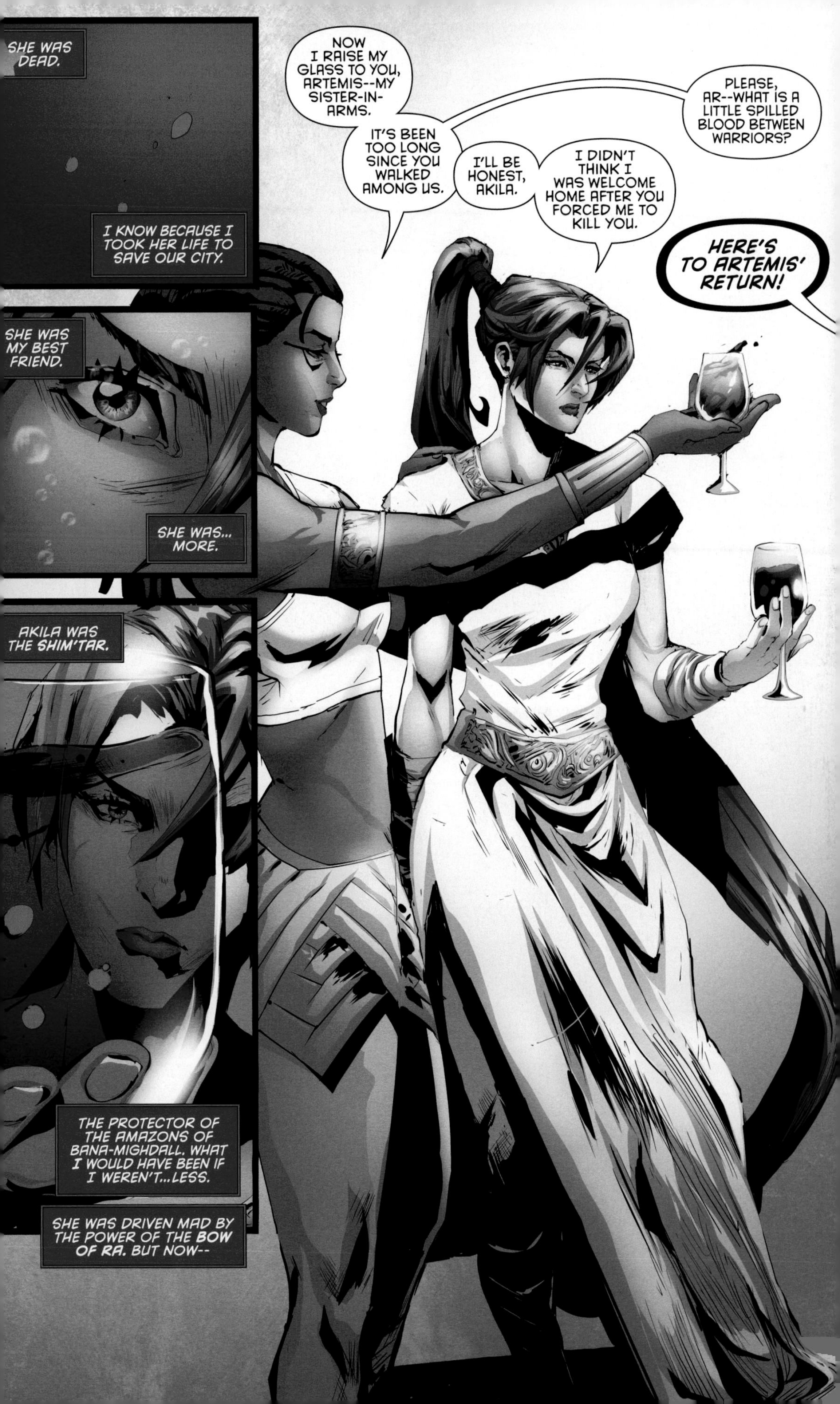
SHE WAS DEAD.
I KNOW BECAUSE I TOOK HER LIFE TO SAVE OUR CITY.
SHE WAS MY BEST FRIEND.
SHE WAS... MORE.
AKILA WAS THE SHIM'TAR.
THE PROTECTOR OF THE AMAZONS OF BANA-MIGHDALL. WHAT I WOULD HAVE BEEN IF I WEREN'T...LESS.
SHE WAS DRIVEN MAD BY THE POWER OF THE BOW OF RA. BUT NOW--
NOW I RAISE MY GLASS TO YOU, ARTEMIS--MY SISTER-IN-ARMS.
IT'S BEEN TOO LONG SINCE YOU WALKED AMONG US.
I'LL BE HONEST, AKILA.
I DIDN'T THINK I WAS WELCOME HOME AFTER YOU FORCED ME TO KILL YOU.
PLEASE, AR--WHAT IS A LITTLE SPILLED BLOOD BETWEEN WARRIORS?
HERE'S TO ARTEMIS' RETURN!

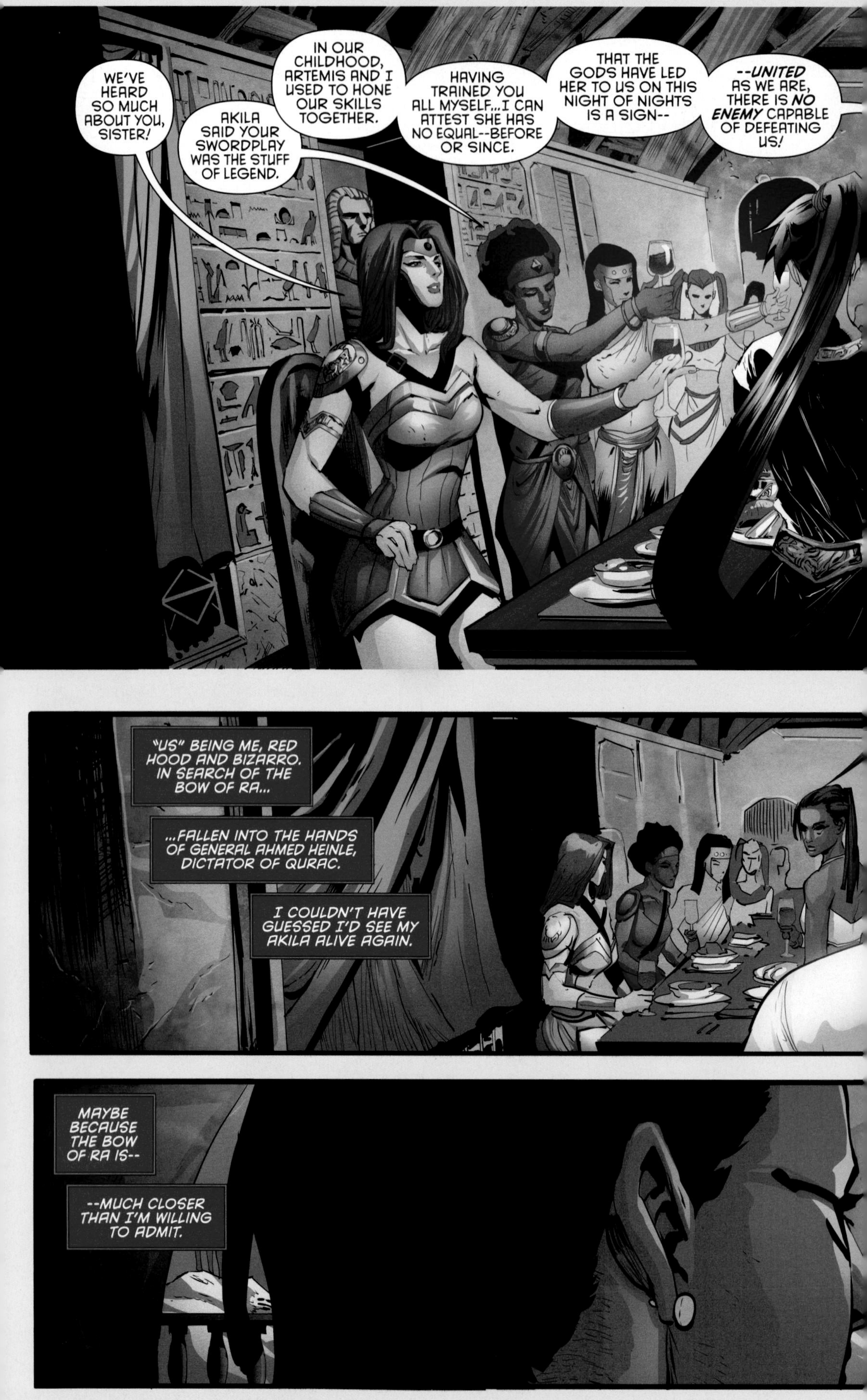
WE'VE HEARD SO MUCH ABOUT YOU, SISTER!
AKILA SAID YOUR SWORDPLAY WAS THE STUFF OF LEGEND.
IN OUR CHILDHOOD, ARTEMIS AND I USED TO HONE OUR SKILLS TOGETHER.
HAVING TRAINED YOU ALL MYSELF...I CAN ATTEST SHE HAS NO EQUAL--BEFORE OR SINCE.
THAT THE GODS HAVE LED HER TO US ON THIS NIGHT OF NIGHTS IS A SIGN--
--UNITED AS WE ARE, THERE IS NO ENEMY CAPABLE OF DEFEATING US!
"US" BEING ME, RED HOOD AND BIZARRO. IN SEARCH OF THE BOW OF RA...
...FALLEN INTO THE HANDS OF GENERAL AHMED HEINLE, DICTATOR OF QURAC.
I COULDN'T HAVE GUESSED I'D SEE MY AKILA ALIVE AGAIN.
MAYBE BECAUSE THE BOW OF RA IS--
--MUCH CLOSER THAN I'M WILLING TO ADMIT.

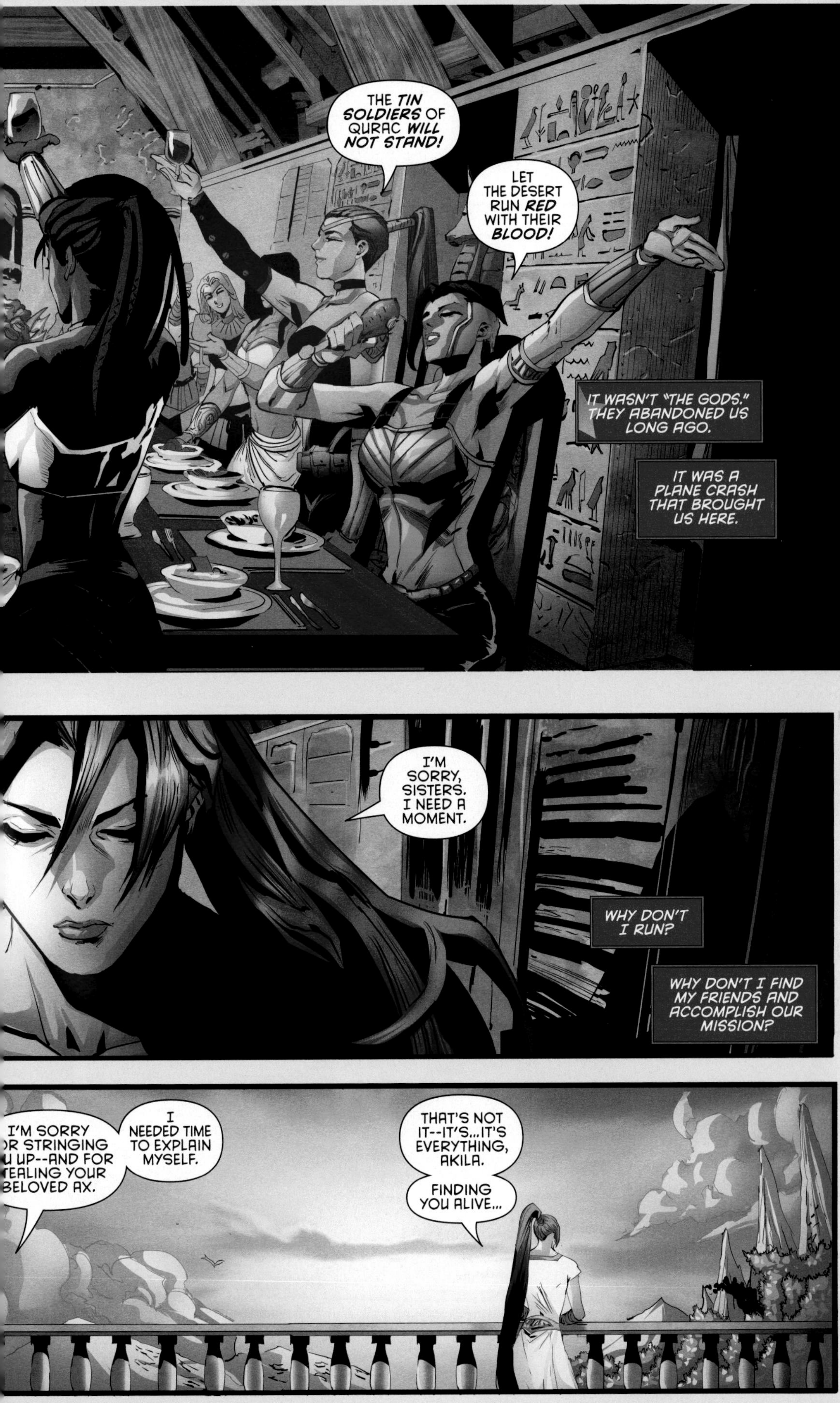
THE TIN SOLDIERS OF QURAC WILL NOT STAND!
LET THE DESERT RUN RED WITH THEIR BLOOD!
IT WASN'T "THE GODS." THEY ABANDONED US LONG AGO.
IT WAS A PLANE CRASH THAT BROUGHT US HERE.
I'M SORRY, SISTERS. I NEED A MOMENT.
WHY DON'T I RUN?
WHY DON'T I FIND MY FRIENDS AND ACCOMPLISH OUR MISSION?
I'M SORRY
OR STRINGING
U UP--AND FOR
TEALING YOUR
BELOVED AX.
I NEEDED TIME TO EXPLAIN MYSELF.
THAT'S NOT IT--IT'S...IT'S EVERYTHING, AKILA.
FINDING YOU ALIVE...

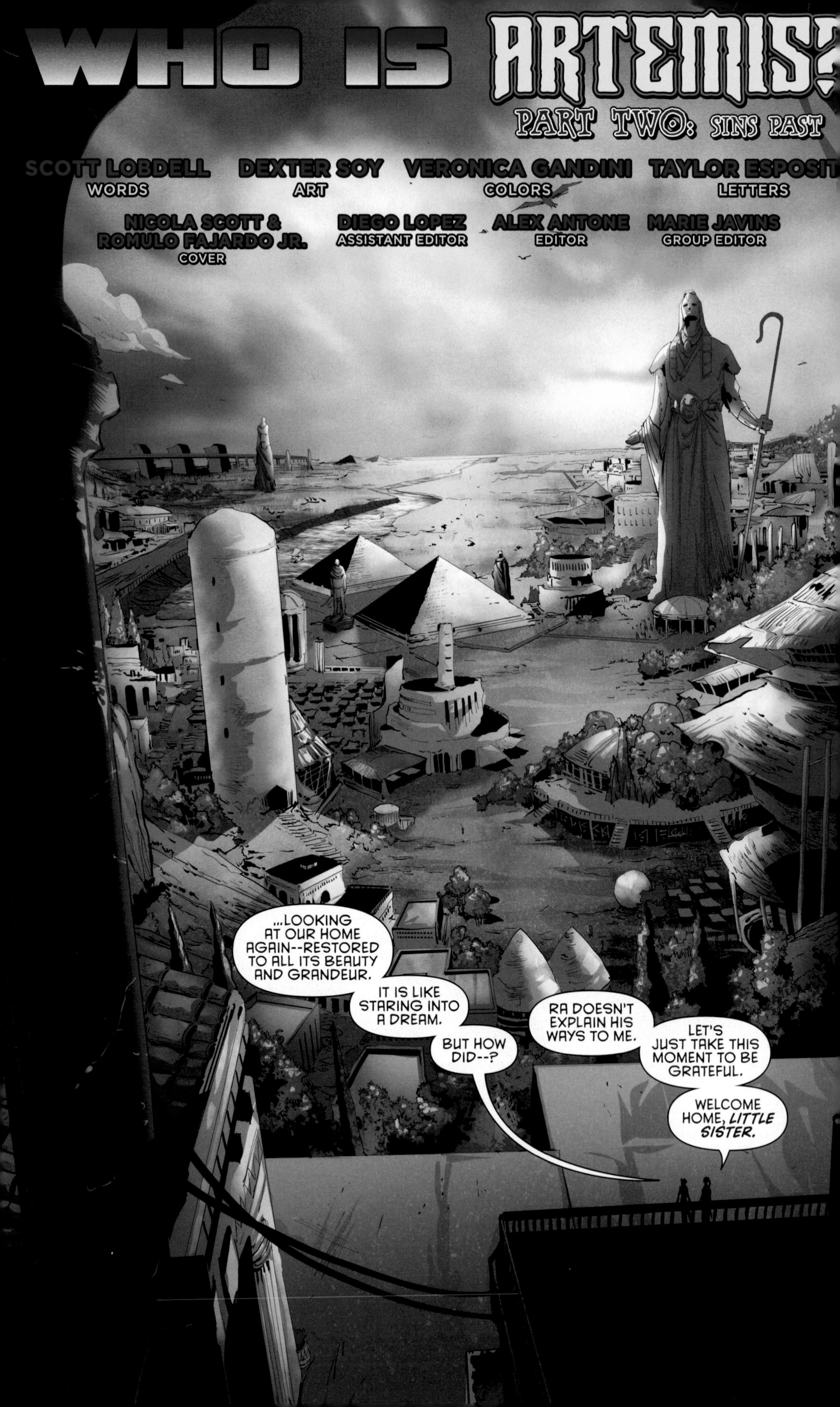

WHO IS ARTEMIS?
PART TWO: SINS PAST
SCOTT LOBDELL WORDS
DEXTER SOY ART
VERONICA GANDINI COLORS
TAYLOR ESPOSIT LETTERS
NICOLA SCOTT & ROMULO FAJARDO JR. COVER
DIEGO LOPEZ ASSISTANT EDITOR
ALEX ANTONE EDITOR
MARIE JAVINS GROUP EDITOR
...LOOKING AT OUR HOME AGAIN--RESTORED TO ALL ITS BEAUTY AND GRANDEUR.
IT IS LIKE STARING INTO A DREAM.
BUT HOW DID--?
RA DOESN'T EXPLAIN HIS WAYS TO ME.
LET'S JUST TAKE THIS MOMENT TO BE GRATEFUL.
WELCOME HOME, *LITTLE SISTER.*

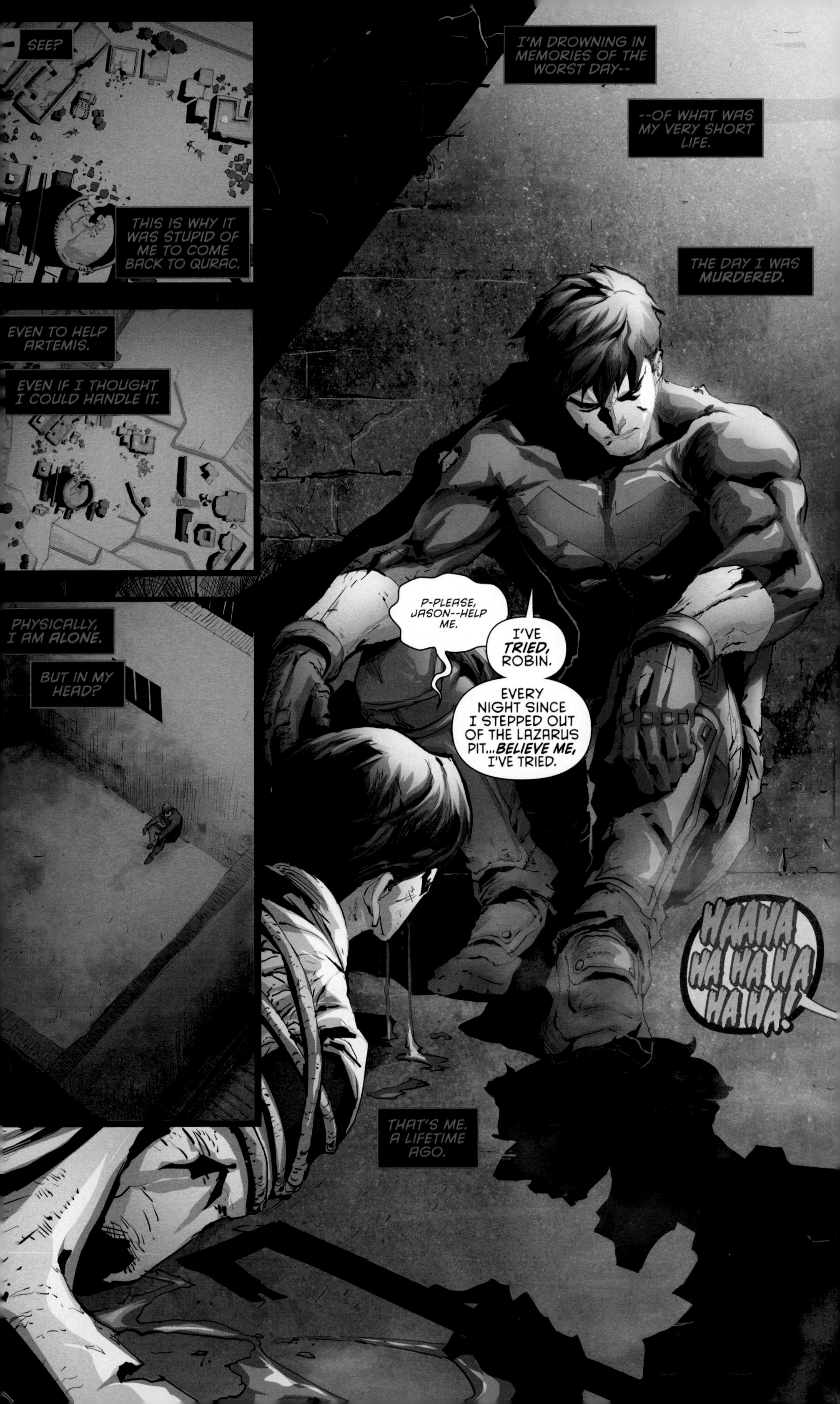
SEE?
THIS IS WHY IT WAS STUPID OF ME TO COME BACK TO QURAC.
EVEN TO HELP ARTEMIS.
EVEN IF I THOUGHT I COULD HANDLE IT.
PHYSICALLY, I AM ALONE.
BUT IN MY HEAD?
I'M DROWNING IN MEMORIES OF THE WORST DAY--
--OF WHAT WAS MY VERY SHORT LIFE.
THE DAY I WAS MURDERED.
P-PLEASE, JASON--HELP ME.
I'VE TRIED, ROBIN.
EVERY NIGHT SINCE I STEPPED OUT OF THE LAZARUS PIT...BELIEVE ME, I'VE TRIED.
HAAHA HA HA HA HA HA!
THAT'S ME. A LIFETIME AGO.

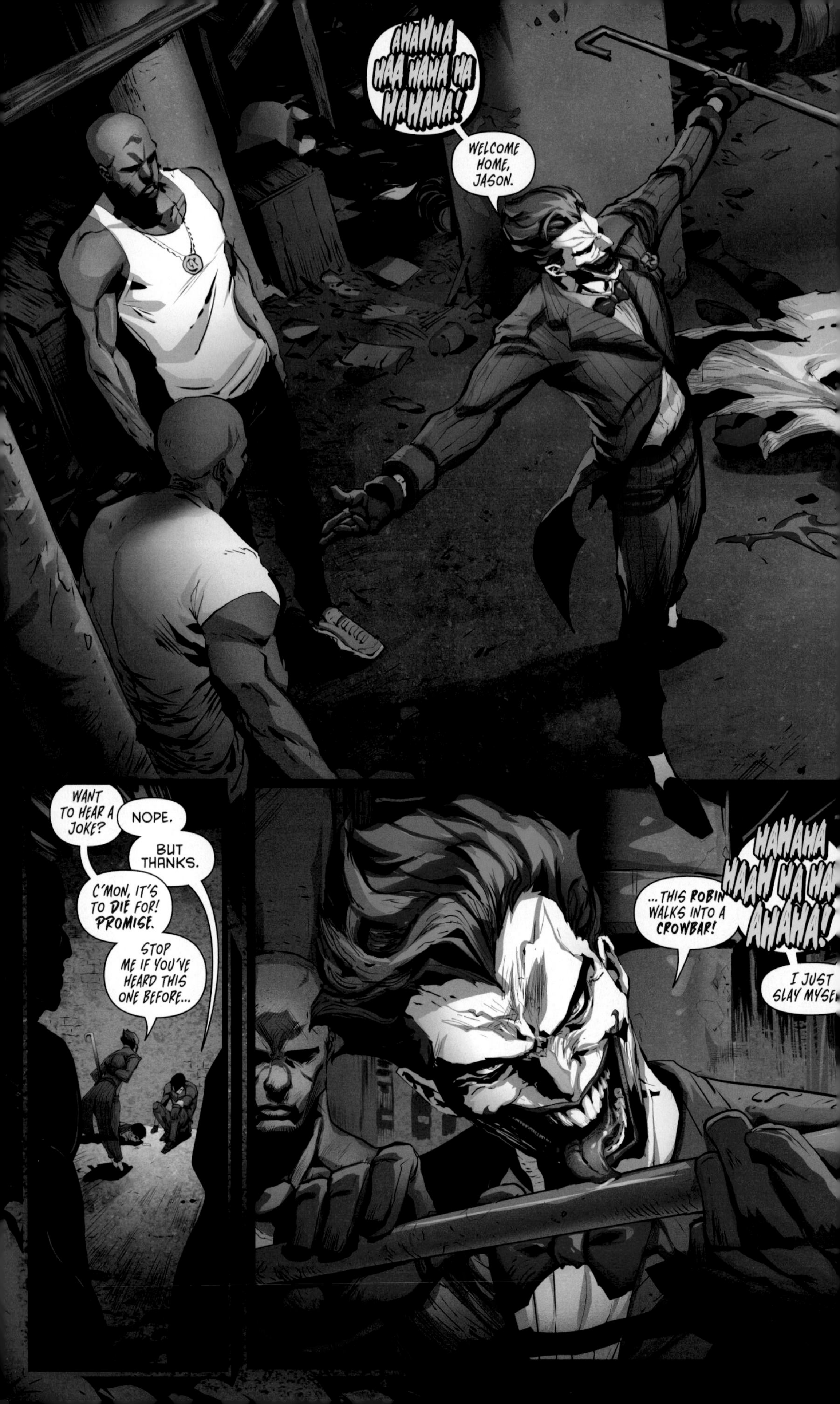

AHAHHA HAA HAHA HA HAHAHA!
WELCOME HOME, JASON.
WANT TO HEAR A JOKE?
NOPE.
BUT THANKS.
C'MON, IT'S TO **DIE** FOR! **PROMISE.**
STOP ME IF YOU'VE HEARD THIS ONE BEFORE...
...THIS **ROBIN** WALKS INTO A **CROWBAR**!
HAHAHA HAAH HA HA AHAHA!
I JUST SLAY MYSE

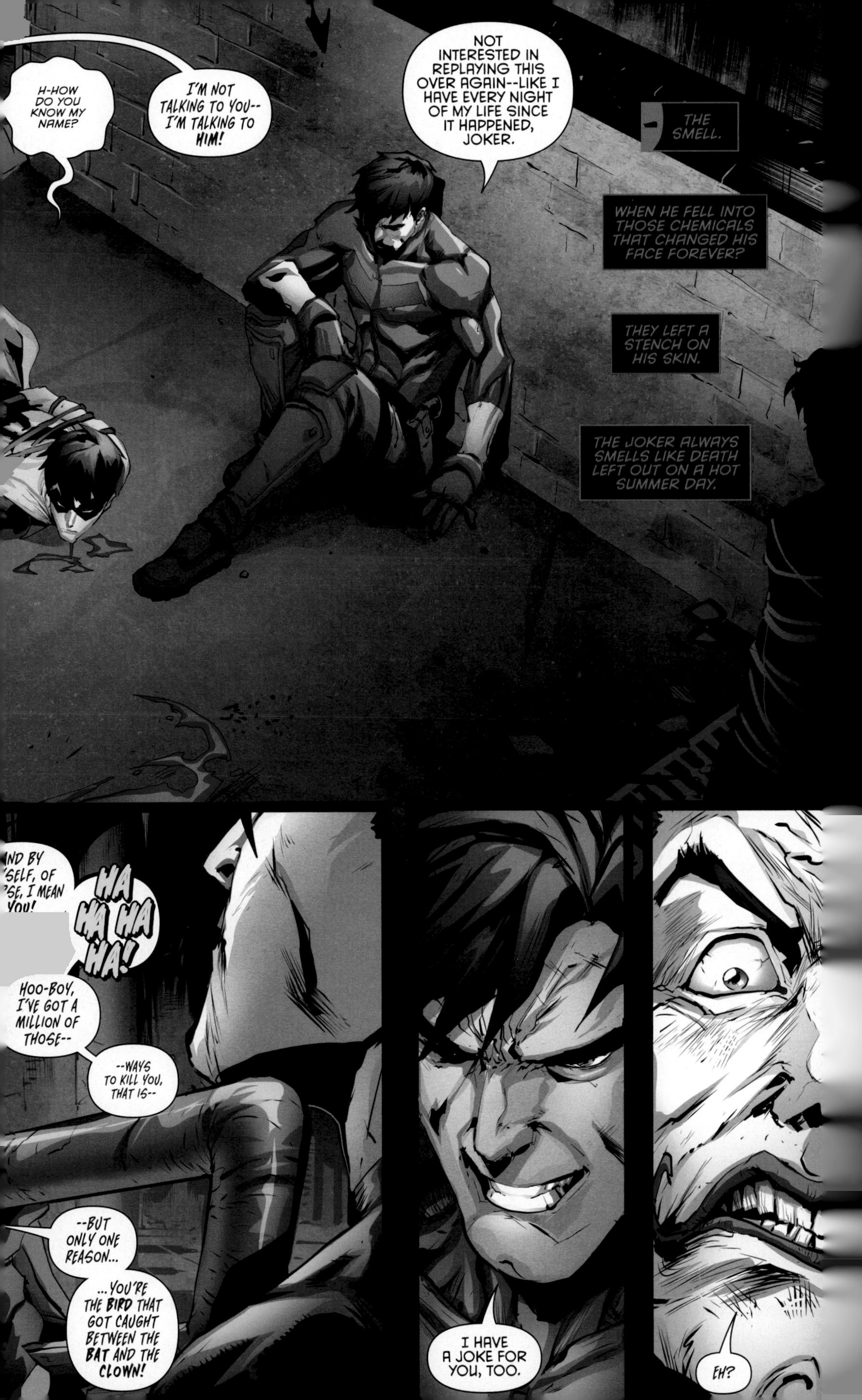
H-HOW DO YOU KNOW MY NAME?
I'M NOT TALKING TO YOU-- I'M TALKING TO HIM!
NOT INTERESTED IN REPLAYING THIS OVER AGAIN--LIKE I HAVE EVERY NIGHT OF MY LIFE SINCE IT HAPPENED, JOKER.
THE SMELL.
WHEN HE FELL INTO THOSE CHEMICALS THAT CHANGED HIS FACE FOREVER?
THEY LEFT A STENCH ON HIS SKIN.
THE JOKER ALWAYS SMELLS LIKE DEATH LEFT OUT ON A HOT SUMMER DAY.
HA HA HA HA!
HOO-BOY, I'VE GOT A MILLION OF THOSE--
--WAYS TO KILL YOU, THAT IS--
--BUT ONLY ONE REASON...
...YOU'RE THE BIRD THAT GOT CAUGHT BETWEEN THE BAT AND THE CLOWN!
I HAVE A JOKE FOR YOU, TOO.
EH?

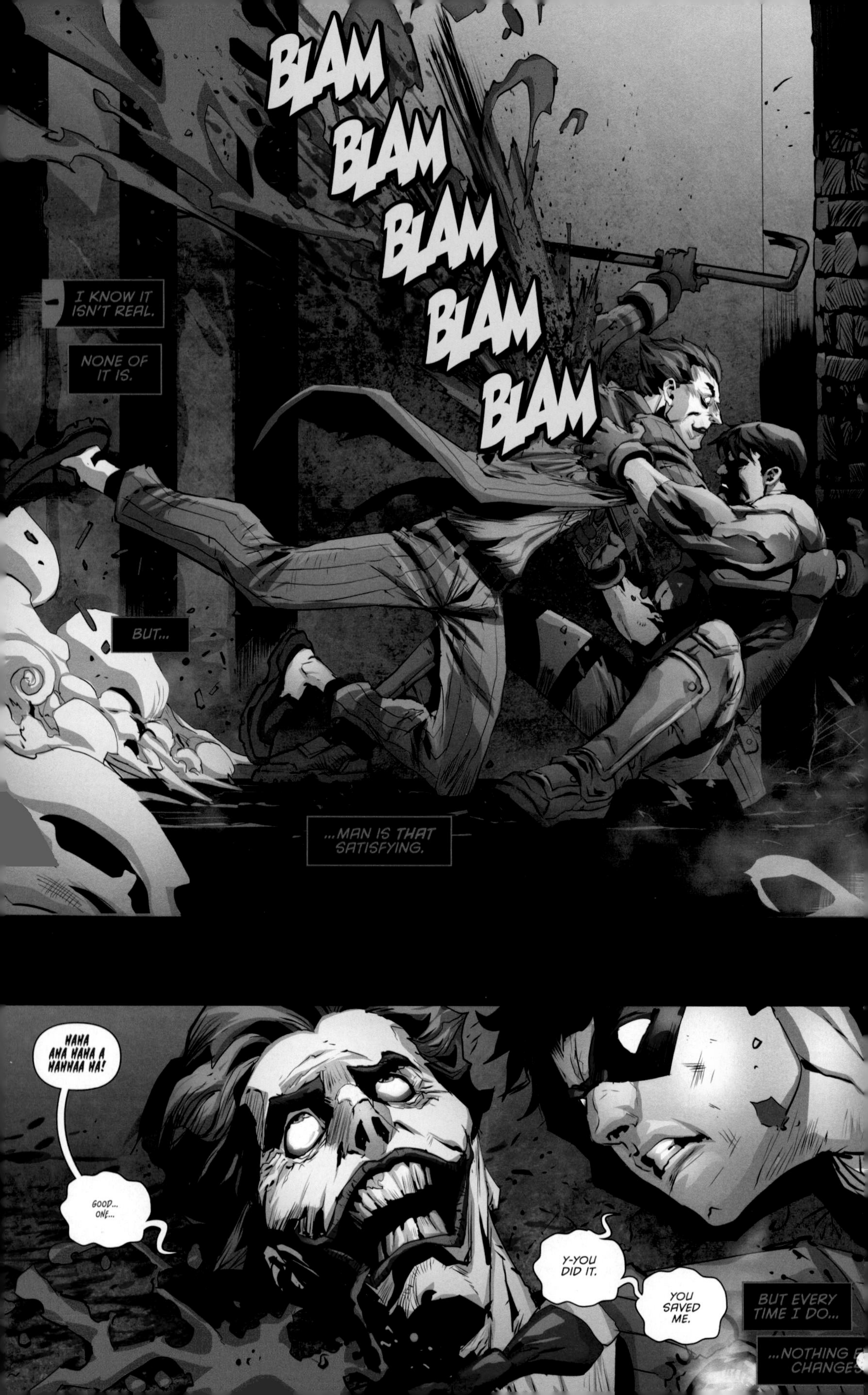
BLAM BLAM BLAM BLAM BLAM
I KNOW IT ISN'T REAL.
NONE OF IT IS.
BUT...
...MAN IS THAT SATISFYING.
HAHA AHA HAHA A HAHHAA HA!
GOOD... ONE...
Y-YOU DID IT.
YOU SAVED ME.
BUT EVERY TIME I DO...
...NOTHING
CHANGES.

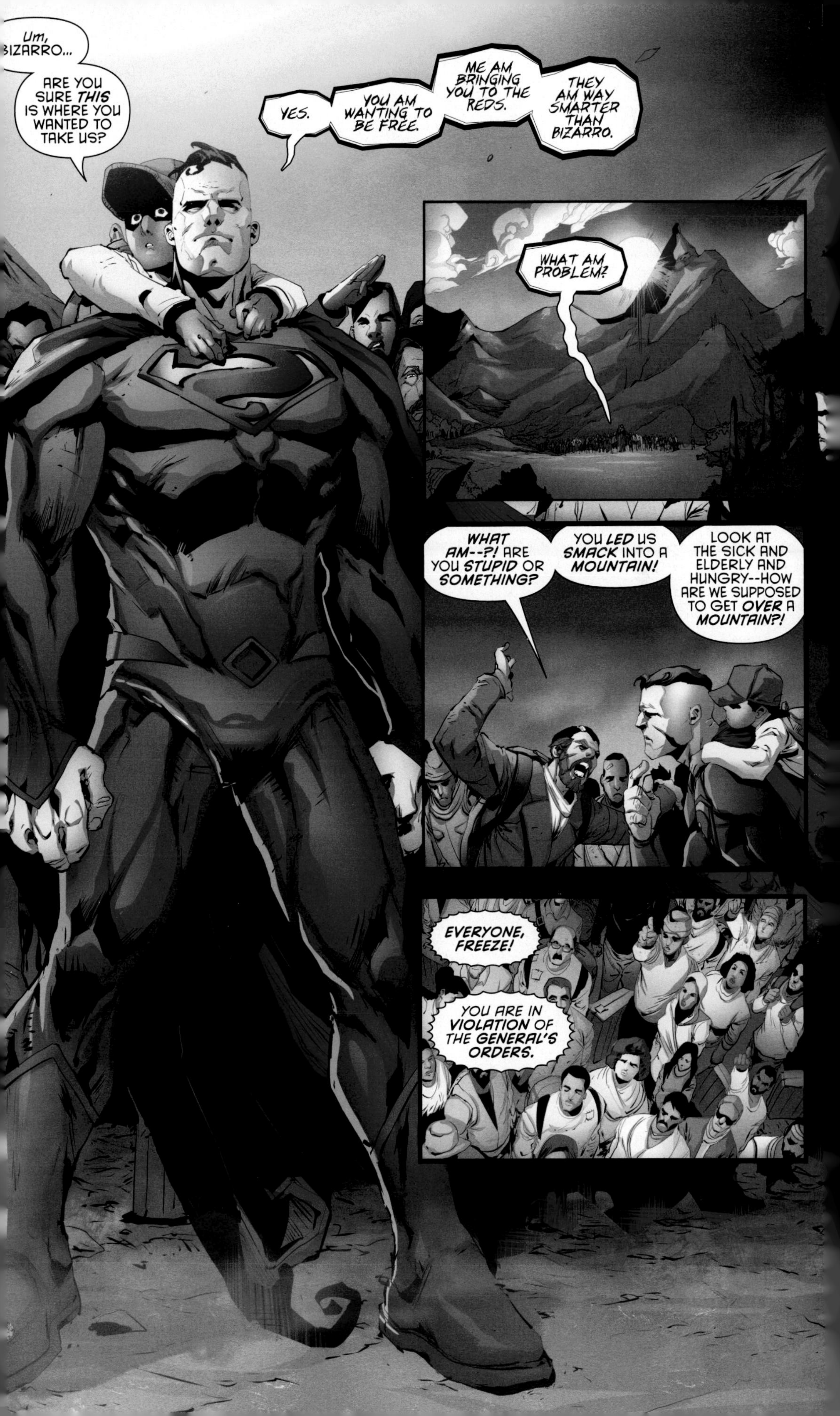

Um, BIZARRO...
ARE YOU SURE THIS IS WHERE YOU WANTED TO TAKE US?
YES.
YOU AM WANTING TO BE FREE.
ME AM BRINGING YOU TO THE REDS.
THEY AM WAY SMARTER THAN BIZARRO.
WHAT AM PROBLEM?
WHAT AM--?! ARE YOU STUPID OR SOMETHING?
YOU LED US SMACK INTO A MOUNTAIN!
LOOK AT THE SICK AND ELDERLY AND HUNGRY--HOW ARE WE SUPPOSED TO GET OVER A MOUNTAIN?!
EVERYONE, FREEZE!
YOU ARE IN VIOLATION OF THE GENERAL'S ORDERS.

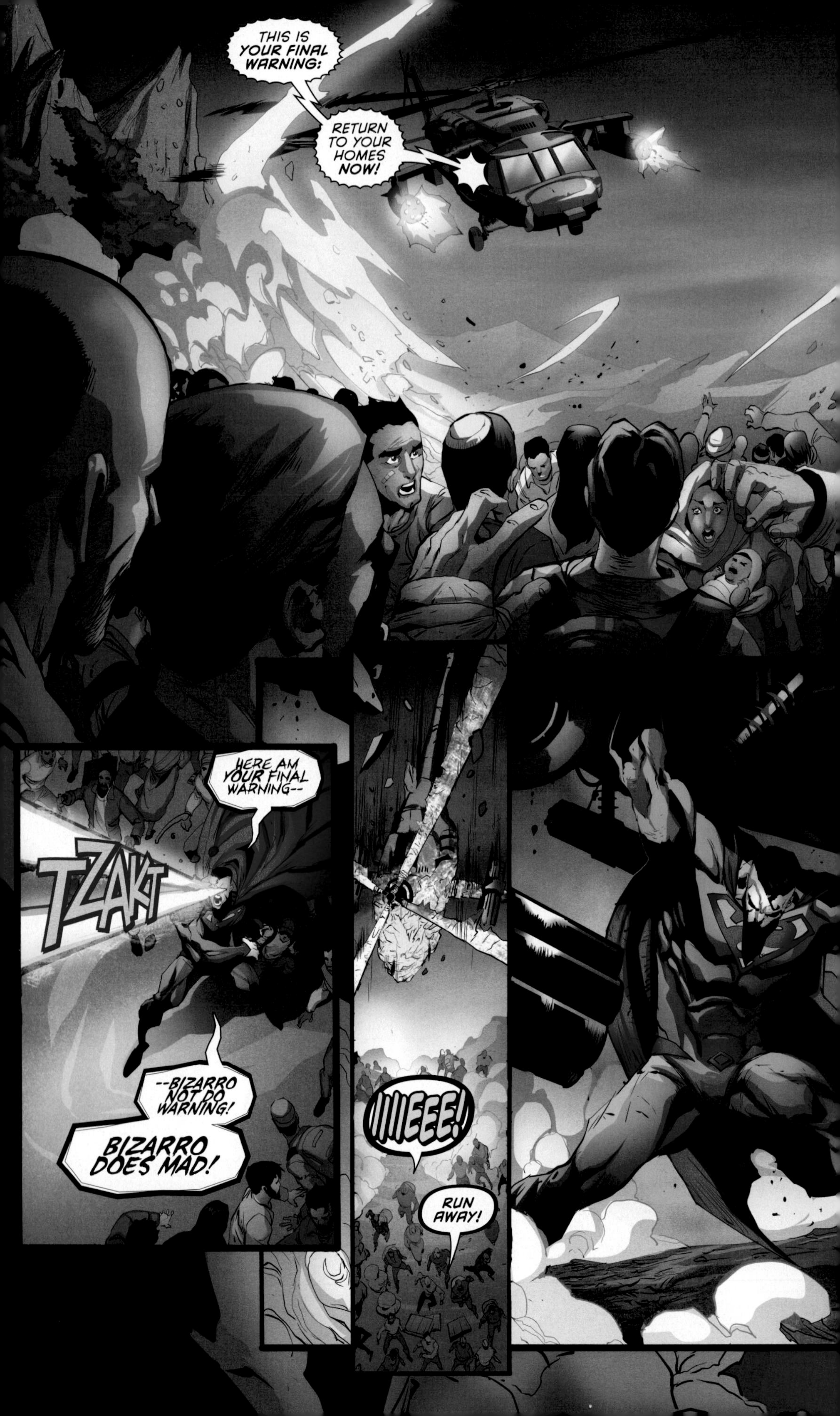
THIS IS YOUR FINAL WARNING:
RETURN TO YOUR HOMES NOW!
HERE AM YOUR FINAL WARNING--
TZAKT
--BIZARRO NOT DO WARNING!
BIZARRO DOES MAD!
IIIIIIEEE!
RUN AWAY!

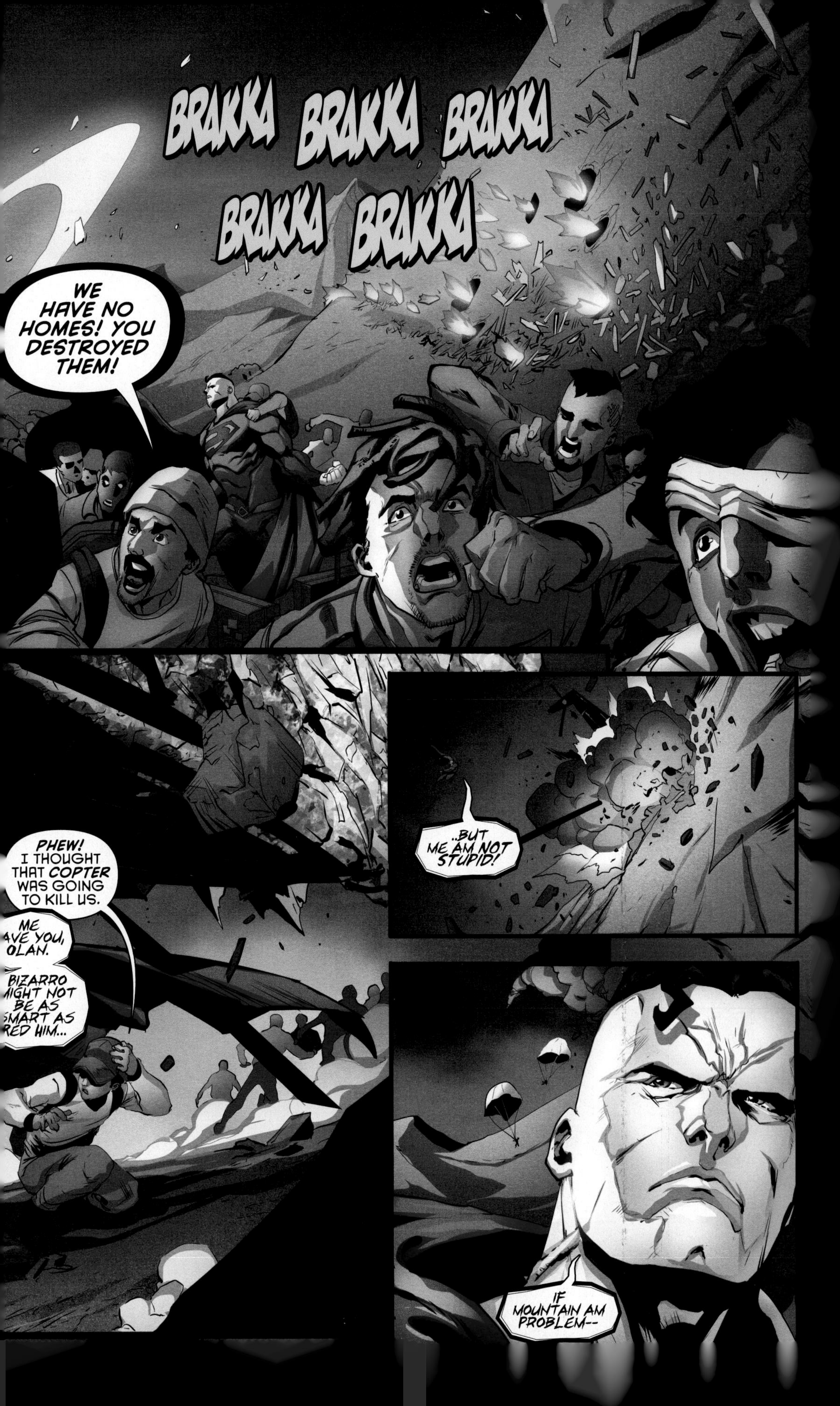

BRAKKA BRAKKA BRAKKA
BRAKKA BRAKKA
WE HAVE NO HOMES! YOU DESTROYED THEM!
PHEW! I THOUGHT THAT COPTER WAS GOING TO KILL US.
..BUT ME AM NOT STUPID!
IF MOUNTAIN AM PROBLEM--

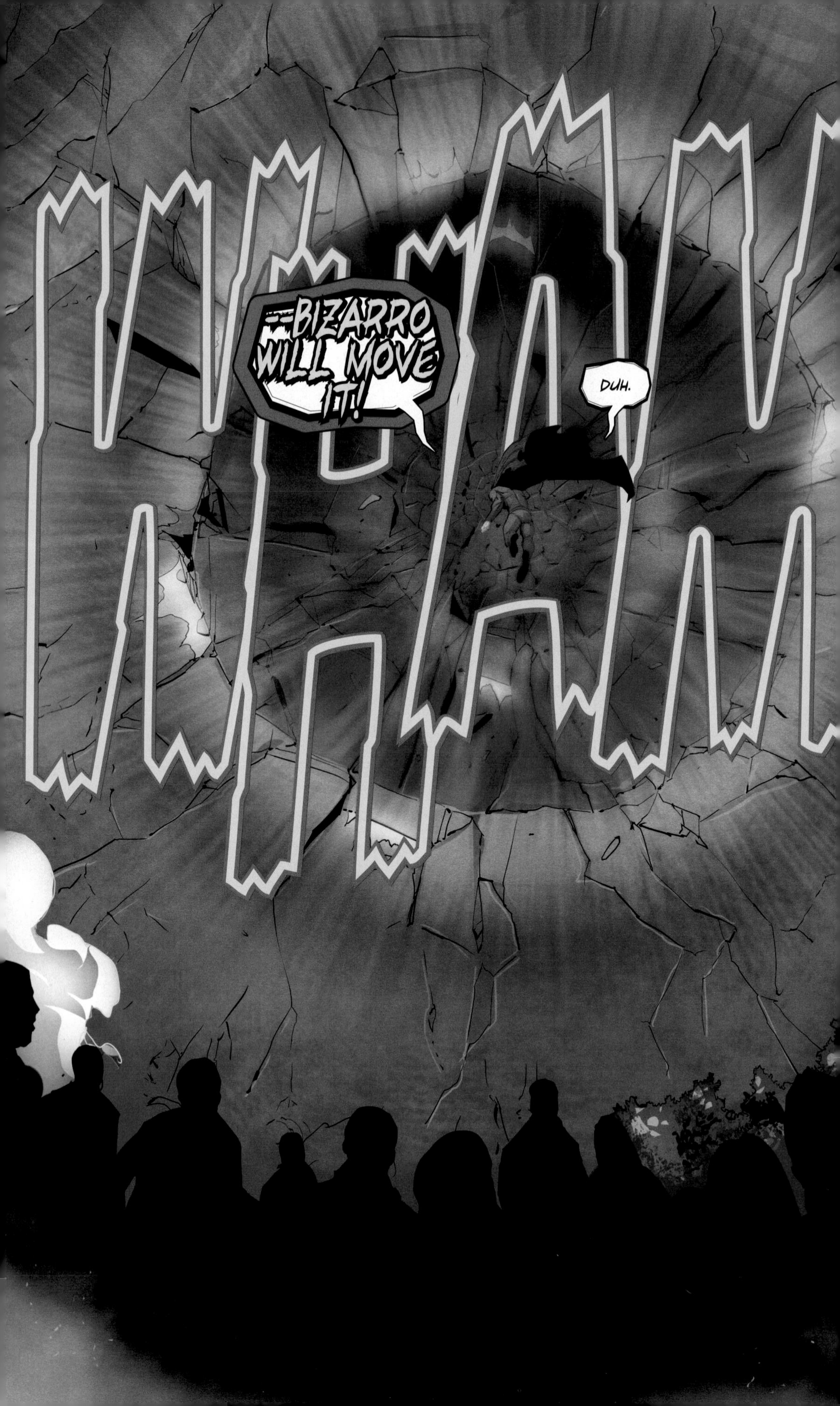
--BIZARRO WILL MOVE IT!
DUH.

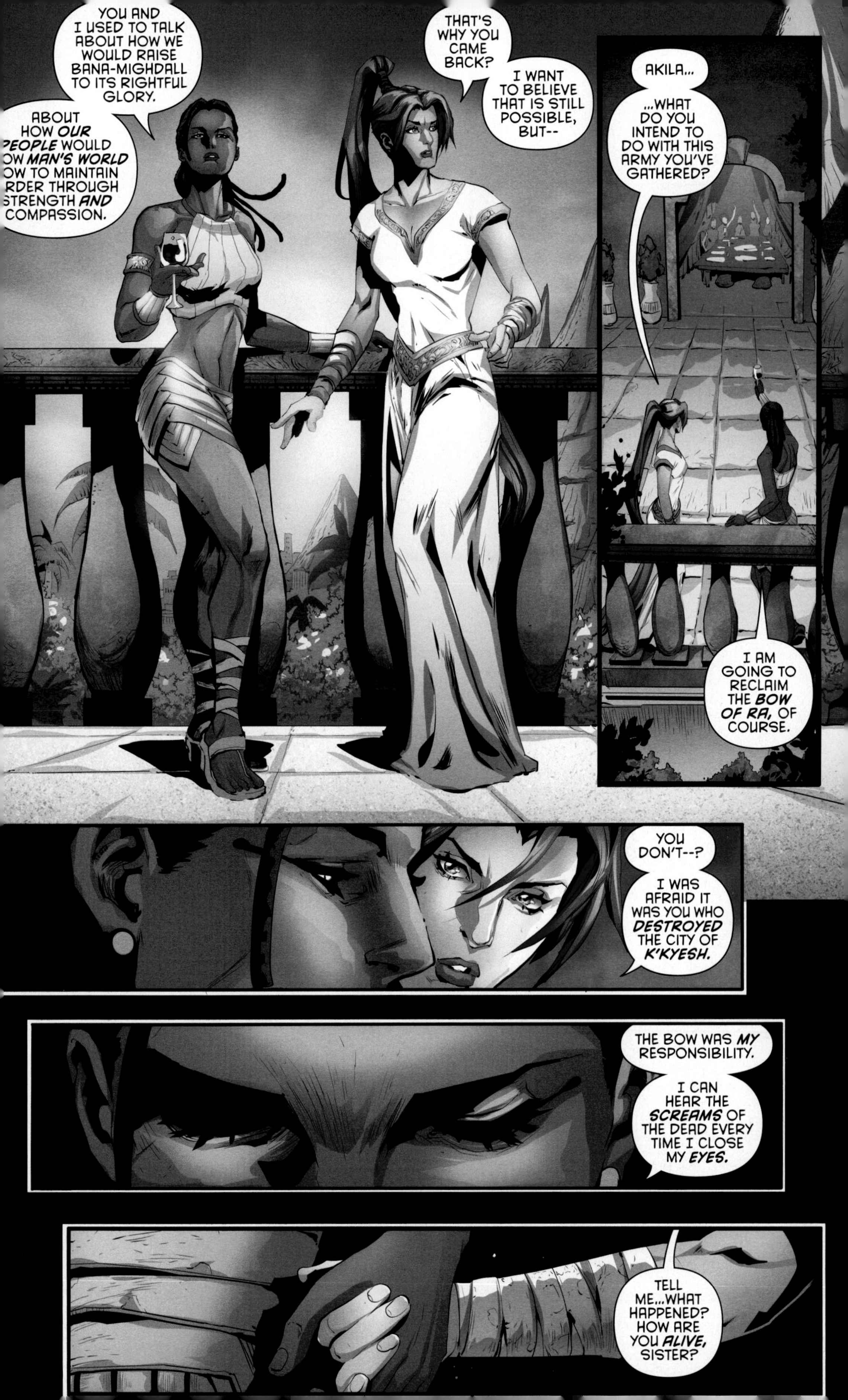
YOU AND I USED TO TALK ABOUT HOW WE WOULD RAISE BANA-MIGHDALL TO ITS RIGHTFUL GLORY.
ABOUT HOW OUR PEOPLE WOULD OW MAN'S WORLD OW TO MAINTAIN RDER THROUGH STRENGTH AND COMPASSION.
THAT'S WHY YOU CAME BACK?
I WANT TO BELIEVE THAT IS STILL POSSIBLE, BUT--
AKILA...
...WHAT DO YOU INTEND TO DO WITH THIS ARMY YOU'VE GATHERED?
I AM GOING TO RECLAIM THE BOW OF RA, OF COURSE.
YOU DON'T--?
I WAS AFRAID IT WAS YOU WHO DESTROYED THE CITY OF K'KYESH.
THE BOW WAS MY RESPONSIBILITY.
I CAN HEAR THE SCREAMS OF THE DEAD EVERY TIME I CLOSE MY EYES.
TELL ME...WHAT HAPPENED? HOW ARE YOU ALIVE, SISTER?

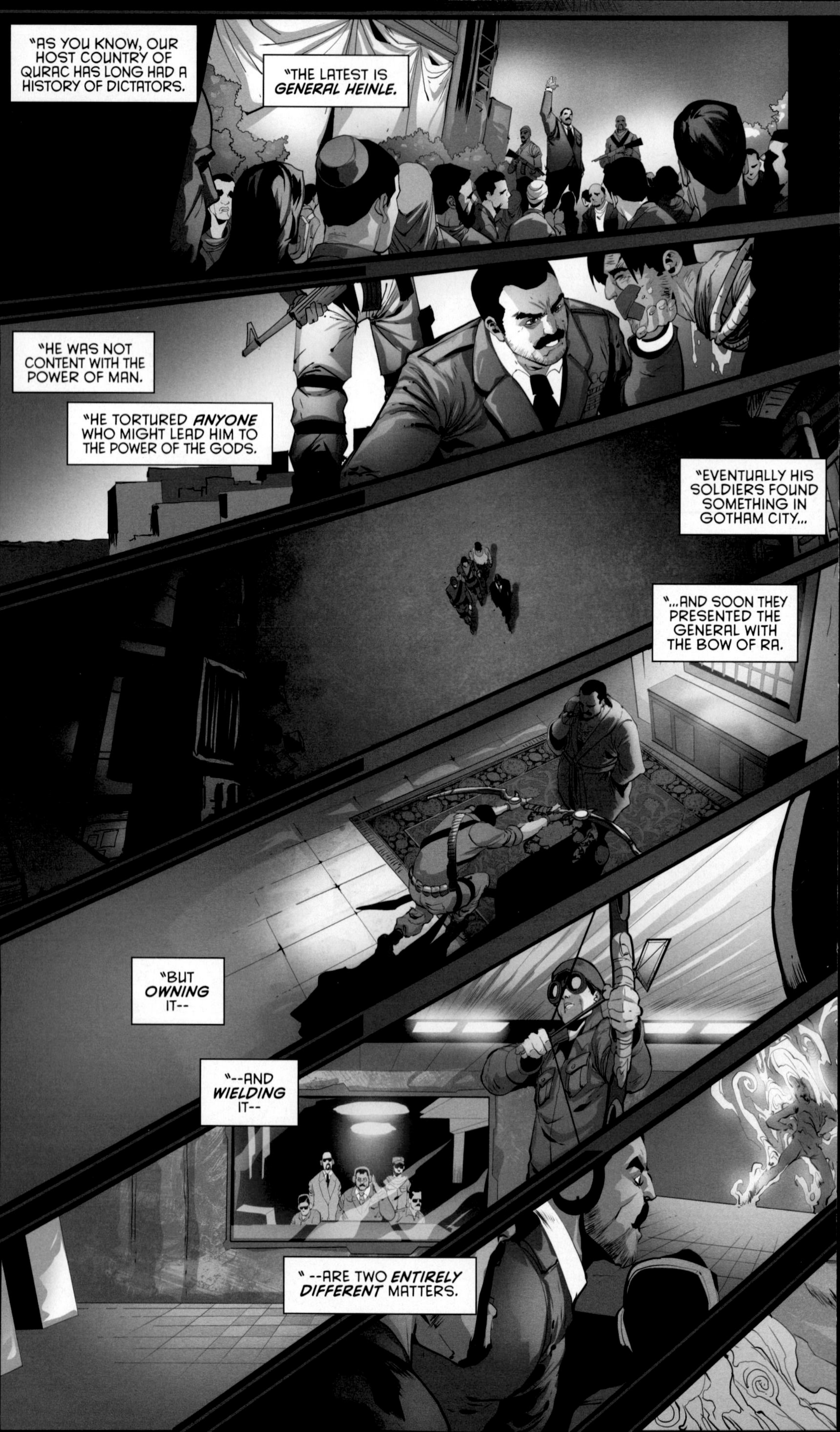
"AS YOU KNOW, OUR HOST COUNTRY OF QURAC HAS LONG HAD A HISTORY OF DICTATORS.
"THE LATEST IS *GENERAL HEINLE.*
"HE WAS NOT CONTENT WITH THE POWER OF MAN.
"HE TORTURED *ANYONE* WHO MIGHT LEAD HIM TO THE POWER OF THE GODS.
"EVENTUALLY HIS SOLDIERS FOUND SOMETHING IN GOTHAM CITY...
"...AND SOON THEY PRESENTED THE GENERAL WITH THE BOW OF RA.
"BUT *OWNING* IT--
"--AND *WIELDING* IT--
" --ARE TWO *ENTIRELY DIFFERENT* MATTERS.

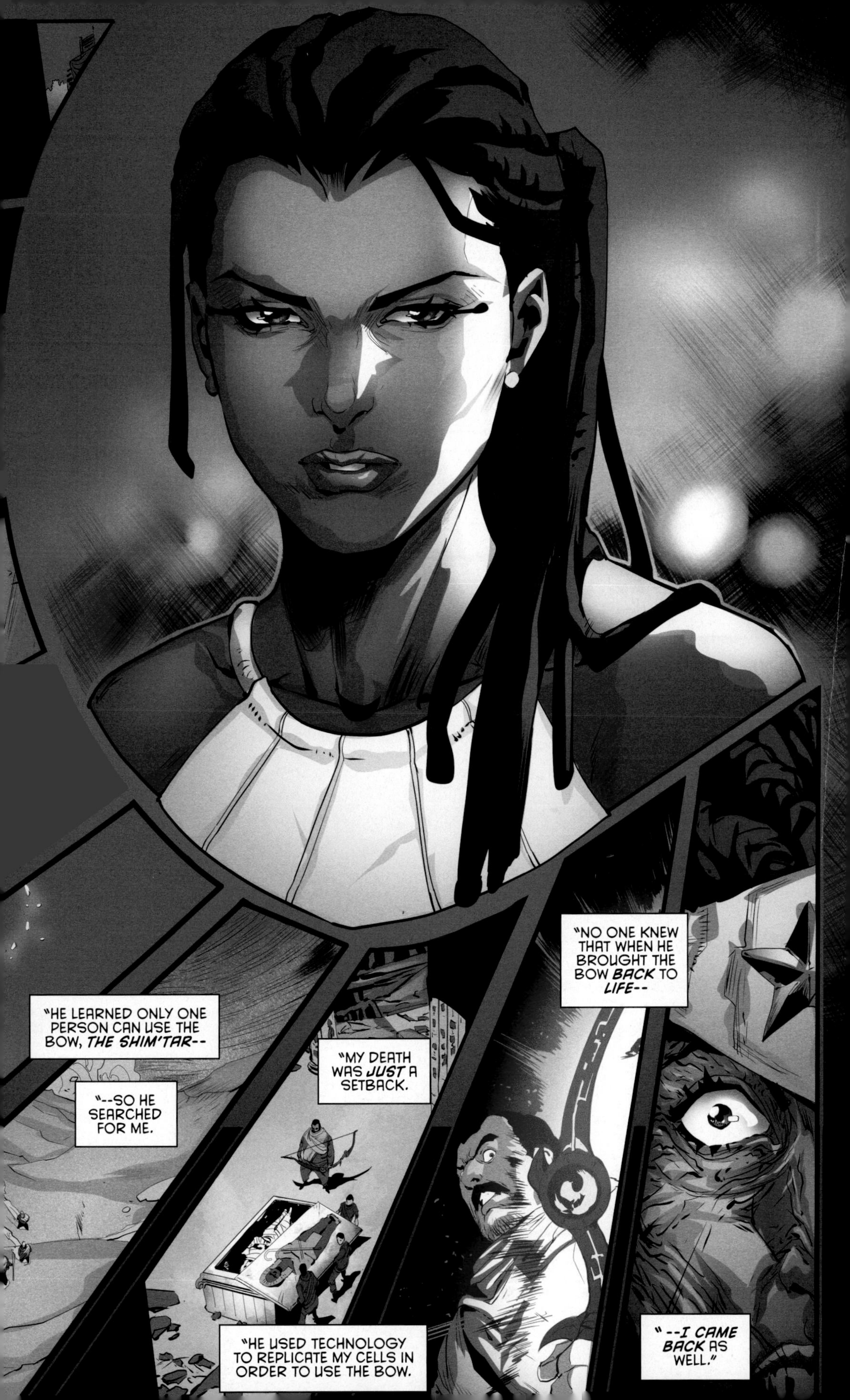
"HE LEARNED ONLY ONE PERSON CAN USE THE BOW, *THE SHIM'TAR*--
"--SO HE SEARCHED FOR ME.
"MY DEATH WAS *JUST* A SETBACK.
"HE USED TECHNOLOGY TO REPLICATE MY CELLS IN ORDER TO USE THE BOW.
"NO ONE KNEW THAT WHEN HE BROUGHT THE BOW *BACK* TO *LIFE*--
"--*I CAME BACK* AS WELL."

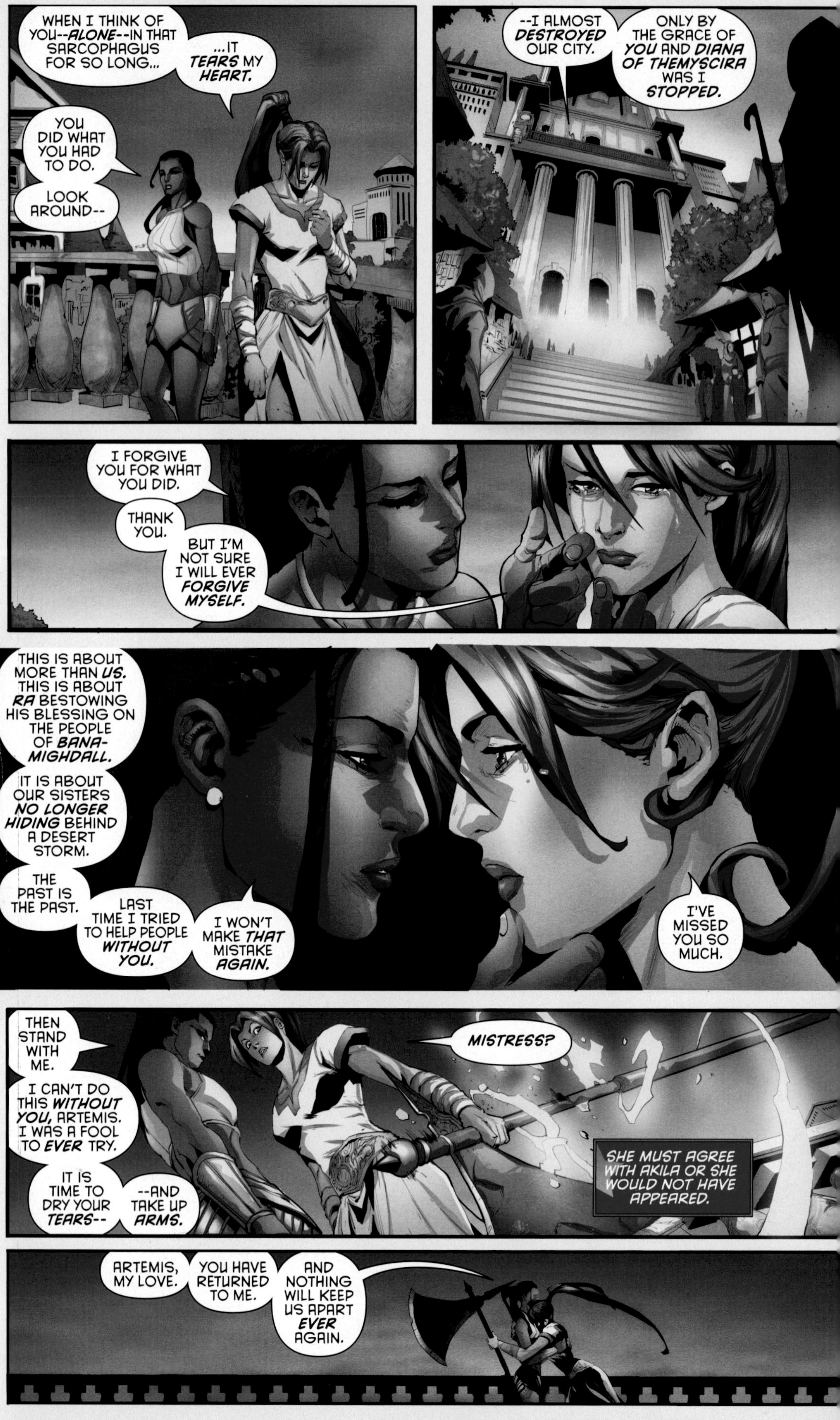
WHEN I THINK OF YOU--ALONE--IN THAT SARCOPHAGUS FOR SO LONG...
...IT TEARS MY HEART.
YOU DID WHAT YOU HAD TO DO.
LOOK AROUND--
--I ALMOST DESTROYED OUR CITY.
ONLY BY THE GRACE OF YOU AND DIANA OF THEMYSCIRA WAS I STOPPED.
I FORGIVE YOU FOR WHAT YOU DID.
THANK YOU.
BUT I'M NOT SURE I WILL EVER FORGIVE MYSELF.
THIS IS ABOUT MORE THAN US. THIS IS ABOUT RA BESTOWING HIS BLESSING ON THE PEOPLE OF BANA-MIGHDALL.
IT IS ABOUT OUR SISTERS NO LONGER HIDING BEHIND A DESERT STORM.
THE PAST IS THE PAST.
LAST TIME I TRIED TO HELP PEOPLE WITHOUT YOU.
I WON'T MAKE THAT MISTAKE AGAIN.
I'VE MISSED YOU SO MUCH.
THEN STAND WITH ME.
I CAN'T DO THIS WITHOUT YOU, ARTEMIS. I WAS A FOOL TO EVER TRY.
IT IS TIME TO DRY YOUR TEARS--
--AND TAKE UP ARMS.
MISTRESS?
SHE MUST AGREE WITH AKILA OR SHE WOULD NOT HAVE APPEARED.
ARTEMIS, MY LOVE.
YOU HAVE RETURNED TO ME.
AND NOTHING WILL KEEP US APART EVER AGAIN.

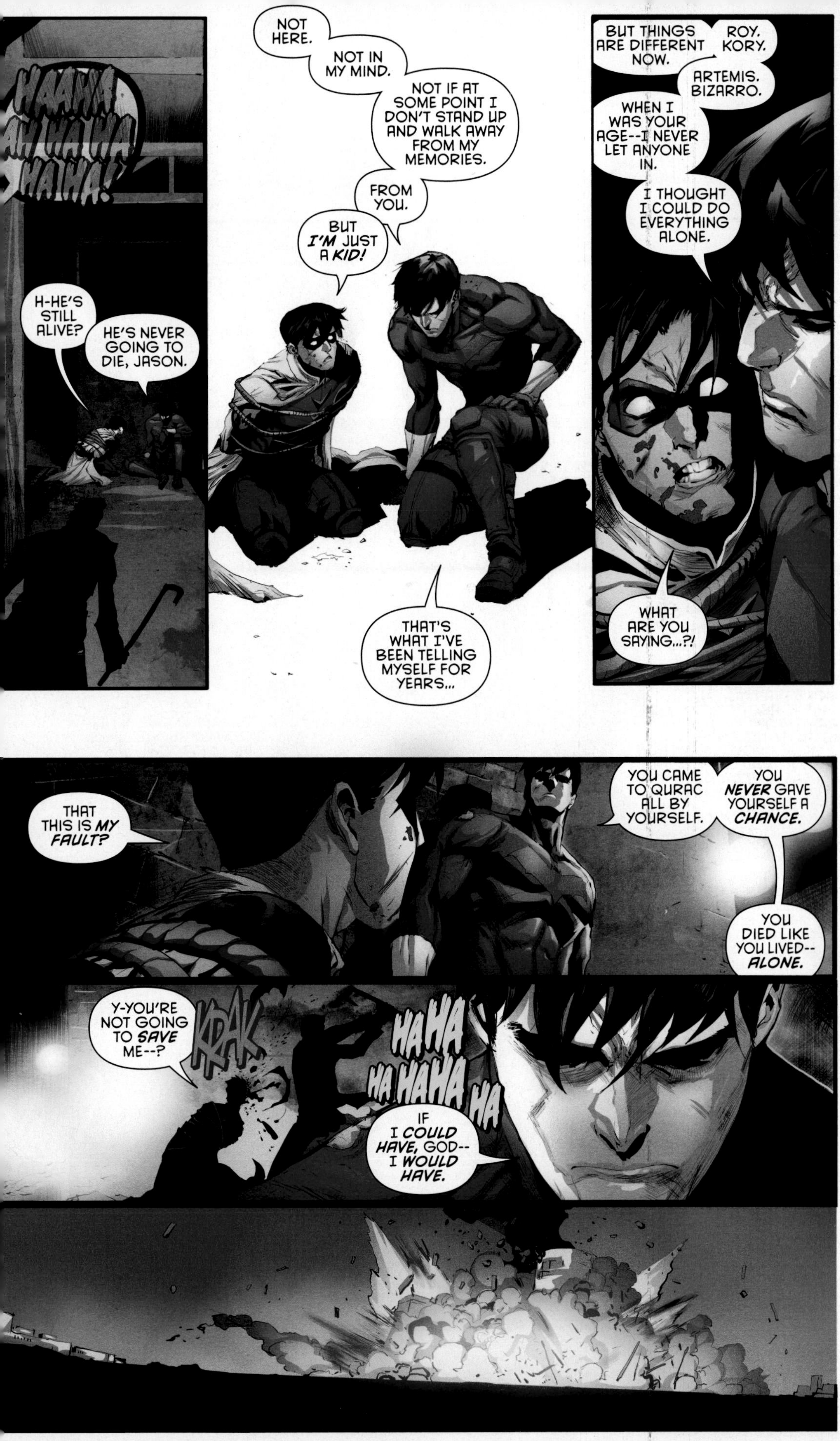
HAAHA AH HAHA HAHA!
H-HE'S STILL ALIVE?
HE'S NEVER GOING TO DIE, JASON.
NOT HERE.
NOT IN MY MIND.
NOT IF AT SOME POINT I DON'T STAND UP AND WALK AWAY FROM MY MEMORIES.
FROM YOU.
BUT I'M JUST A KID!
THAT'S WHAT I'VE BEEN TELLING MYSELF FOR YEARS...
BUT THINGS ARE DIFFERENT NOW.
ROY. KORY.
ARTEMIS. BIZARRO.
WHEN I WAS YOUR AGE--I NEVER LET ANYONE IN.
I THOUGHT I COULD DO EVERYTHING ALONE.
WHAT ARE YOU SAYING...?!
THAT THIS IS MY FAULT?
YOU CAME TO QURAC ALL BY YOURSELF.
YOU NEVER GAVE YOURSELF A CHANCE.
YOU DIED LIKE YOU LIVED--ALONE.
Y-YOU'RE NOT GOING TO SAVE ME--?
KRAK
HAHA HA HAHA HA HA
IF I COULD HAVE, GOD--I WOULD HAVE.

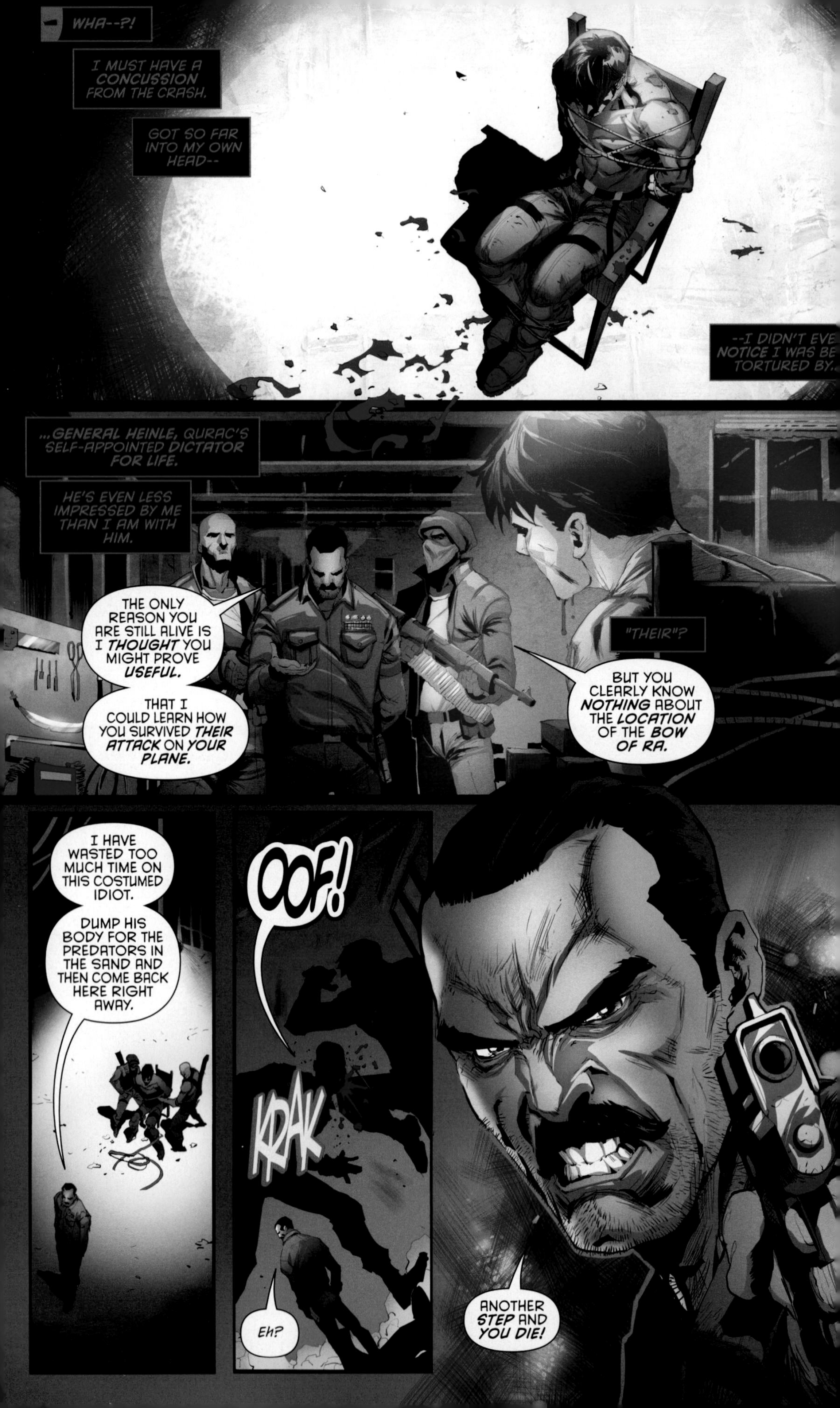
WHA--?!
I MUST HAVE A CONCUSSION FROM THE CRASH.
GOT SO FAR INTO MY OWN HEAD--
--I DIDN'T EVE NOTICE I WAS BE TORTURED BY.
...GENERAL HEINLE, QURAC'S SELF-APPOINTED DICTATOR FOR LIFE.
HE'S EVEN LESS IMPRESSED BY ME THAN I AM WITH HIM.
THE ONLY REASON YOU ARE STILL ALIVE IS I THOUGHT YOU MIGHT PROVE USEFUL.
THAT I COULD LEARN HOW YOU SURVIVED THEIR ATTACK ON YOUR PLANE.
"THEIR"?
BUT YOU CLEARLY KNOW NOTHING ABOUT THE LOCATION OF THE BOW OF RA.
I HAVE WASTED TOO MUCH TIME ON THIS COSTUMED IDIOT.
DUMP HIS BODY FOR THE PREDATORS IN THE SAND AND THEN COME BACK HERE RIGHT AWAY.
OOF!
KRAK
Eh?
ANOTHER STEP AND YOU DIE!

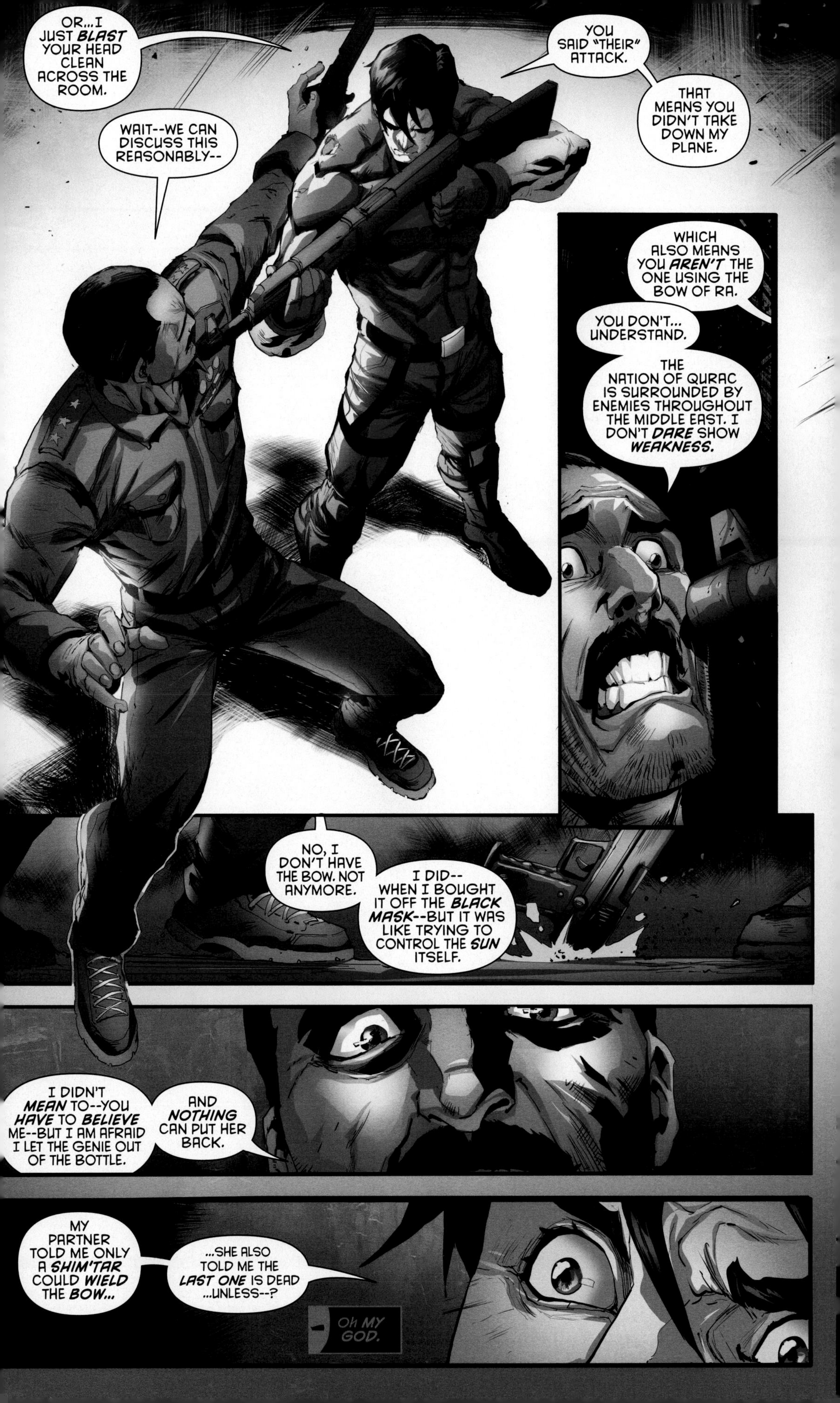

OR...I JUST BLAST YOUR HEAD CLEAN ACROSS THE ROOM.
WAIT--WE CAN DISCUSS THIS REASONABLY--
YOU SAID "THEIR" ATTACK.
THAT MEANS YOU DIDN'T TAKE DOWN MY PLANE.
WHICH ALSO MEANS YOU AREN'T THE ONE USING THE BOW OF RA.
YOU DON'T... UNDERSTAND.
THE NATION OF QURAC IS SURROUNDED BY ENEMIES THROUGHOUT THE MIDDLE EAST. I DON'T DARE SHOW WEAKNESS.
NO, I DON'T HAVE THE BOW. NOT ANYMORE.
I DID-- WHEN I BOUGHT IT OFF THE BLACK MASK--BUT IT WAS LIKE TRYING TO CONTROL THE SUN ITSELF.
I DIDN'T MEAN TO--YOU HAVE TO BELIEVE ME--BUT I AM AFRAID I LET THE GENIE OUT OF THE BOTTLE.
AND NOTHING CAN PUT HER BACK.
MY PARTNER TOLD ME ONLY A SHIM'TAR COULD WIELD THE BOW...
...SHE ALSO TOLD ME THE LAST ONE IS DEAD ...UNLESS--?
Oh MY GOD.

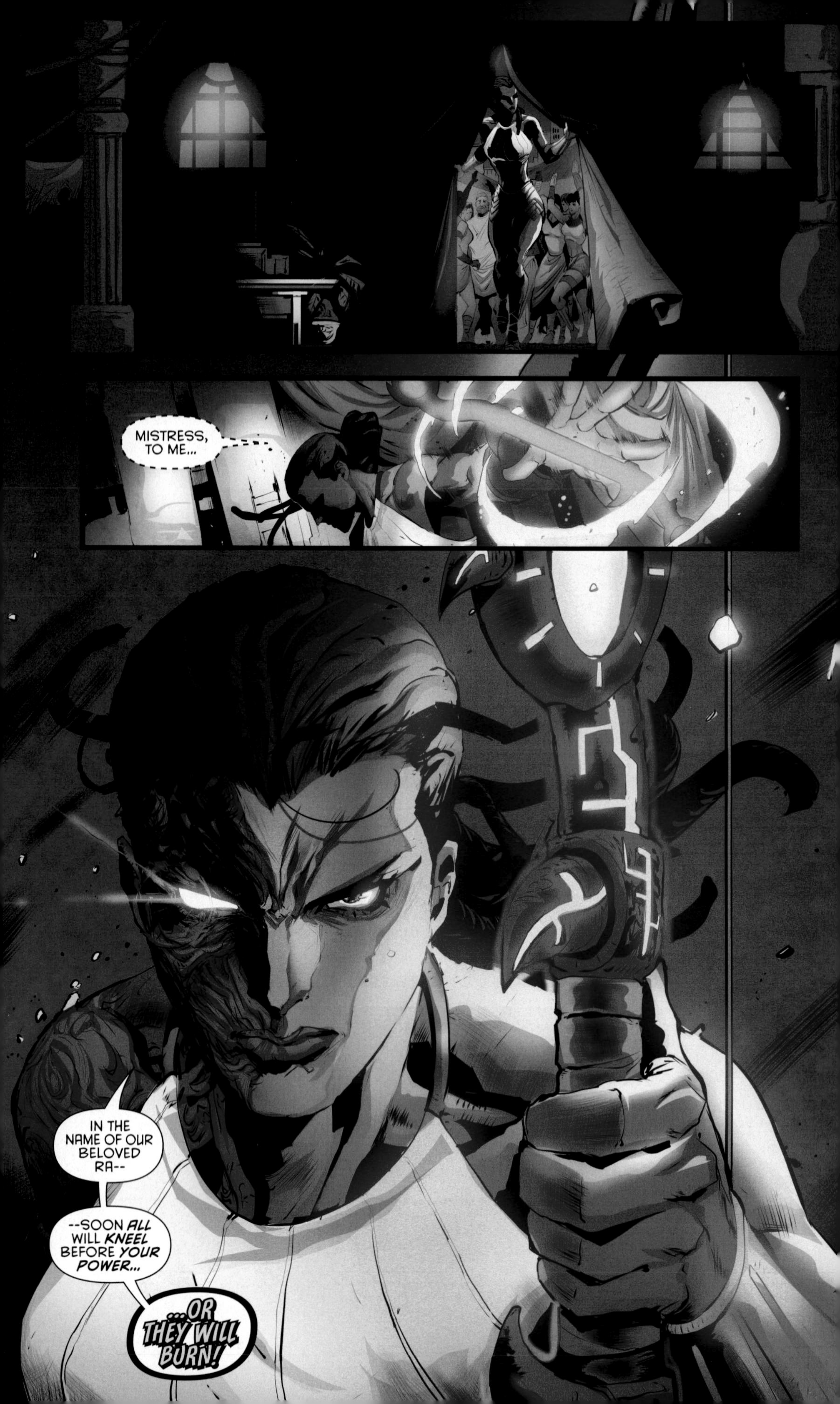
MISTRESS, TO ME...
IN THE NAME OF OUR BELOVED RA--
--SOON ALL WILL KNEEL BEFORE YOUR POWER...
...OR THEY WILL BURN!

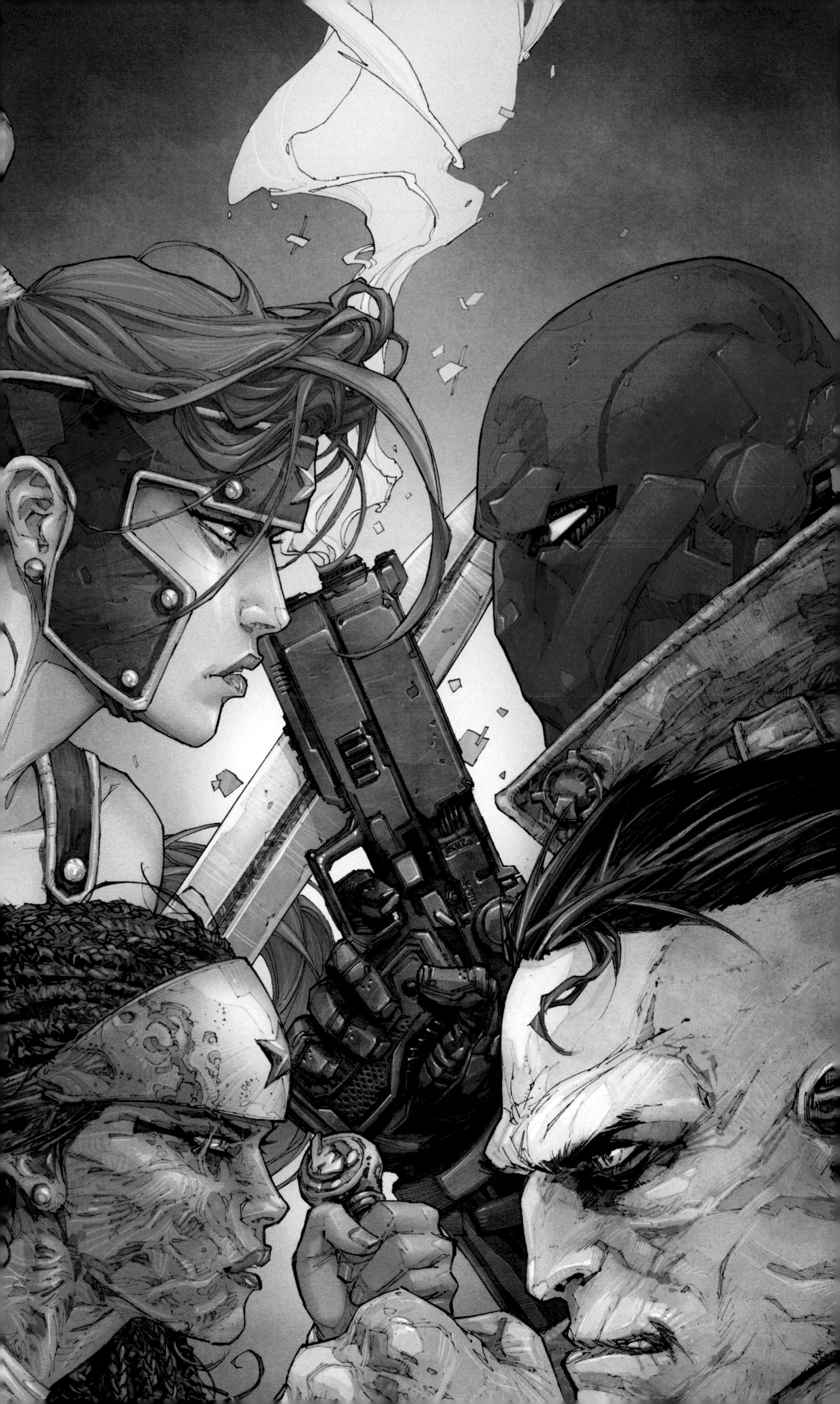

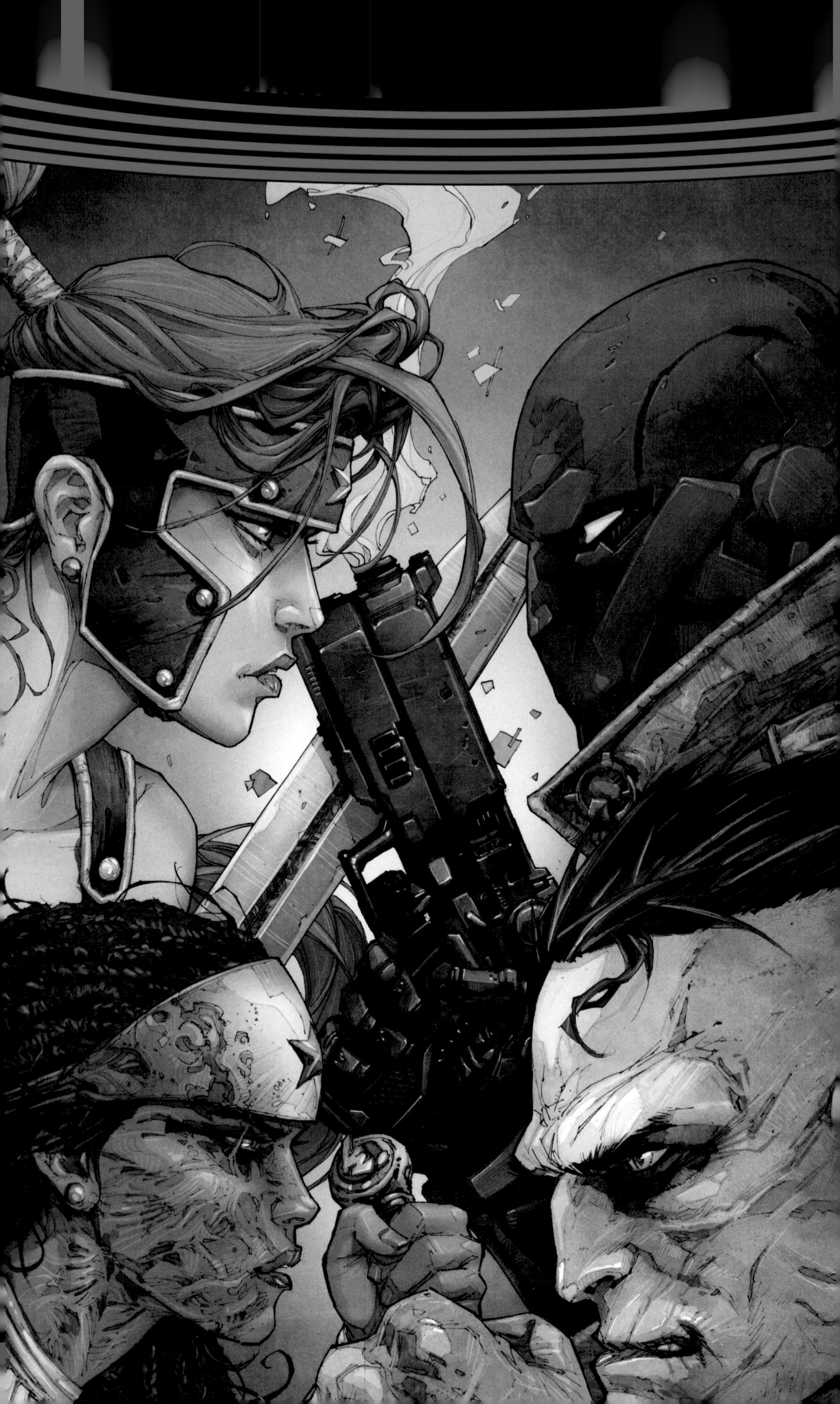

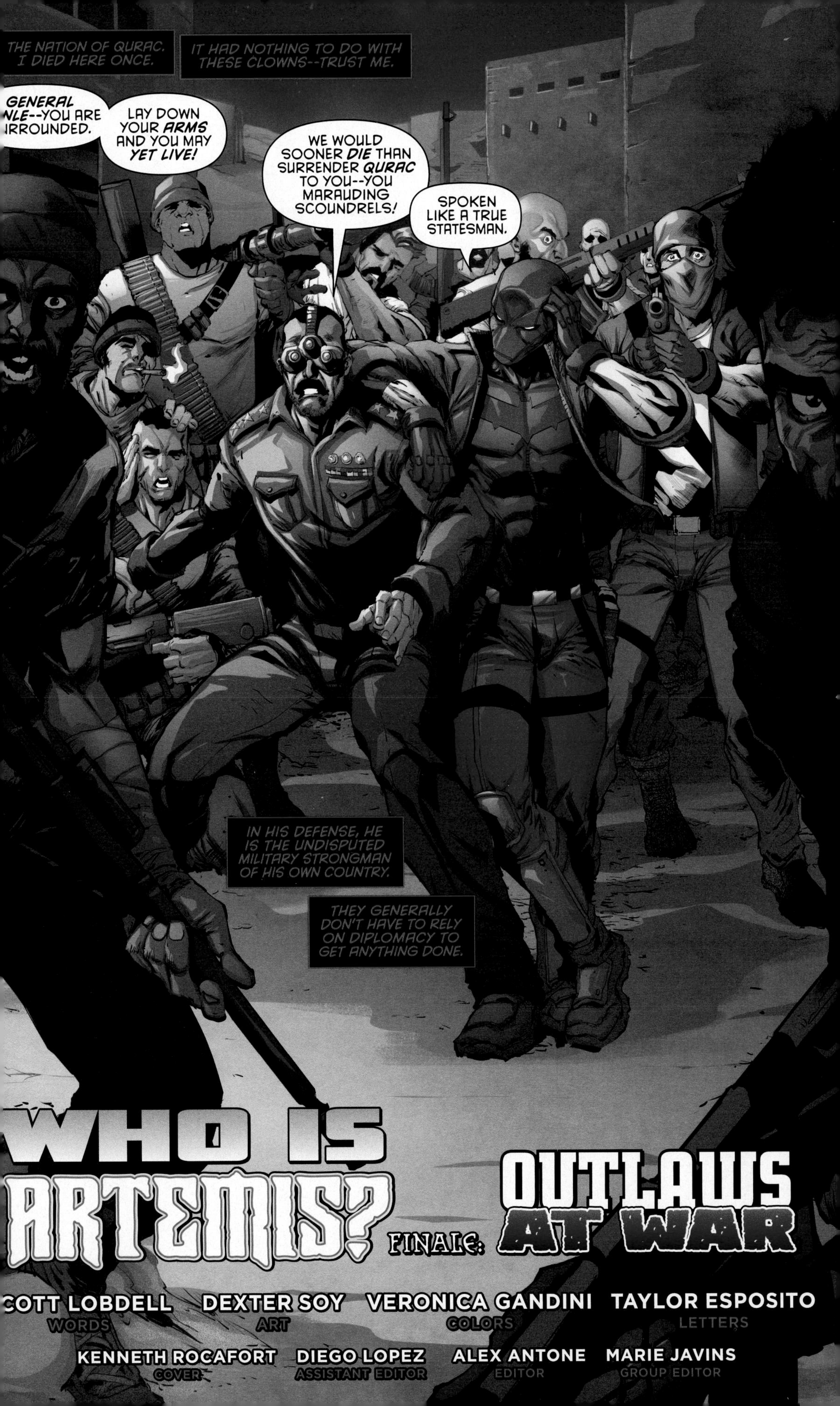
THE NATION OF QURAC. I DIED HERE ONCE.
IT HAD NOTHING TO DO WITH THESE CLOWNS--TRUST ME.
GENERAL NLE--YOU ARE RROUNDED.
LAY DOWN YOUR ARMS AND YOU MAY YET LIVE!
WE WOULD SOONER DIE THAN SURRENDER QURAC TO YOU--YOU MARAUDING SCOUNDRELS!
SPOKEN LIKE A TRUE STATESMAN.
IN HIS DEFENSE, HE IS THE UNDISPUTED MILITARY STRONGMAN OF HIS OWN COUNTRY.
THEY GENERALLY DON'T HAVE TO RELY ON DIPLOMACY TO GET ANYTHING DONE.
WHO IS ARTEMIS? FINALE: OUTLAWS AT WAR
COTT LOBDELL WORDS
DEXTER SOY ART
VERONICA GANDINI COLORS
TAYLOR ESPOSITO LETTERS
KENNETH ROCAFORT COVER
DIEGO LOPEZ ASSISTANT EDITOR
ALEX ANTONE EDITOR
MARIE JAVINS GROUP EDITOR

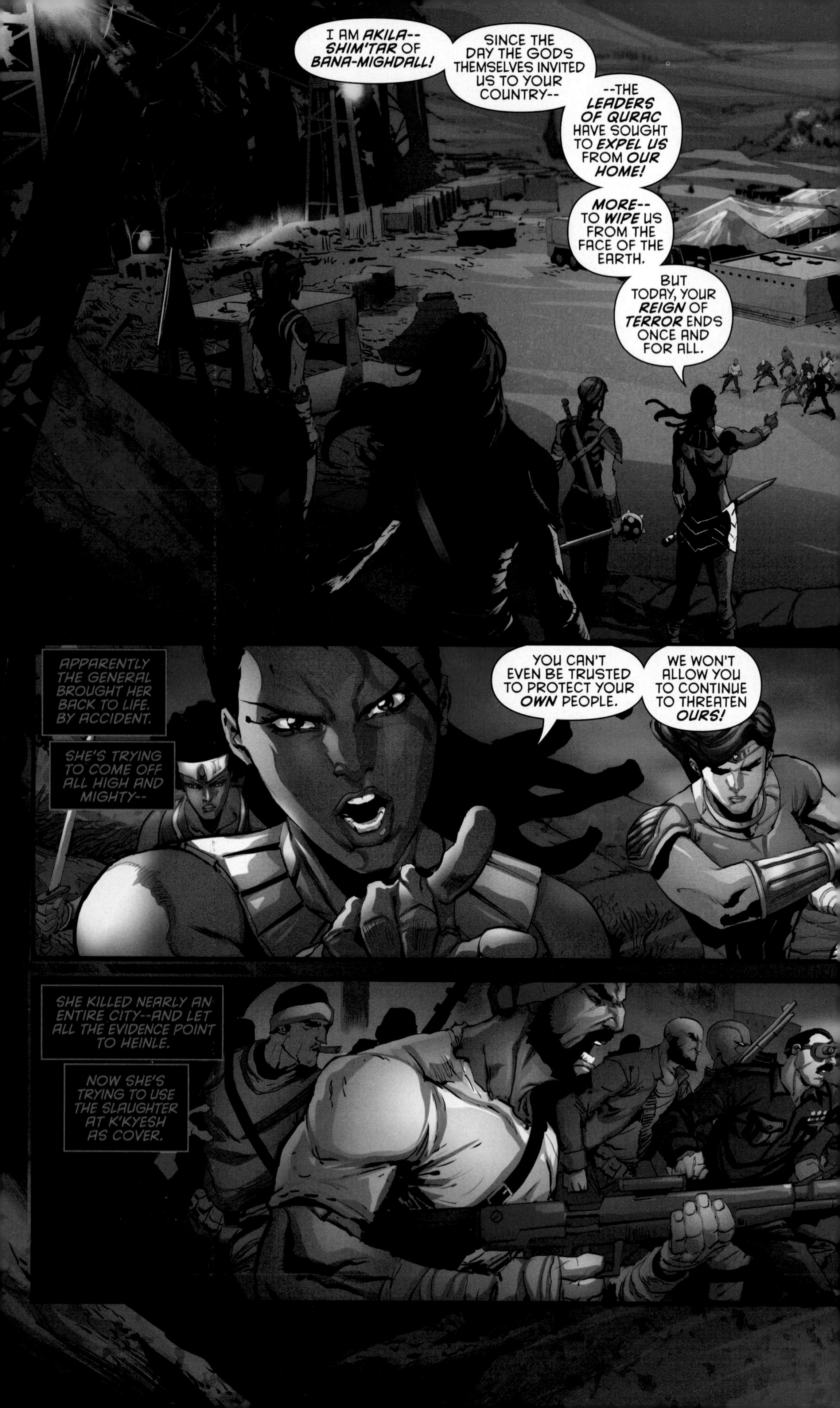

I AM AKILA--SHIM'TAR OF BANA-MIGHDALL!
SINCE THE DAY THE GODS THEMSELVES INVITED US TO YOUR COUNTRY--
--THE LEADERS OF QURAC HAVE SOUGHT TO EXPEL US FROM OUR HOME!
MORE--TO WIPE US FROM THE FACE OF THE EARTH.
BUT TODAY, YOUR REIGN OF TERROR ENDS ONCE AND FOR ALL.
APPARENTLY THE GENERAL BROUGHT HER BACK TO LIFE. BY ACCIDENT.
SHE'S TRYING TO COME OFF ALL HIGH AND MIGHTY--
YOU CAN'T EVEN BE TRUSTED TO PROTECT YOUR OWN PEOPLE.
WE WON'T ALLOW YOU TO CONTINUE TO THREATEN OURS!
SHE KILLED NEARLY AN ENTIRE CITY--AND LET ALL THE EVIDENCE POINT TO HEINLE.
NOW SHE'S TRYING TO USE THE SLAUGHTER AT K'KYESH AS COVER.

DAMN, SHE'S GOOD.
AT TELLING ONLY HALF THE STORY.
THIS IS AKILA. DEAD LIKE ME, ONCE.
KILLED BY A MUTUAL FRIEND OF OURS--ARTEMIS--WHEN AKILA WAS DRIVEN MAD BY THE BOW OF RA.
BUT I'M NOT BUYING IT.
ACCORDING TO THE LESSER OF TWO EVILS HERE, THE GENERAL--
SHE DIDN'T SPEND A MINUTE UNDER
S CONTROL WHEN SHE RETURNED TO THE LAND OF THE LIVING.
ONWARD, FOR THE GLORY THAT IS QURAC!
WAS HOPING ARTEMIS ALREADY HOOKED UP WITH HER BESTIE--
--AND DIFFUSED THE SITUATION BY NOW.
A FEW THOUSAND MILES FROM GOTHAM, I DON'T FEEL LIKE MY PROMISE TO BRUCE HAS A ZIP CODE EXCEPTION.
EVEN IF I AM IN THE MIDDLE OF A WAR.

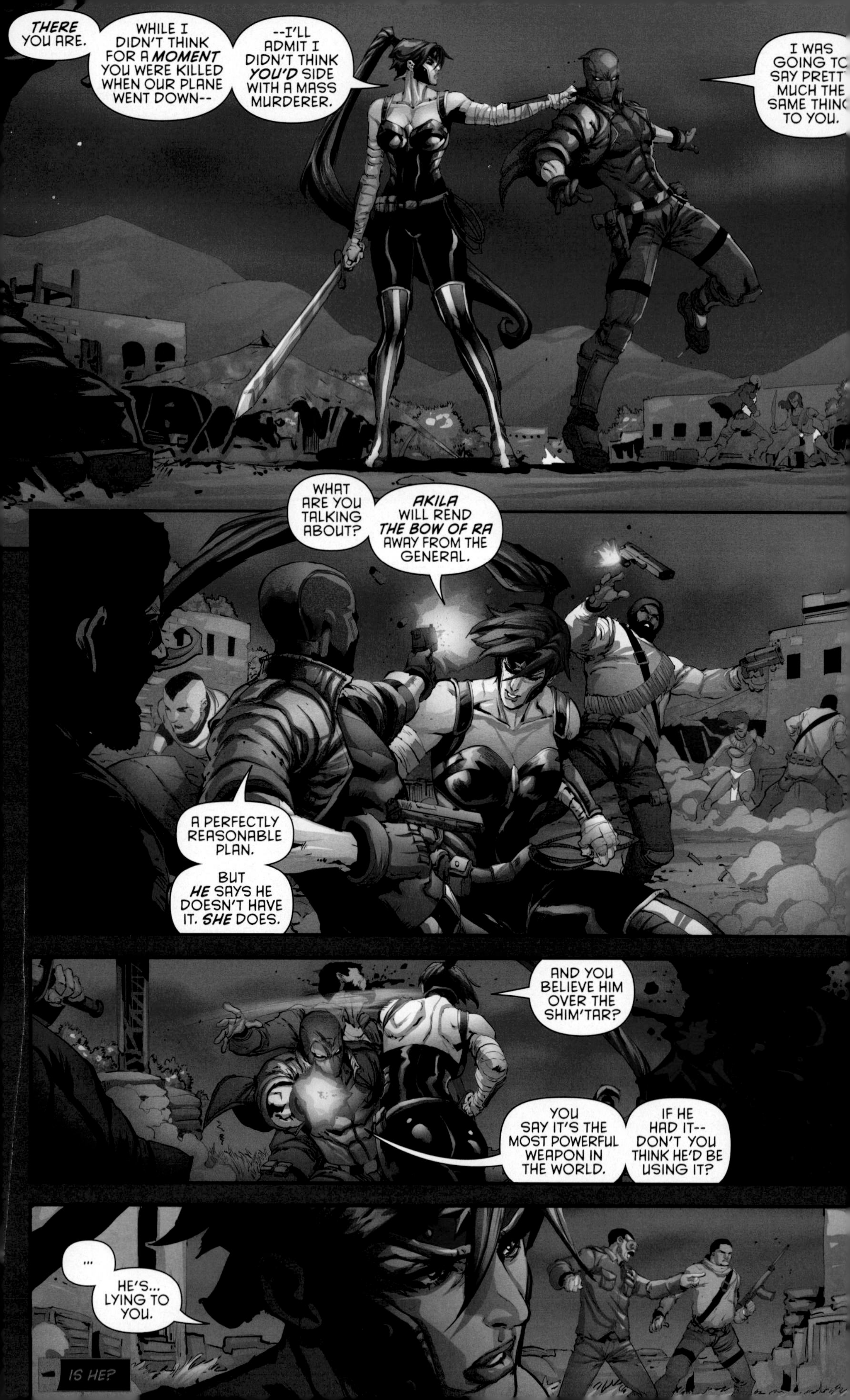
THERE YOU ARE.
WHILE I DIDN'T THINK FOR A MOMENT YOU WERE KILLED WHEN OUR PLANE WENT DOWN--
--I'LL ADMIT I DIDN'T THINK YOU'D SIDE WITH A MASS MURDERER.
I WAS GOING TO SAY PRETT MUCH THE SAME THING TO YOU.
WHAT ARE YOU TALKING ABOUT?
AKILA WILL REND THE BOW OF RA AWAY FROM THE GENERAL.
A PERFECTLY REASONABLE PLAN.
BUT HE SAYS HE DOESN'T HAVE IT. SHE DOES.
AND YOU BELIEVE HIM OVER THE SHIM'TAR?
YOU SAY IT'S THE MOST POWERFUL WEAPON IN THE WORLD.
IF HE HAD IT-- DON'T YOU THINK HE'D BE USING IT?
...
HE'S... LYING TO YOU.
IS HE?

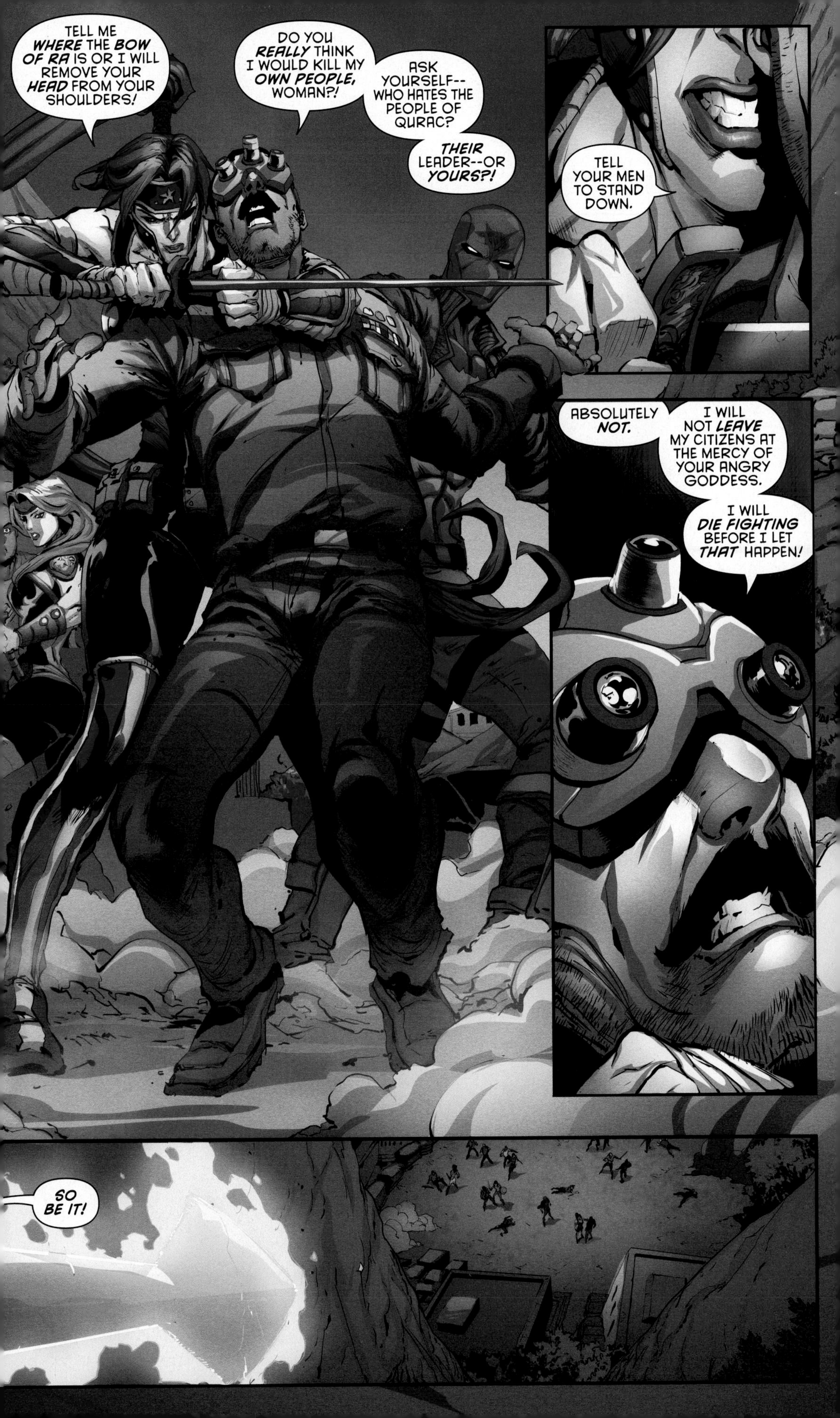
TELL ME WHERE THE BOW OF RA IS OR I WILL REMOVE YOUR HEAD FROM YOUR SHOULDERS!
DO YOU REALLY THINK I WOULD KILL MY OWN PEOPLE, WOMAN?!
ASK YOURSELF-- WHO HATES THE PEOPLE OF QURAC?
THEIR LEADER--OR YOURS?!
TELL YOUR MEN TO STAND DOWN.
ABSOLUTELY NOT.
I WILL NOT LEAVE MY CITIZENS AT THE MERCY OF YOUR ANGRY GODDESS.
I WILL DIE FIGHTING BEFORE I LET THAT HAPPEN!
SO BE IT!

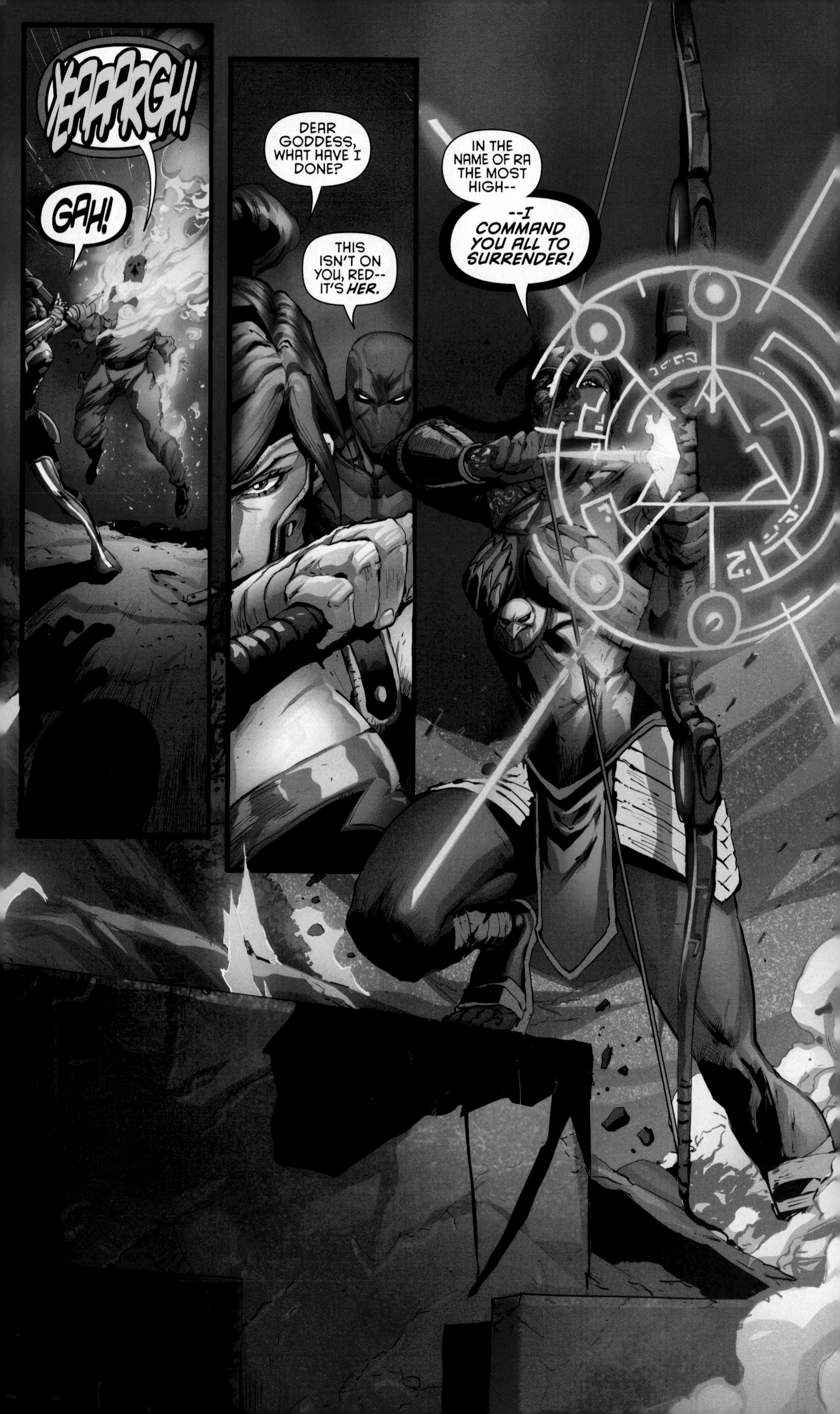
YEAARGH!
GAH!
DEAR GODDESS, WHAT HAVE I DONE?
THIS ISN'T ON YOU, RED-- IT'S *HER.*
IN THE NAME OF RA THE MOST HIGH--
--I COMMAND YOU ALL TO SURRENDER!

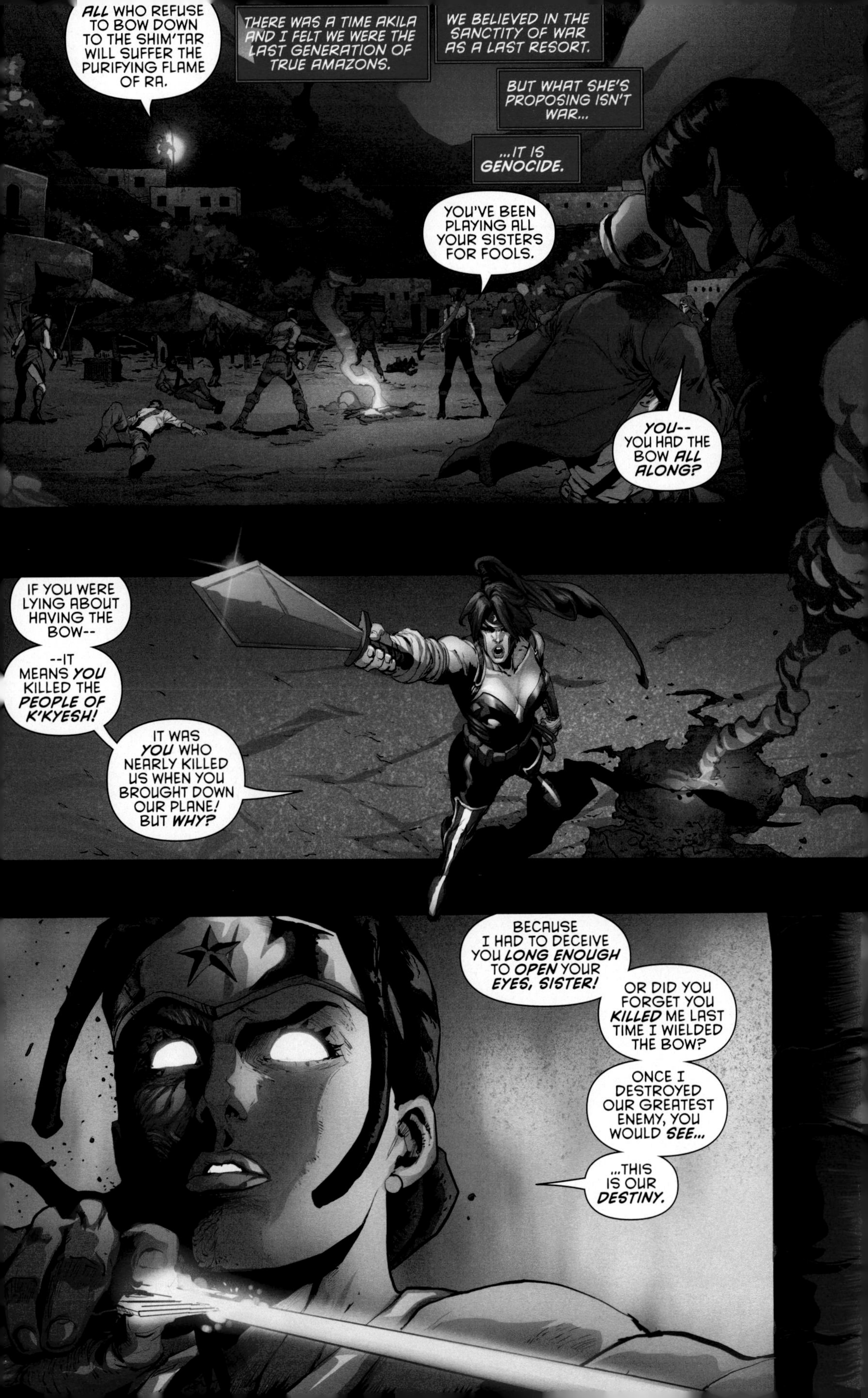
ALL WHO REFUSE TO BOW DOWN TO THE SHIM'TAR WILL SUFFER THE PURIFYING FLAME OF RA.
THERE WAS A TIME AKILA AND I FELT WE WERE THE LAST GENERATION OF TRUE AMAZONS.
WE BELIEVED IN THE SANCTITY OF WAR AS A LAST RESORT.
BUT WHAT SHE'S PROPOSING ISN'T WAR...
...IT IS GENOCIDE.
YOU'VE BEEN PLAYING ALL YOUR SISTERS FOR FOOLS.
YOU-- YOU HAD THE BOW ALL ALONG?
IF YOU WERE LYING ABOUT HAVING THE BOW--
--IT MEANS YOU KILLED THE PEOPLE OF K'KYESH!
IT WAS YOU WHO NEARLY KILLED US WHEN YOU BROUGHT DOWN OUR PLANE! BUT WHY?
BECAUSE I HAD TO DECEIVE YOU LONG ENOUGH TO OPEN YOUR EYES, SISTER!
OR DID YOU FORGET YOU KILLED ME LAST TIME I WIELDED THE BOW?
ONCE I DESTROYED OUR GREATEST ENEMY, YOU WOULD SEE...
...THIS IS OUR DESTINY.

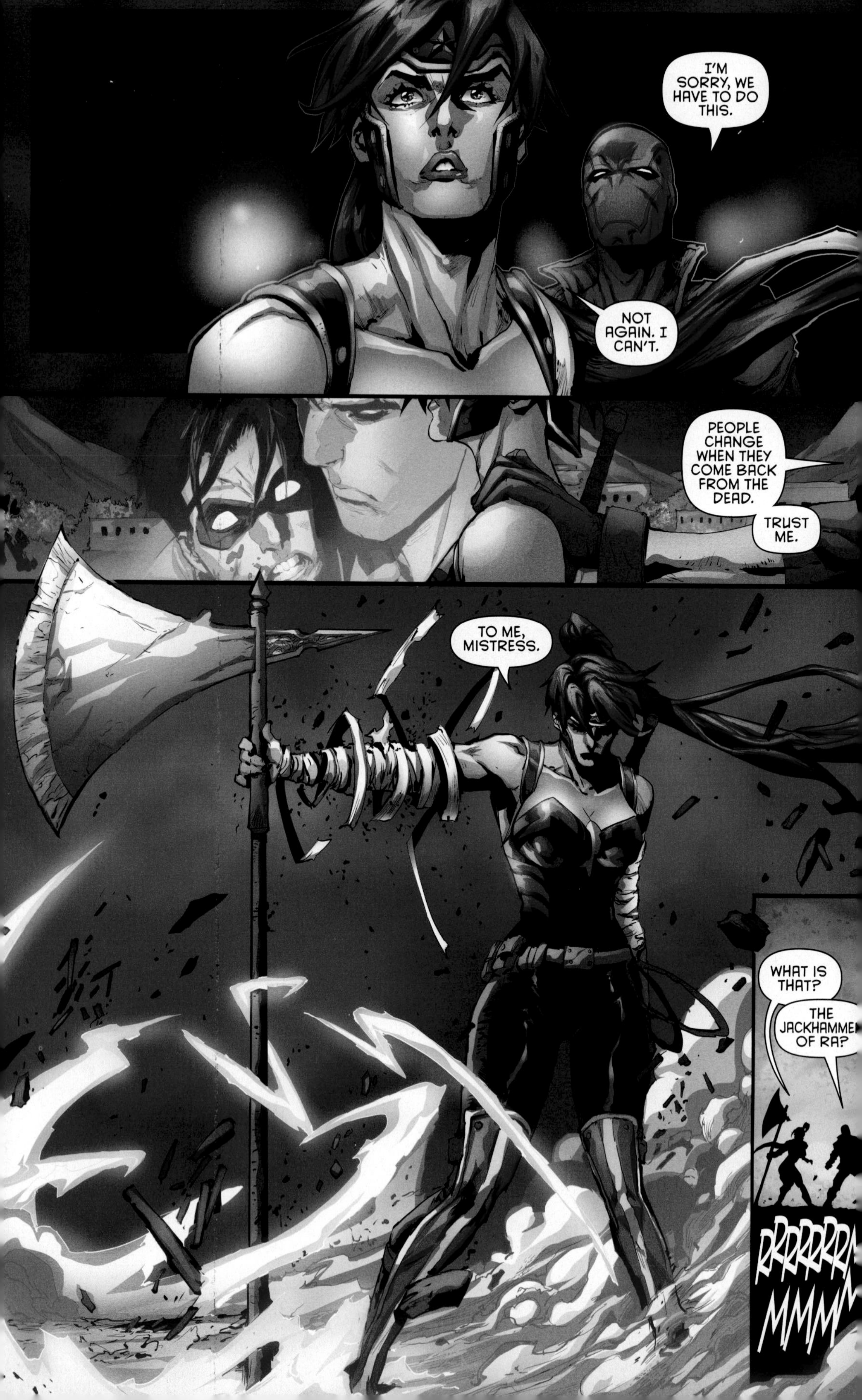

I'M SORRY, WE HAVE TO DO THIS.
NOT AGAIN. I CAN'T.
PEOPLE CHANGE WHEN THEY COME BACK FROM THE DEAD.
TRUST ME.
TO ME, MISTRESS.
WHAT IS THAT?
THE JACKHAMME OF RA?
RRRRRRRR MMMM

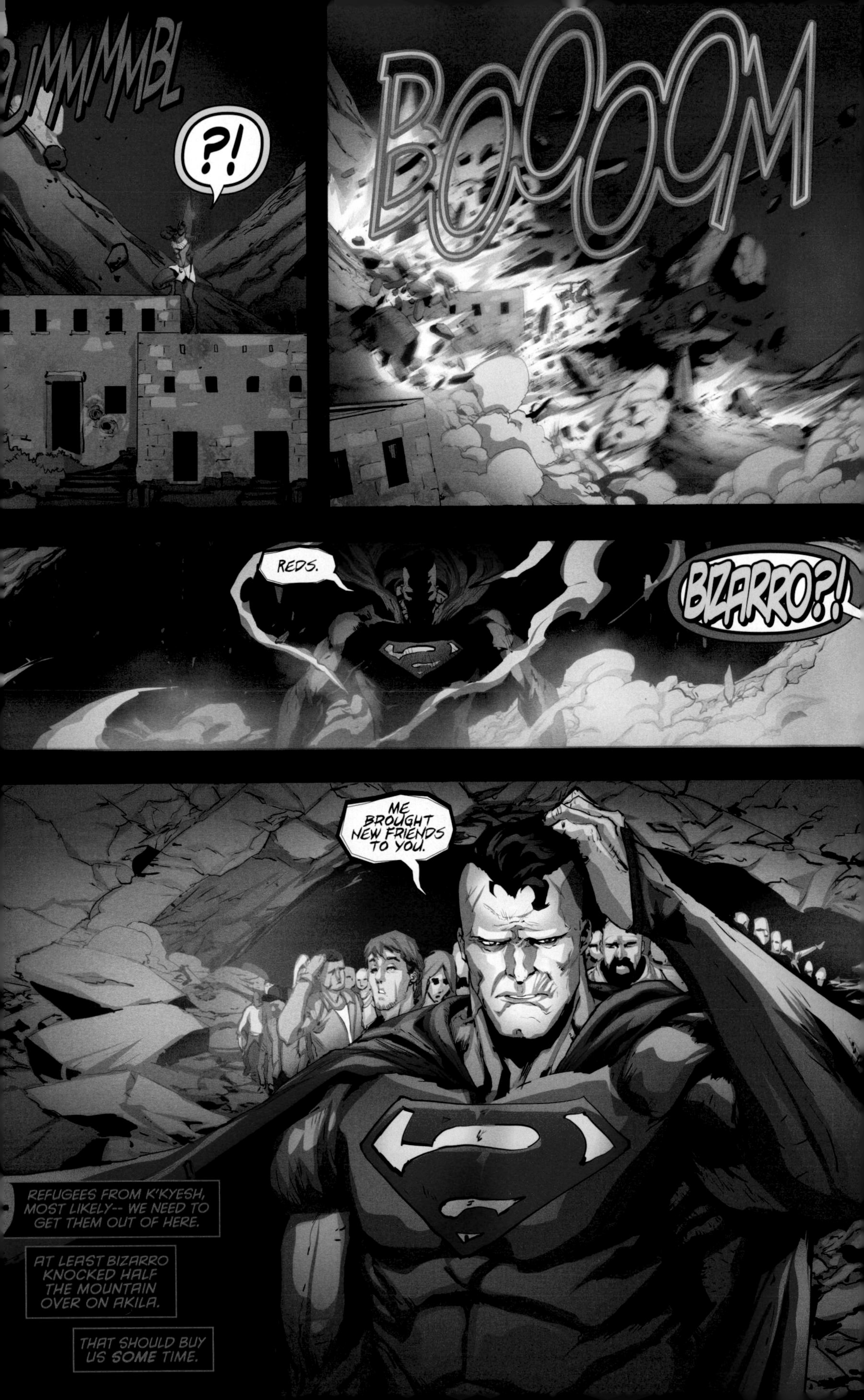
RUMMMMBL
?!
BOOOOOM
REDS.
BIZARRO?!
ME BROUGHT NEW FRIENDS TO YOU.
REFUGEES FROM K'KYESH, MOST LIKELY-- WE NEED TO GET THEM OUT OF HERE.
AT LEAST BIZARRO KNOCKED HALF THE MOUNTAIN OVER ON AKILA.
THAT SHOULD BUY US SOME TIME.

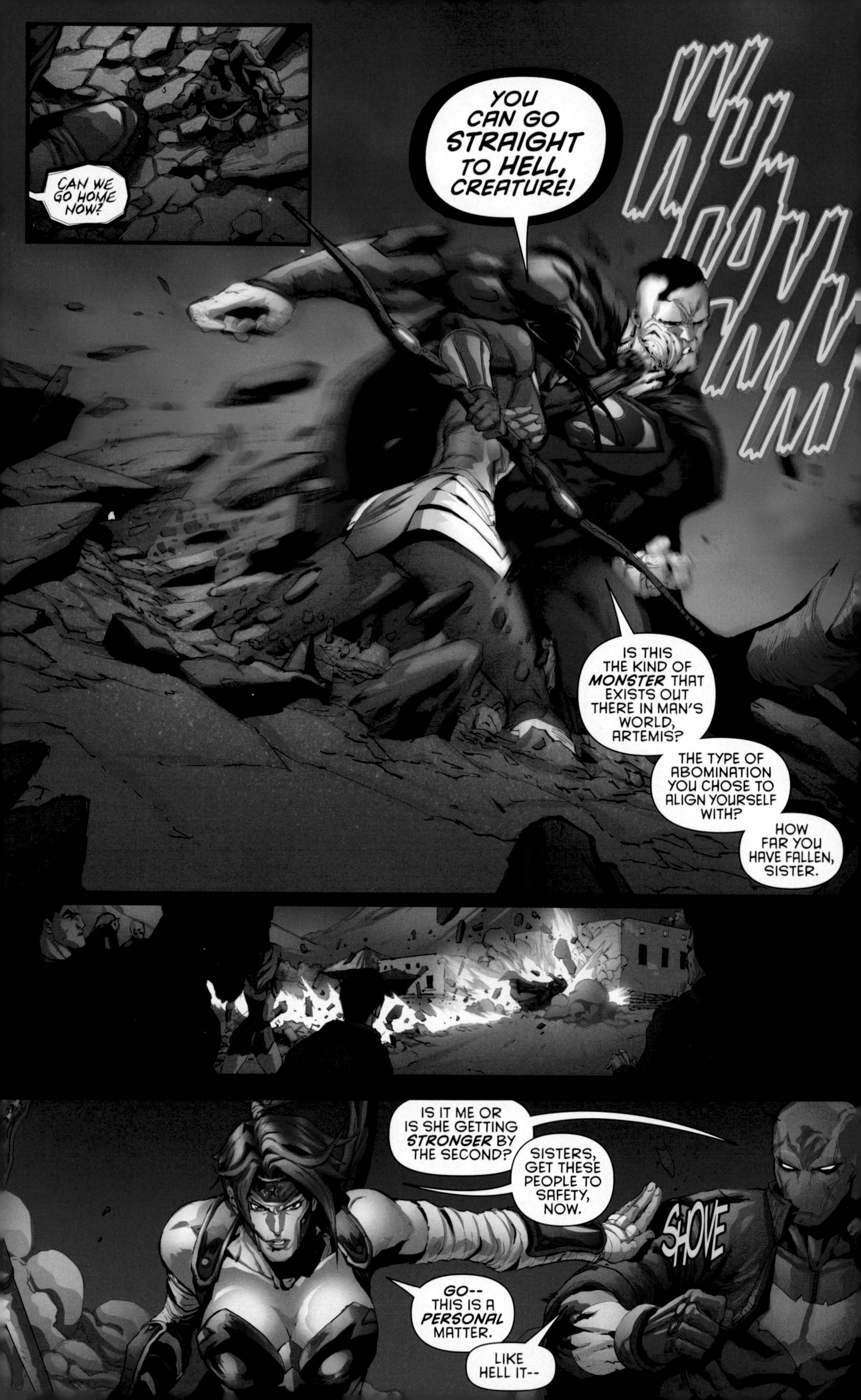
CAN WE GO HOME NOW?
YOU CAN GO STRAIGHT TO HELL, CREATURE!
IS THIS THE KIND OF MONSTER THAT EXISTS OUT THERE IN MAN'S WORLD, ARTEMIS?
THE TYPE OF ABOMINATION YOU CHOSE TO ALIGN YOURSELF WITH?
HOW FAR YOU HAVE FALLEN, SISTER.
IS IT ME OR IS SHE GETTING STRONGER BY THE SECOND?
SISTERS, GET THESE PEOPLE TO SAFETY, NOW.
SHOVE
GO-- THIS IS A PERSONAL MATTER.
LIKE HELL IT--

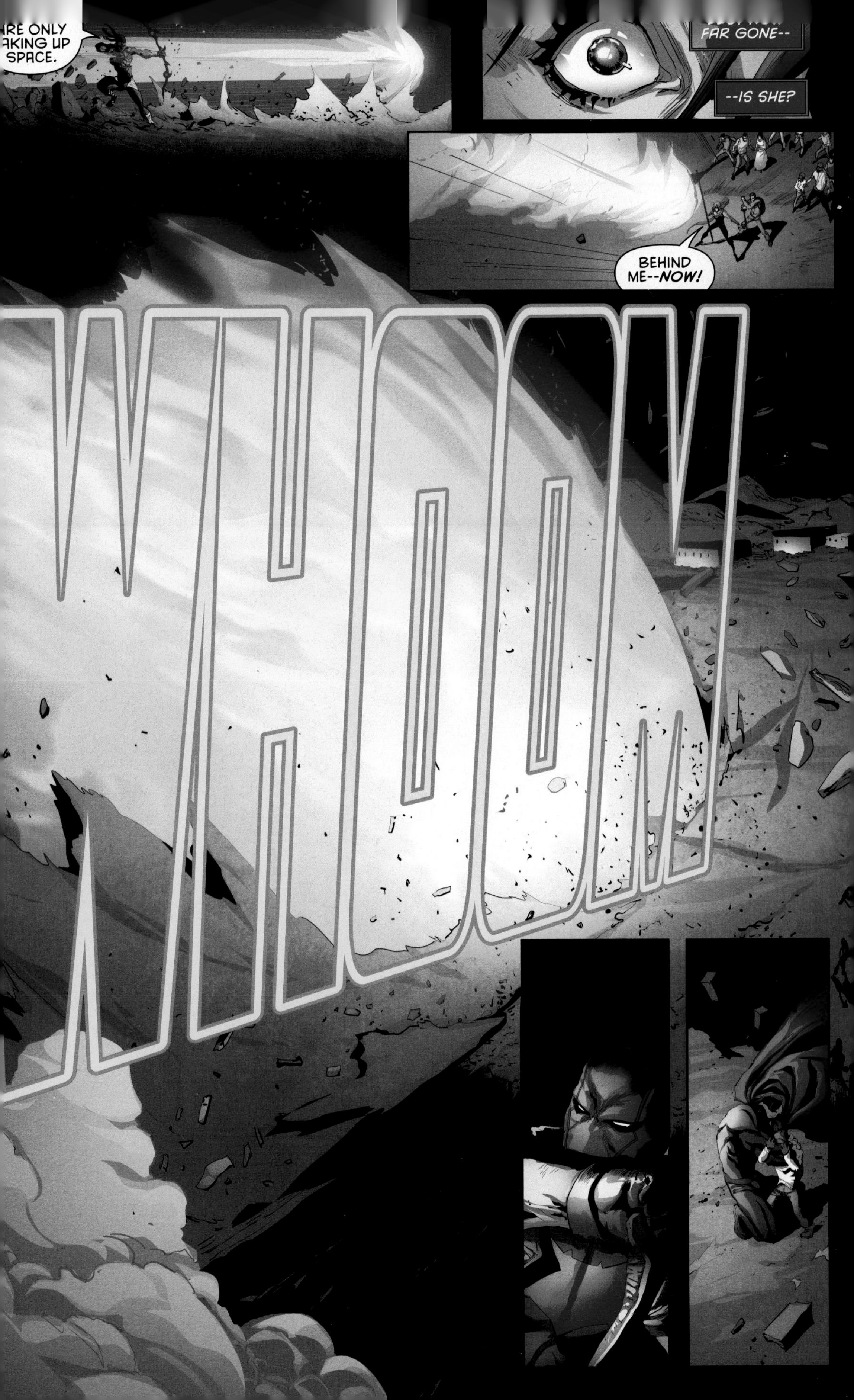

RE ONLY
AKING UP
SPACE.
FAR GONE--
--IS SHE?
BEHIND ME--NOW!
WHOOM

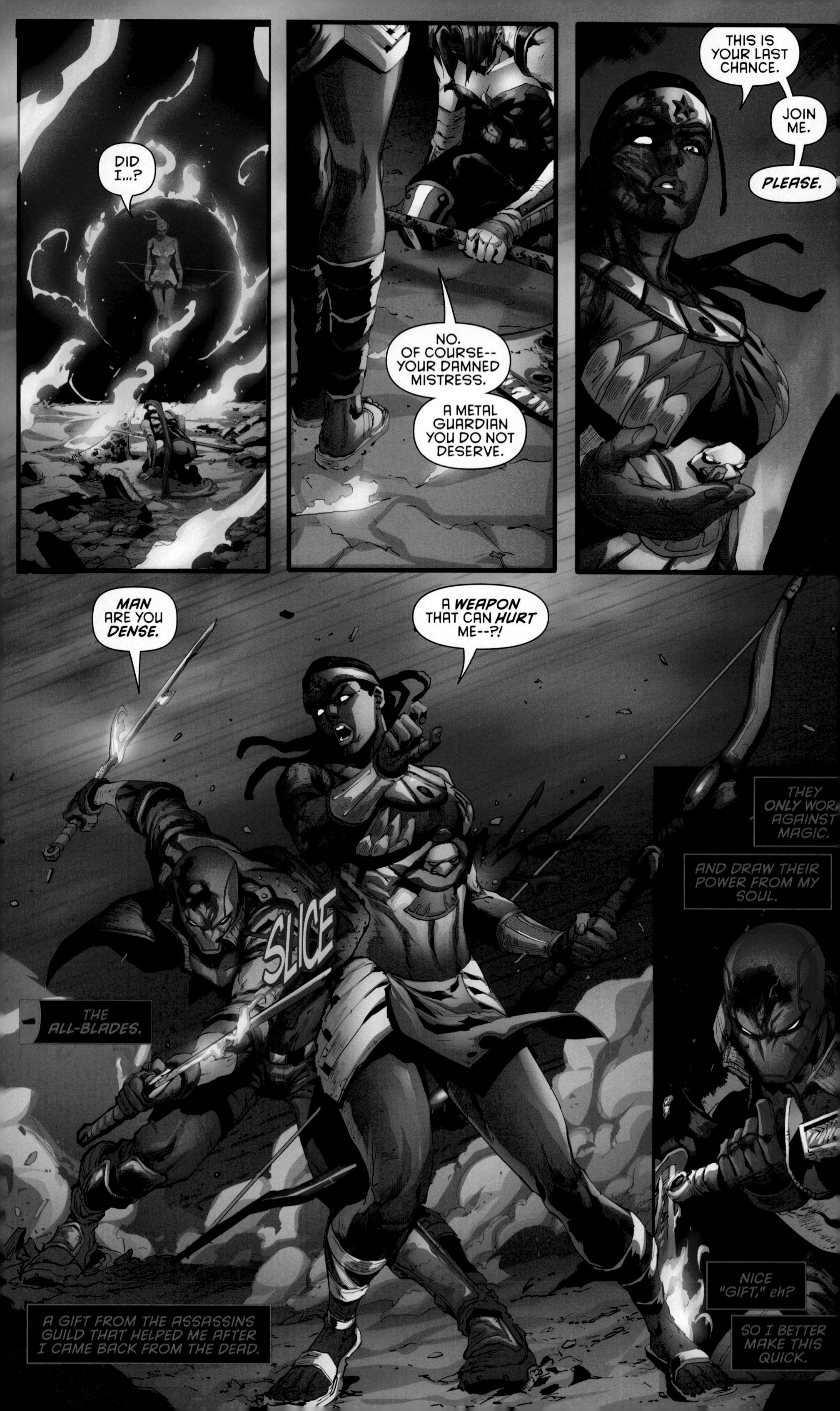

DID I...?
NO. OF COURSE-- YOUR DAMNED MISTRESS.
A METAL GUARDIAN YOU DO NOT DESERVE.
THIS IS YOUR LAST CHANCE.
JOIN ME.
PLEASE.
MAN ARE YOU DENSE.
A WEAPON THAT CAN HURT ME--?!
THE ALL-BLADES.
A GIFT FROM THE ASSASSINS GUILD THAT HELPED ME AFTER I CAME BACK FROM THE DEAD.
SLICE
THEY ONLY WOR AGAINST MAGIC.
AND DRAW THEIR POWER FROM MY SOUL.
NICE "GIFT," eh?
SO I BETTER MAKE THIS QUICK.

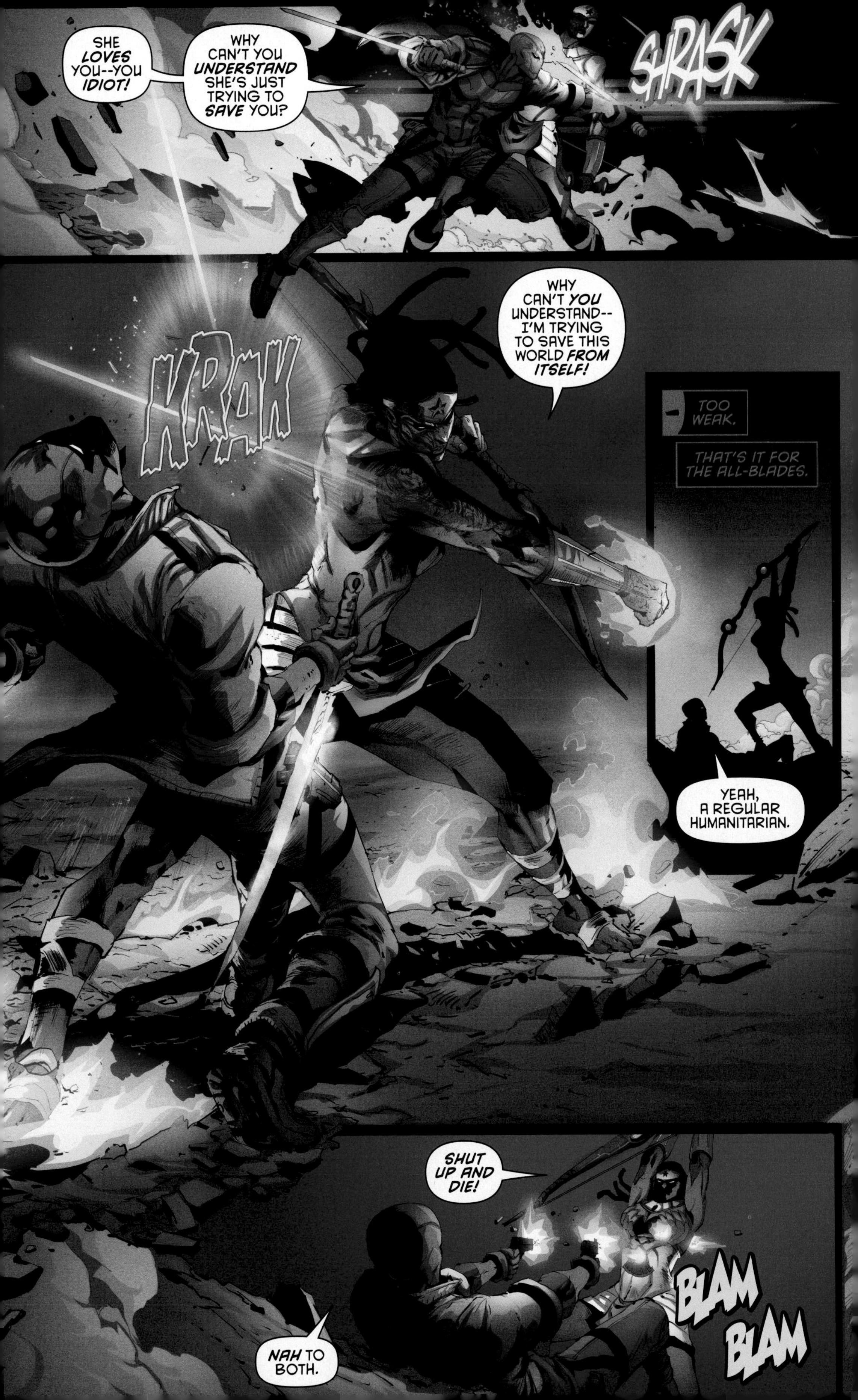
SHE LOVES YOU--YOU IDIOT!
WHY CAN'T YOU UNDERSTAND SHE'S JUST TRYING TO SAVE YOU?
SHRASK
KRAK
WHY CAN'T YOU UNDERSTAND-- I'M TRYING TO SAVE THIS WORLD FROM ITSELF!
TOO WEAK.
THAT'S IT FOR THE ALL-BLADES.
YEAH, A REGULAR HUMANITARIAN.
SHUT UP AND DIE!
BLAM
BLAM
NAH TO BOTH.

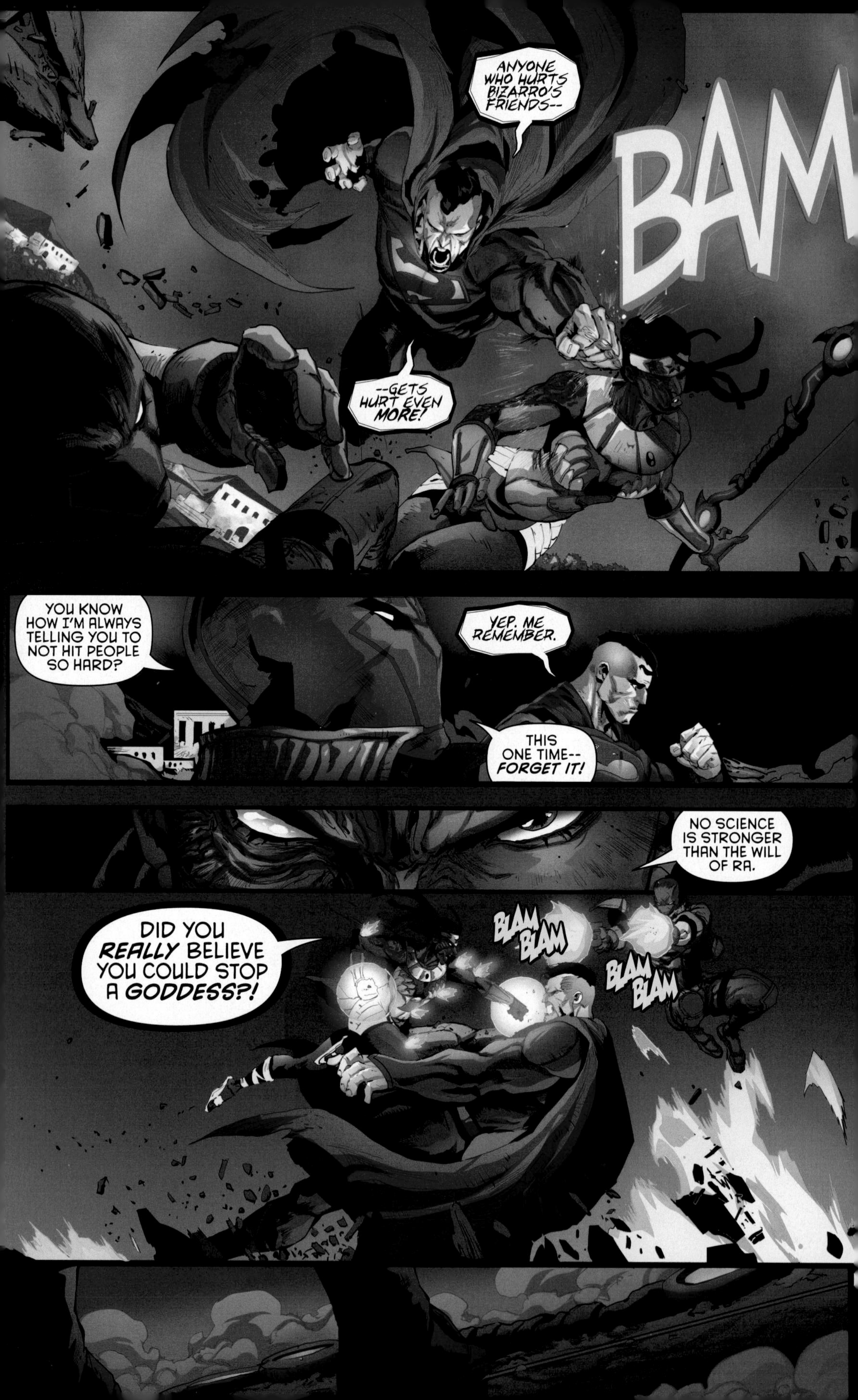
ANYONE WHO HURTS BIZARRO'S FRIENDS--
BAM
--GETS HURT EVEN MORE!
YOU KNOW HOW I'M ALWAYS TELLING YOU TO NOT HIT PEOPLE SO HARD?
YEP. ME REMEMBER.
THIS ONE TIME-- FORGET IT!
NO SCIENCE IS STRONGER THAN THE WILL OF RA.
DID YOU REALLY BELIEVE YOU COULD STOP A GODDESS?!
BLAM BLAM
BLAM BLAM

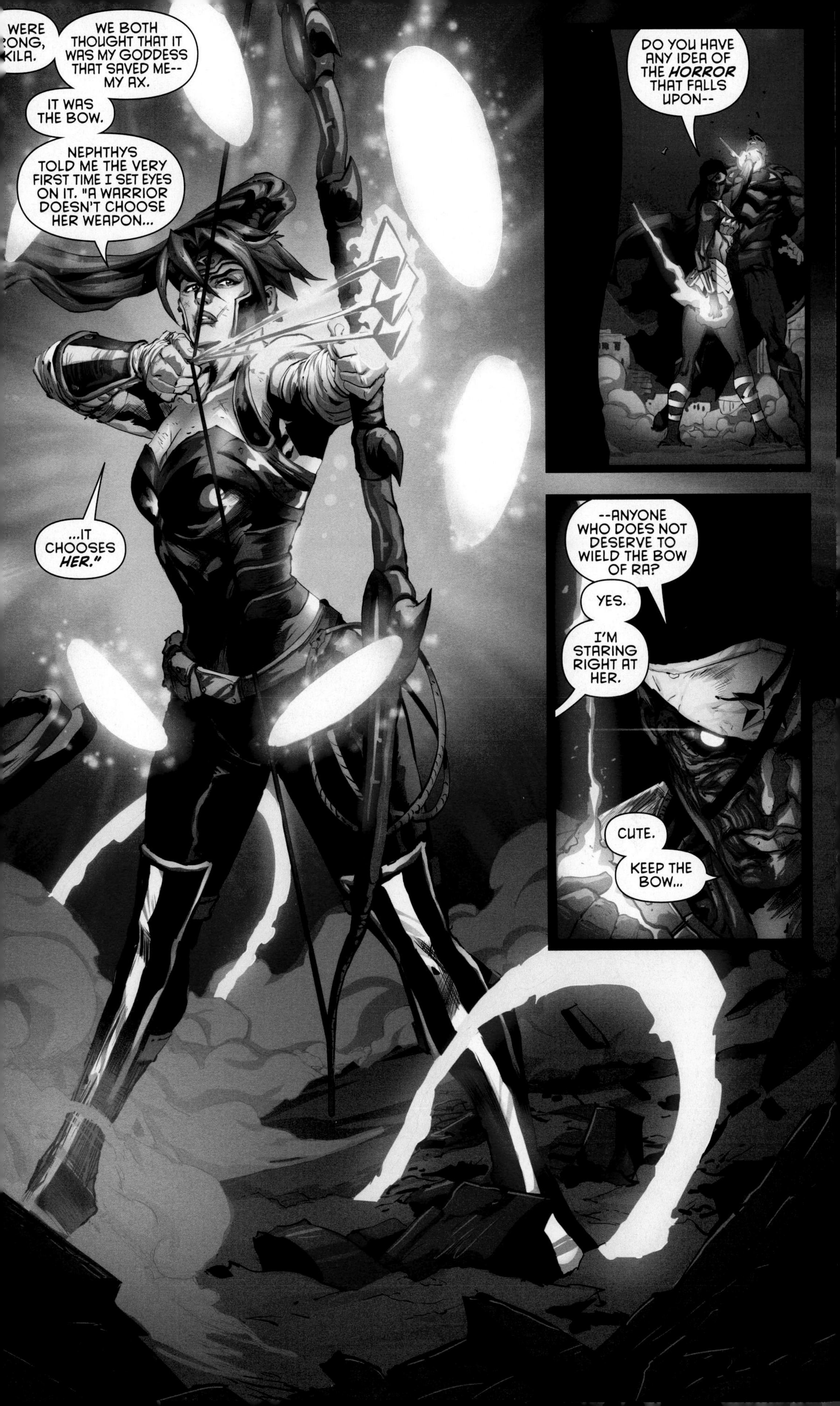

WERE
RONG,
KILA.
WE BOTH THOUGHT THAT IT WAS MY GODDESS THAT SAVED ME-- MY AX.
IT WAS THE BOW.
NEPHTHYS TOLD ME THE VERY FIRST TIME I SET EYES ON IT. "A WARRIOR DOESN'T CHOOSE HER WEAPON...
...IT CHOOSES *HER.*"
DO YOU HAVE ANY IDEA OF THE *HORROR* THAT FALLS UPON--
--ANYONE WHO DOES NOT DESERVE TO WIELD THE BOW OF RA?
YES.
I'M STARING RIGHT AT HER.
CUTE.
KEEP THE BOW...

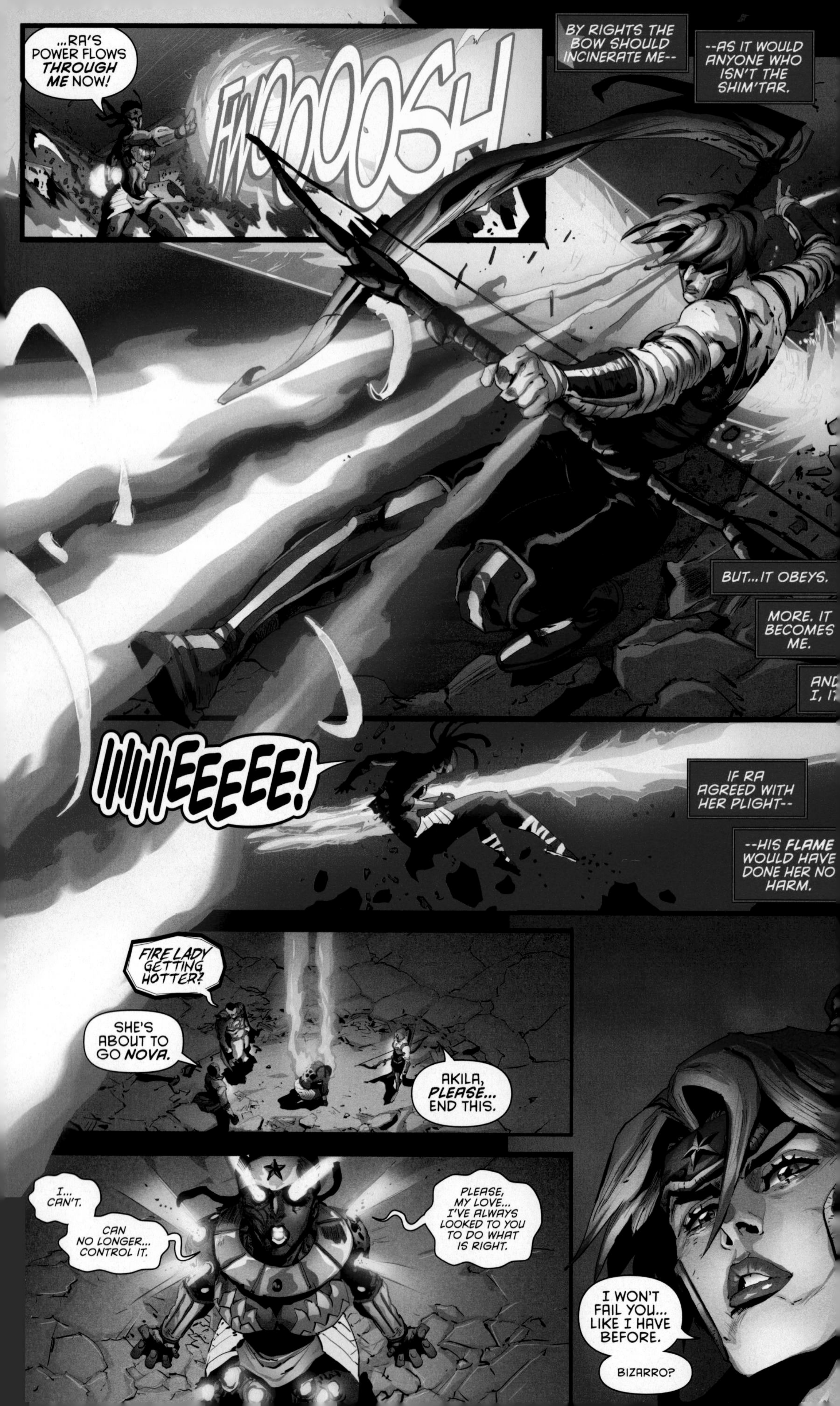
...RA'S POWER FLOWS THROUGH ME NOW!
FWOOOOSH
BY RIGHTS THE BOW SHOULD INCINERATE ME--
--AS IT WOULD ANYONE WHO ISN'T THE SHIM'TAR.
BUT...IT OBEYS.
MORE. IT BECOMES ME.
IIIIIIEEEEEE!
IF RA AGREED WITH HER PLIGHT--
--HIS FLAME WOULD HAVE DONE HER NO HARM.
FIRE LADY GETTING HOTTER?
SHE'S ABOUT TO GO NOVA.
AKILA, PLEASE... END THIS.
I... CAN'T.
CAN NO LONGER... CONTROL IT.
PLEASE, MY LOVE... I'VE ALWAYS LOOKED TO YOU TO DO WHAT IS RIGHT.
I WON'T FAIL YOU... LIKE I HAVE BEFORE.
BIZARRO?

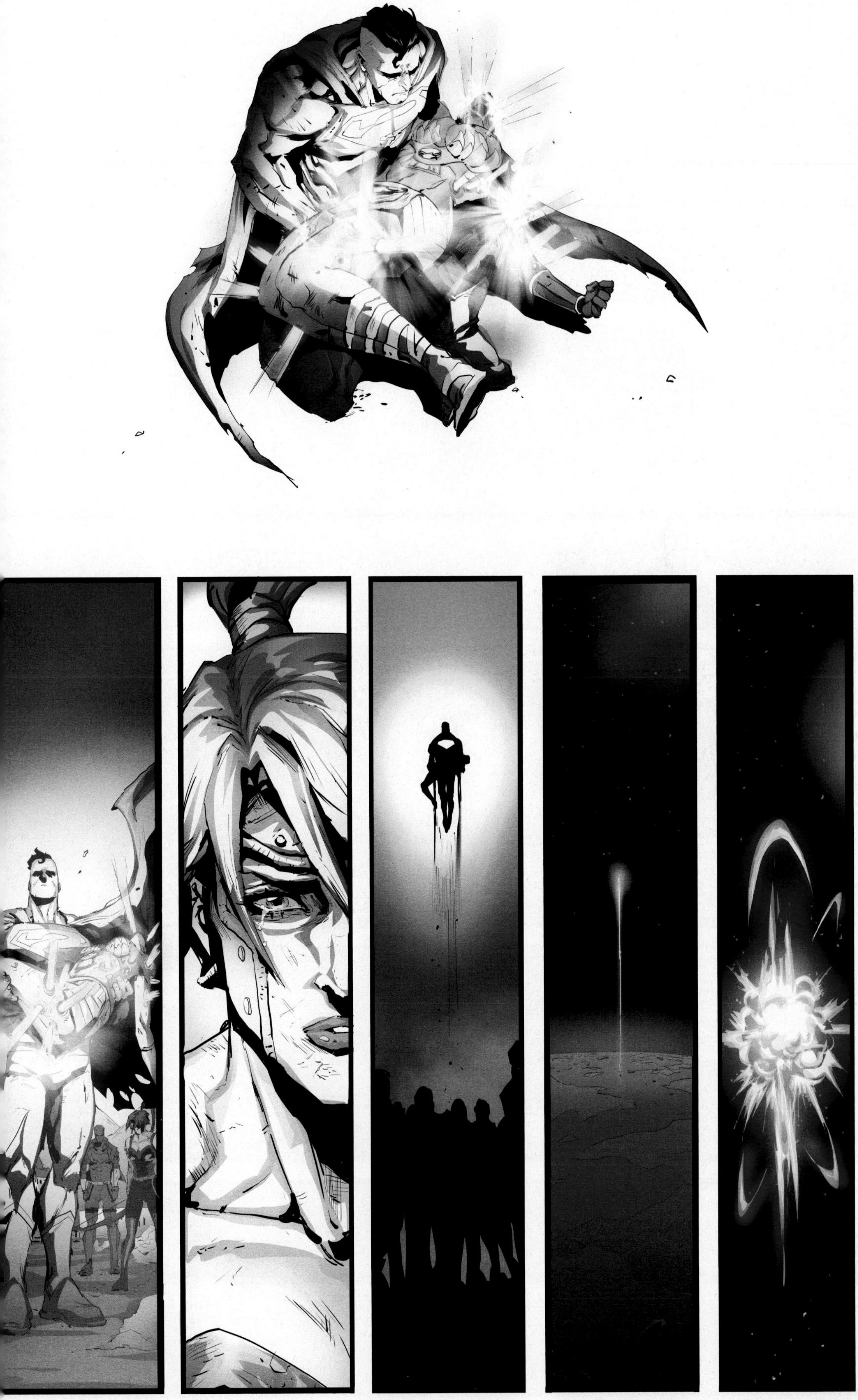

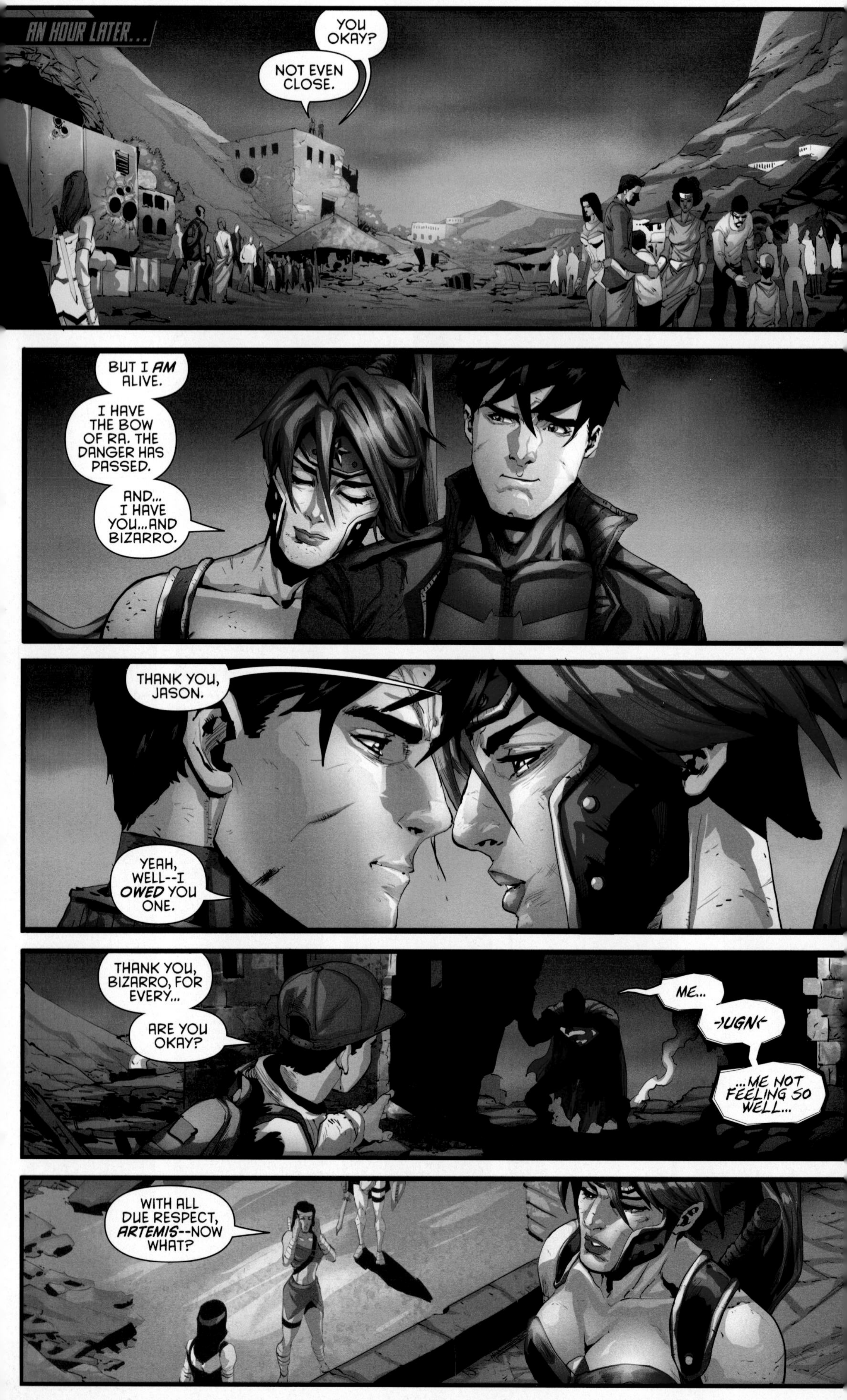
AN HOUR LATER...
YOU OKAY?
NOT EVEN CLOSE.
BUT I AM ALIVE.
I HAVE THE BOW OF RA. THE DANGER HAS PASSED.
AND... I HAVE YOU...AND BIZARRO.
THANK YOU, JASON.
YEAH, WELL--I OWED YOU ONE.
THANK YOU, BIZARRO, FOR EVERY...
ARE YOU OKAY?
ME...
UGN
...ME NOT FEELING SO WELL...
WITH ALL DUE RESPECT, ARTEMIS--NOW WHAT?

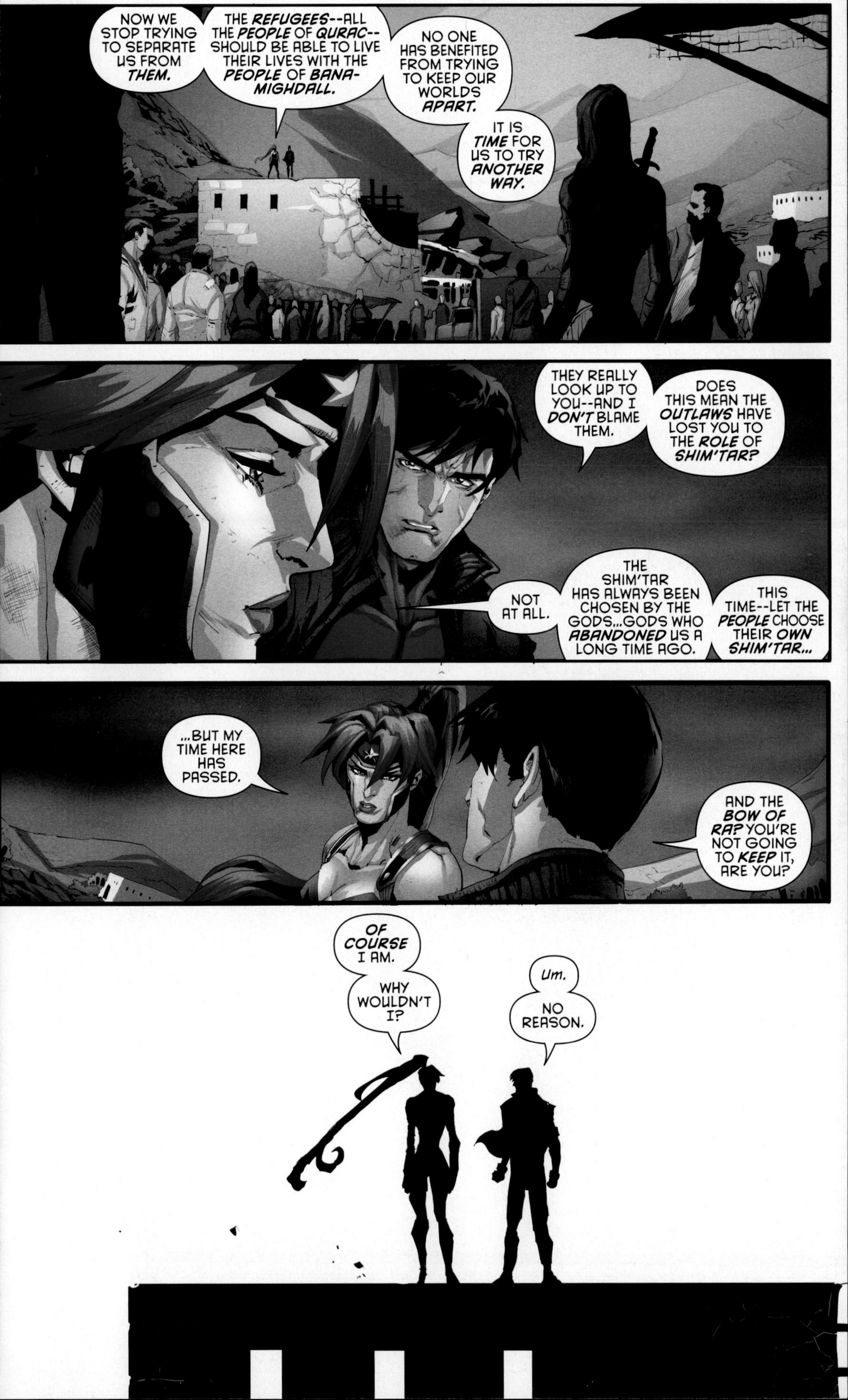
NOW WE STOP TRYING TO SEPARATE US FROM THEM.
THE REFUGEES--ALL THE PEOPLE OF QURAC--SHOULD BE ABLE TO LIVE THEIR LIVES WITH THE PEOPLE OF BANA-MIGHDALL.
NO ONE HAS BENEFITED FROM TRYING TO KEEP OUR WORLDS APART.
IT IS TIME FOR US TO TRY ANOTHER WAY.
THEY REALLY LOOK UP TO YOU--AND I DON'T BLAME THEM.
DOES THIS MEAN THE OUTLAWS HAVE LOST YOU TO THE ROLE OF SHIM'TAR?
NOT AT ALL.
THE SHIM'TAR HAS ALWAYS BEEN CHOSEN BY THE GODS...GODS WHO ABANDONED US A LONG TIME AGO.
THIS TIME--LET THE PEOPLE CHOOSE THEIR OWN SHIM'TAR...
...BUT MY TIME HERE HAS PASSED.
AND THE BOW OF RA? YOU'RE NOT GOING TO KEEP IT, ARE YOU?
OF COURSE I AM.
WHY WOULDN'T I?
Um.
NO REASON.

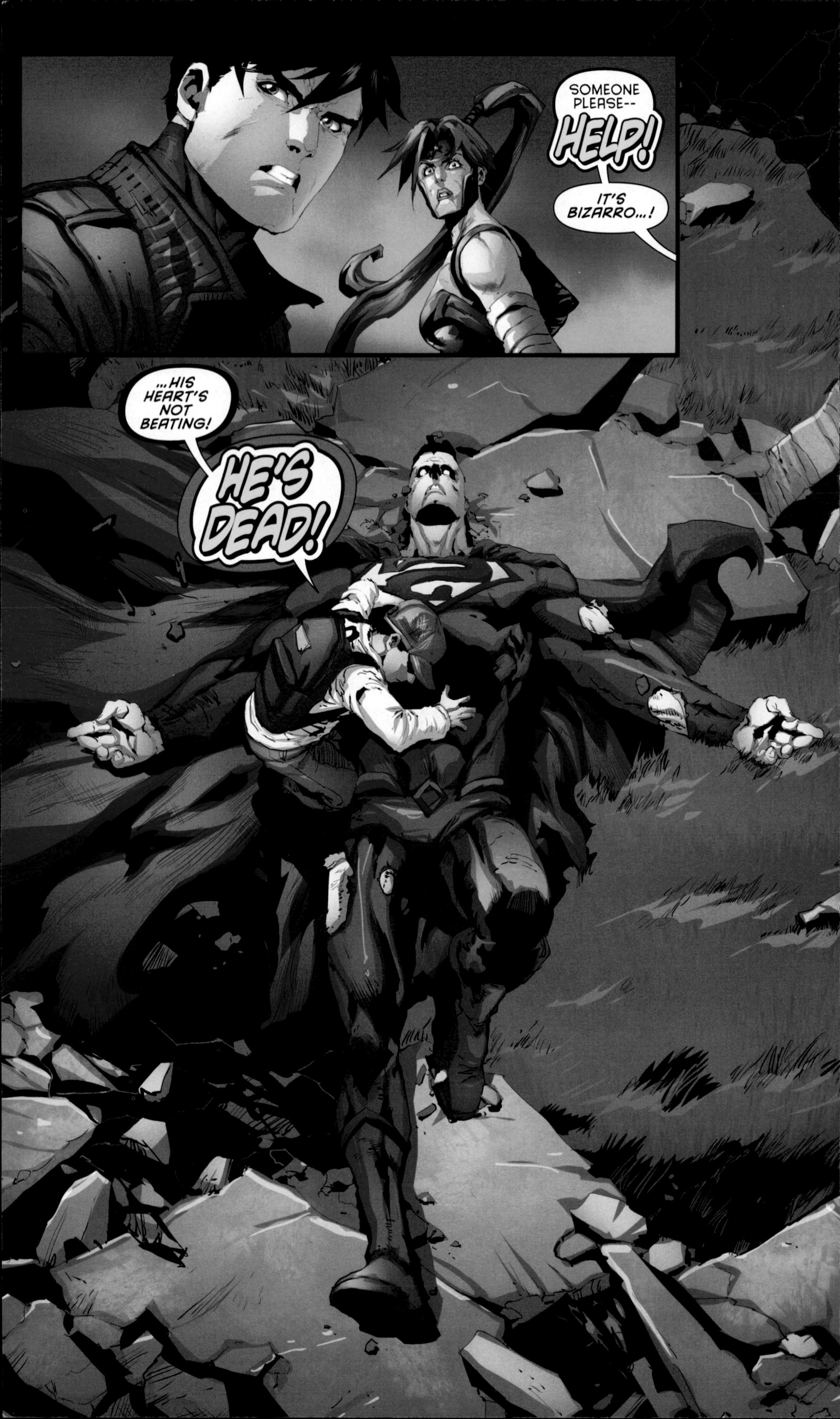
SOMEONE PLEASE--
HELP!
IT'S BIZARRO...!
...HIS HEART'S NOT BEATING!
HE'S DEAD!

RED HOOD AND THE OUTLAWS

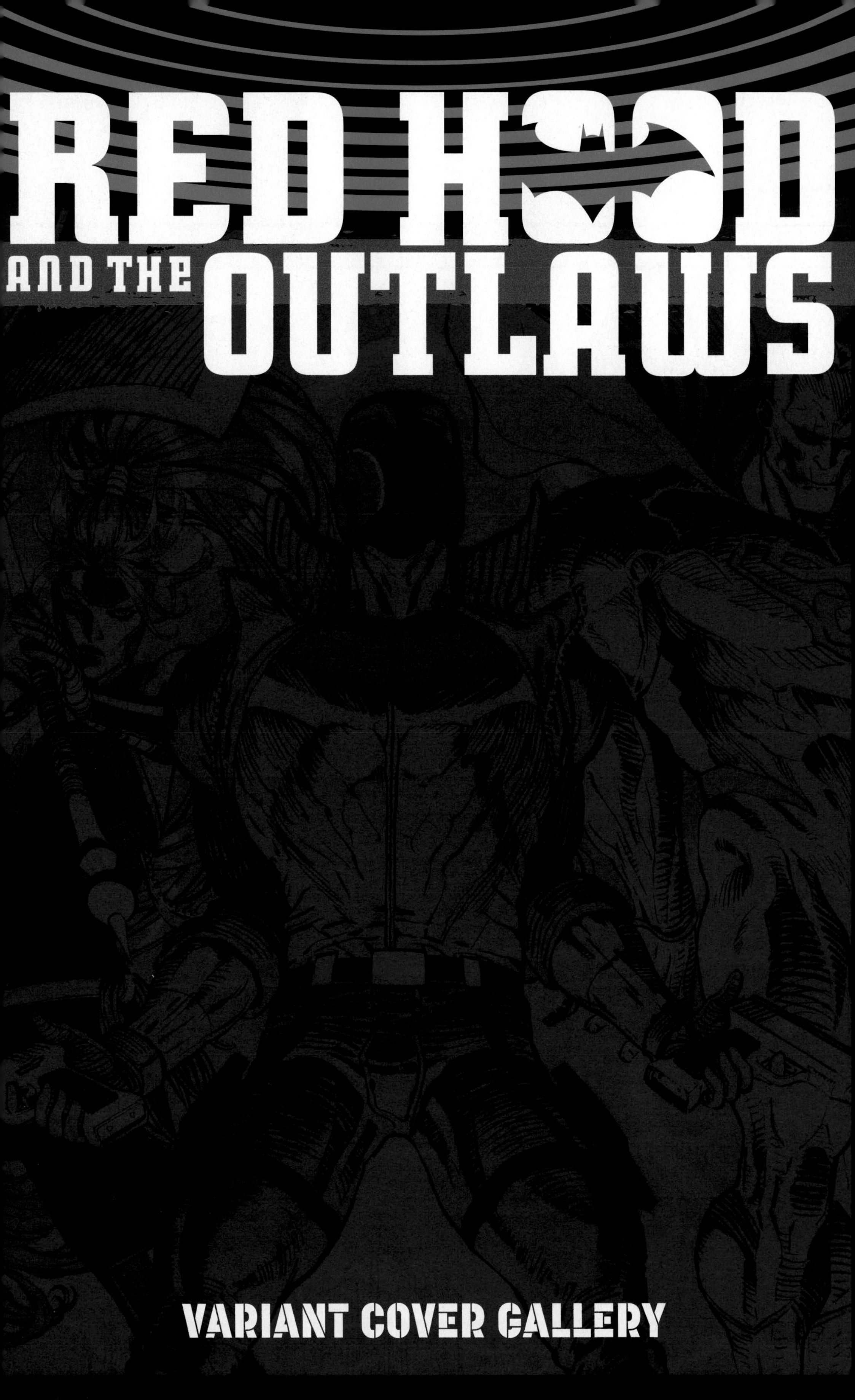

VARIANT COVER GALLERY

RED HOOD AND THE OUTLAWS #7 variant cover by GUILLEM MARCH

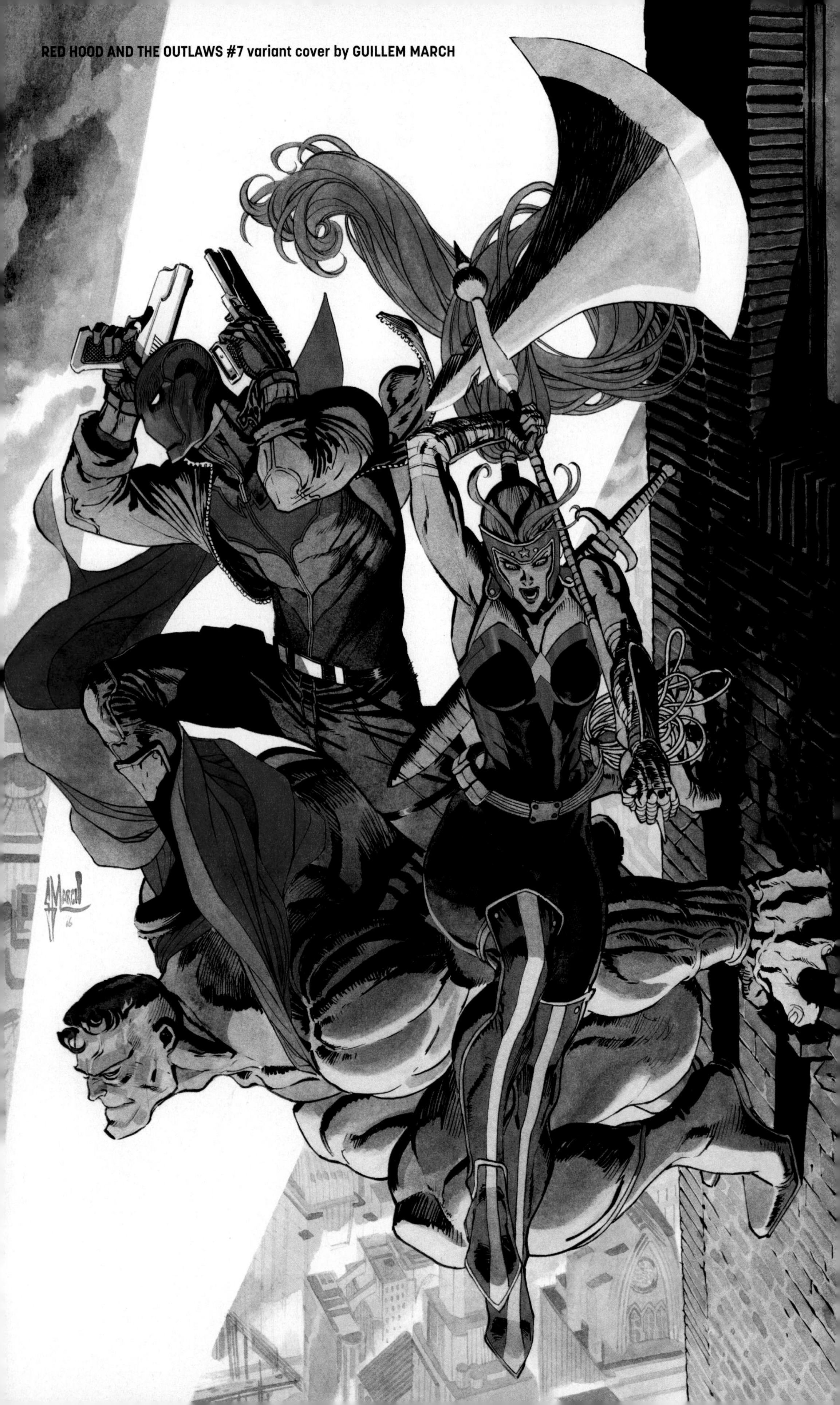

RED HOOD AND THE OUTLAWS #8 variant cover by GUILLEM MARCH

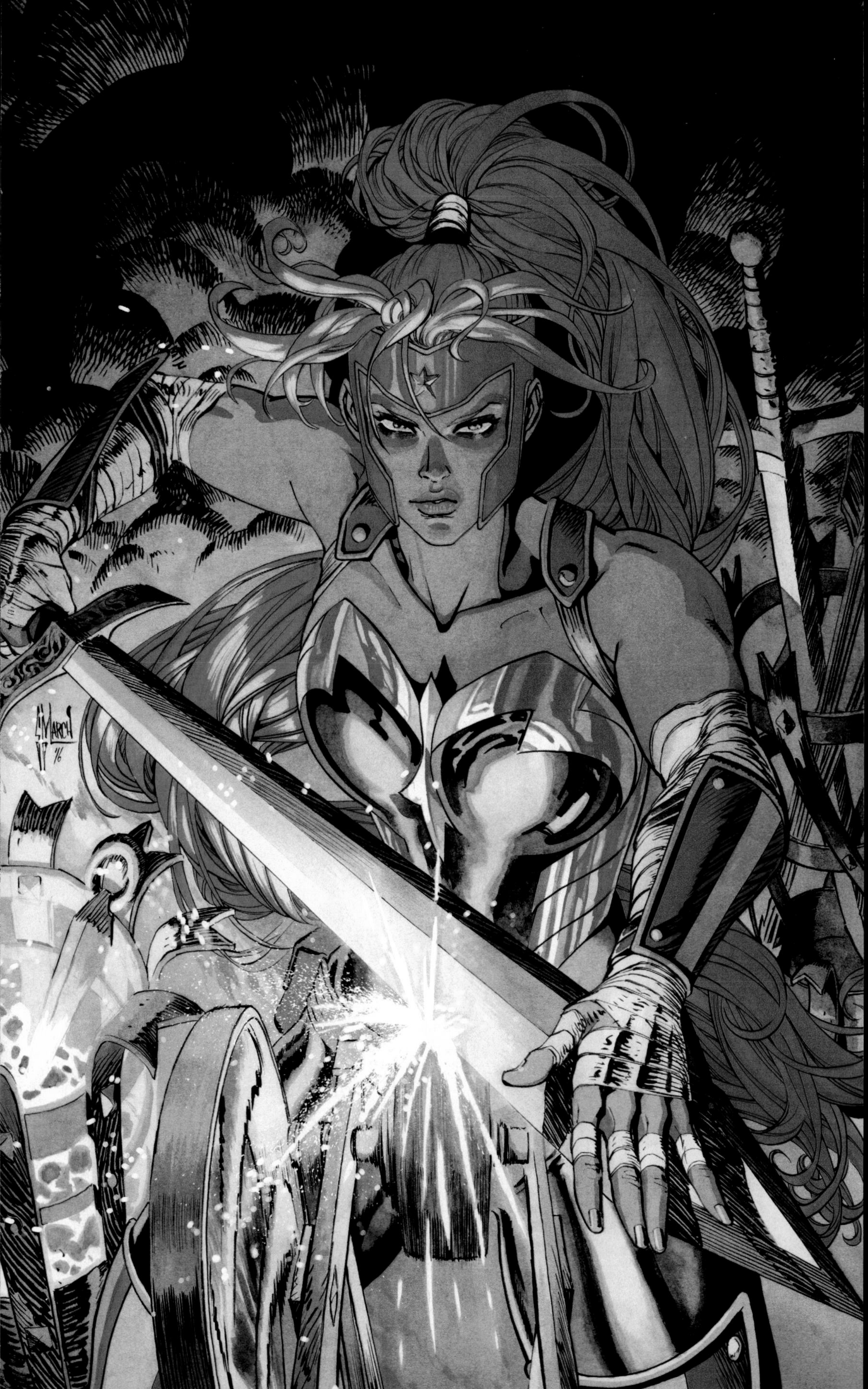

RED HOOD AND THE OUTLAWS #9 variant cover by GUILLEM MARCH

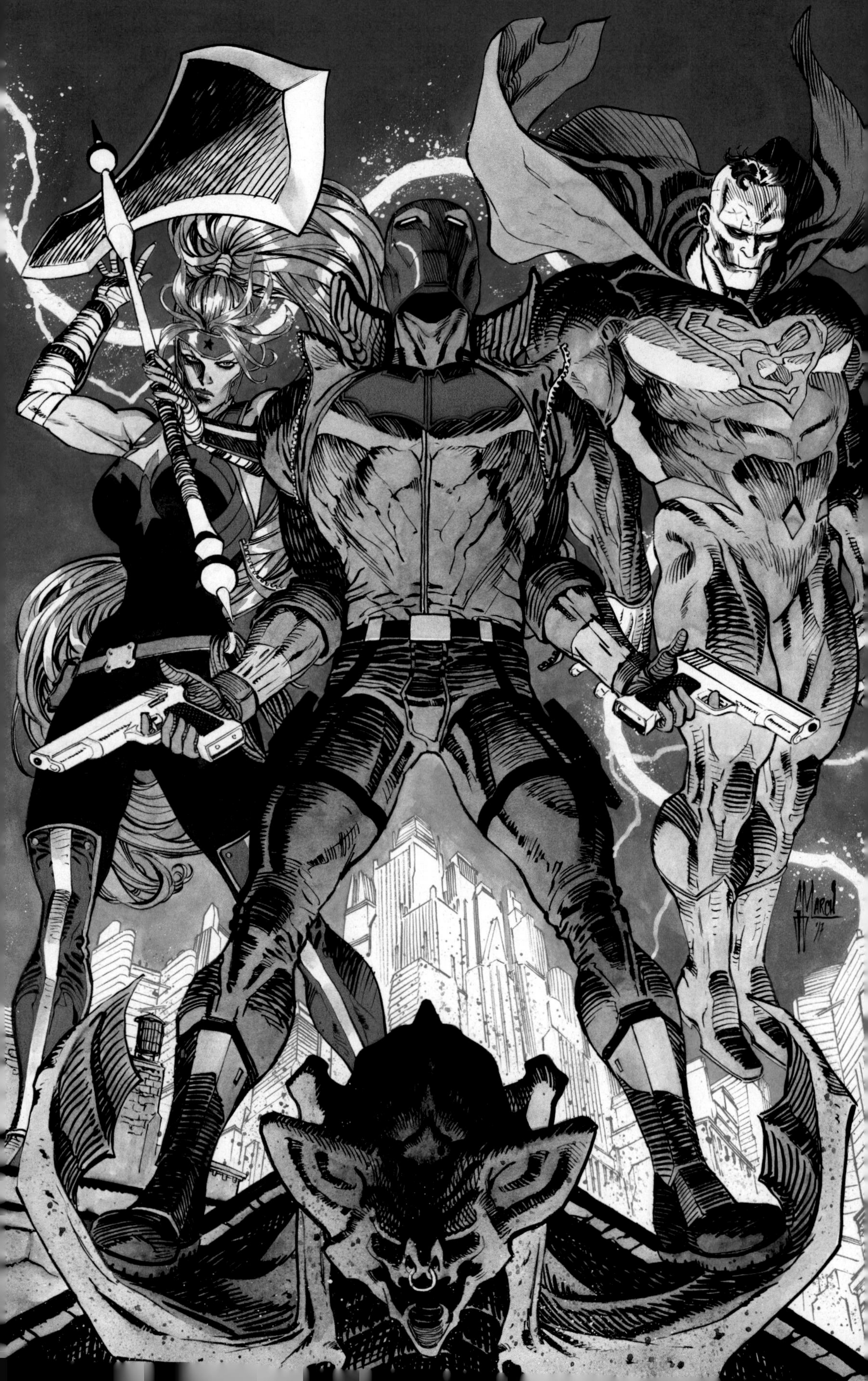

RED HOOD AND THE OUTLAWS #10 variant cover by GUILLEM MARCH

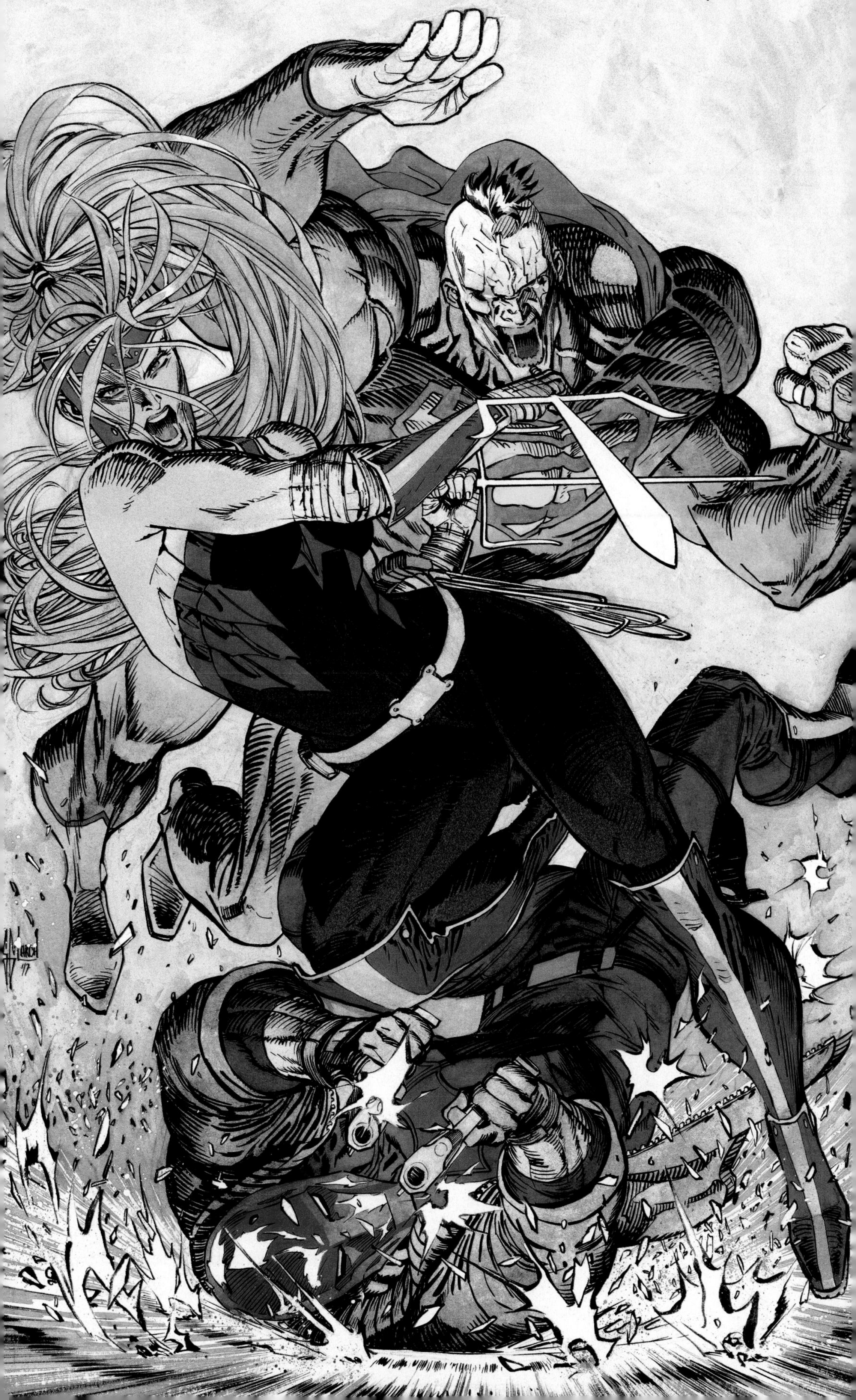

RED HOOD AND THE OUTLAWS #11 variant cover by GUILLEM MARCH

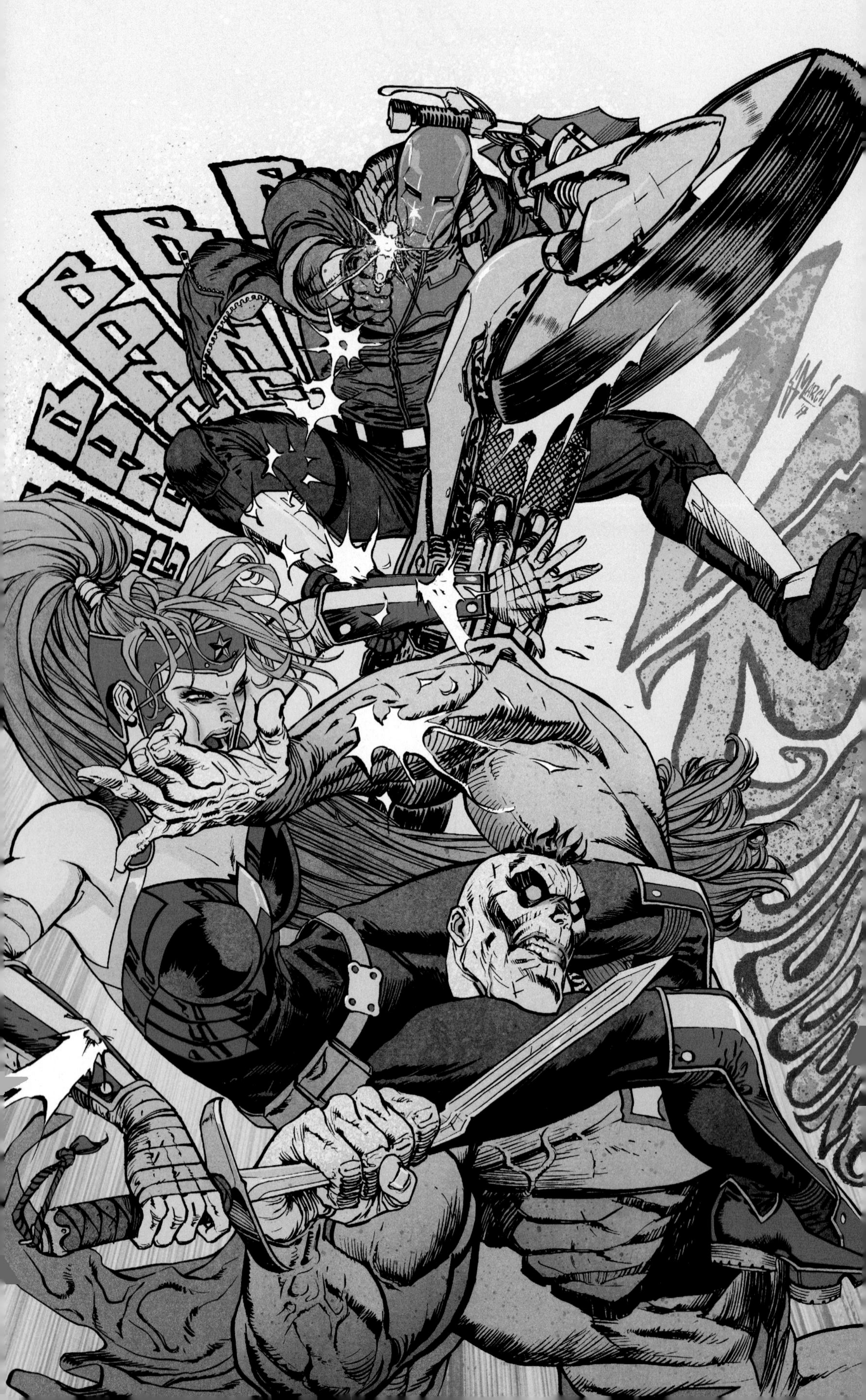

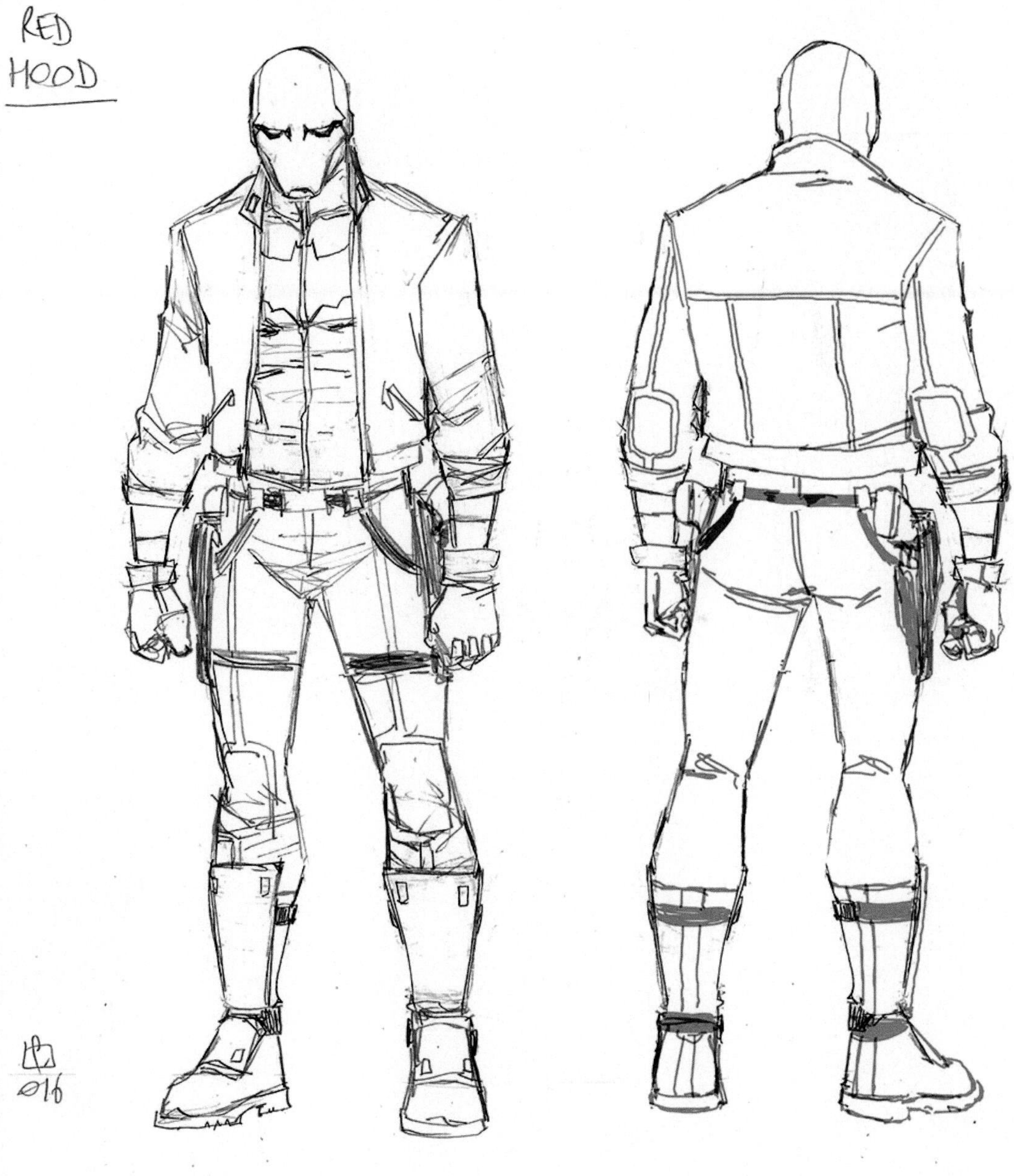
RED
HOOD

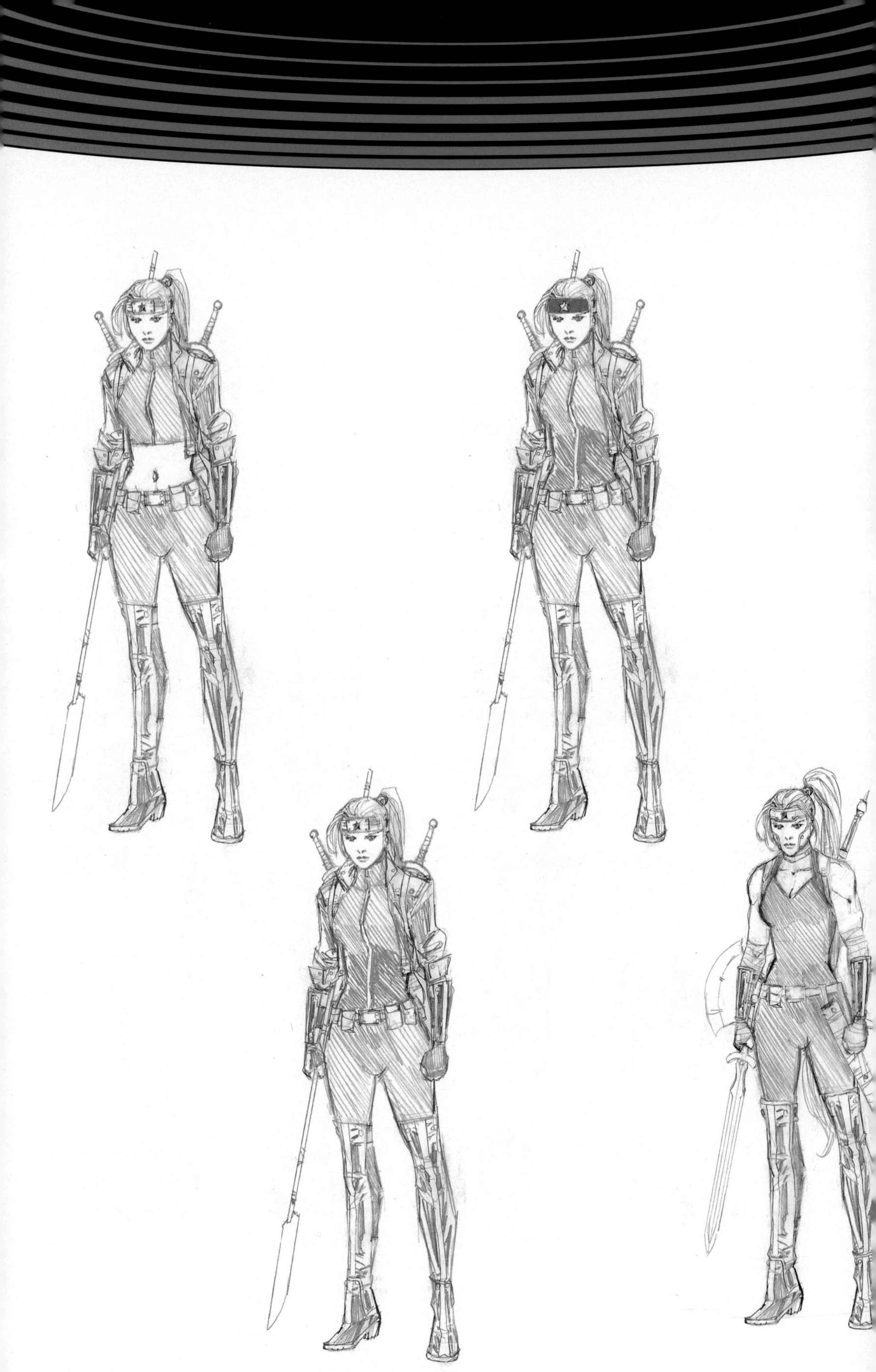

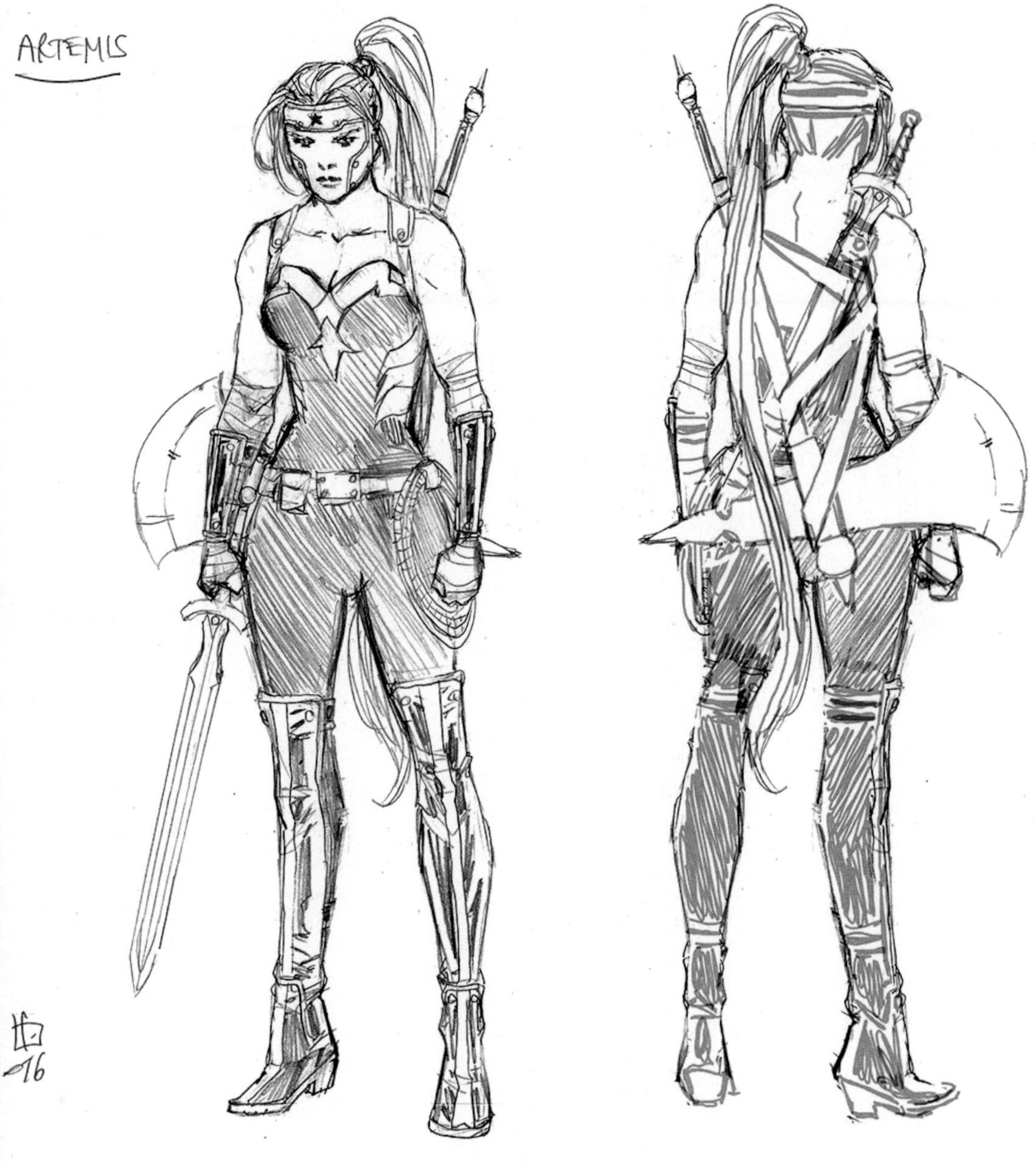
ARTEMIS

BIZARRO

BIZARRO

BIZARRO

DC UNIVERSE REBIRTH

SUICIDE SQUAD

VOL. 1: THE BLACK VAULT

ROB WILLIAMS
with JIM LEE and others

VOL.1 THE BLACK VAULT
ROB WILLIAMS • JIM LEE • PHILIP TAN • JASON FABOK • IVAN REIS • GARY FRANK

**THE HELLBLAZER VOL. 1:
THE POISON TRUTH**

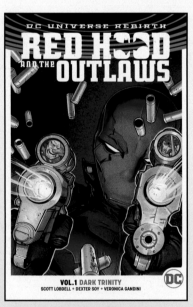

**RED HOOD AND THE OUTLAWS VOL. 1:
DARK TRINITY**

**HARLEY QUINN VOL. 1:
DIE LAUGHING**

Get more DC graphic novels wherever comics and books are sold!

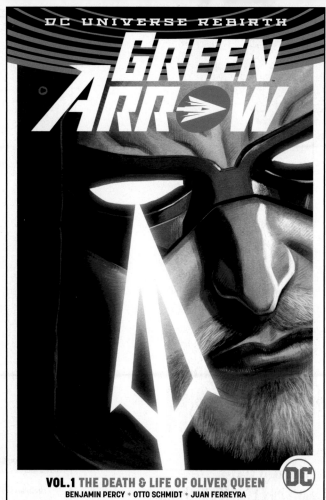